Nihil Unbound

Also by Ray Brassier

ALAIN BADIOU: Theoretical Writings (*co-editor with A. Toscano*)

Nihil Unbound

Enlightenment and Extinction

Ray Brassier

First published 2007 by
PALGRAVE MACMILLAN
Houndmills, Basingstoke, Hampshire RG21 6XS and
175 Fifth Avenue, New York, N.Y. 10010
Companies and representatives throughout the world

PALGRAVE MACMILLAN is the global academic imprint of the Palgrave Macmillan division of St. Martin's Press, LLC and of Palgrave Macmillan Ltd. Macmillan® is a registered trademark in the United States, United Kingdom and other countries. Palgrave is a registered trademark in the European Union and other countries.

ISBN 978-0-230-52205-3   ISBN 978-0-230-59082-3 (eBook)
DOI 10.1007/978-0-230-59082-3

A catalogue record for this book is available from the British Library.

A catalog record for this book is available from the Library of Congress.

10   9   8   7   6   5   4   3   2   1
16   15   14   13   12   11   10   09   08   07

Transferred to Digital Printing in 2009.

There is nothing to do and there is nowhere to go
There is nothing to be and there is no-one to know

Thomas Ligotti

Contents

Preface

> Since Copernicus, man has been rolling from the
> centre toward X.
>
> (Friedrich Nietzsche 1885)[1]
>
> The more the universe seems comprehensible, the
> more it also seems pointless.
>
> (Steven Weinberg 1978)[2]

The term 'nihilism' has a hackneyed quality. Too much has been written on the topic, and any sense of urgency that the word might once have communicated has been dulled by overexposure. The result is a vocable tainted by dreary over-familiarity and nebulous indeterminacy. Nevertheless, few other topics of philosophical debate exert such an immediate grip on people with little or no interest in the problems of philosophy as the claim of nihilism in its most 'naive' acceptation: existence is worthless. This book was spurred by the conviction that this apparently banal assertion harbours hidden depths which have yet to be sounded by philosophers, despite the plethora of learned books and articles on the topic. Although the philosophical literature on nihilism is impressively vast, comprising several important works from which I have learned much, the rationale for writing this book was the conviction that something of fundamental philosophical importance remained unsaid and buried beneath the learned disquisitions on the historical origins, contemporary ramifications, and long-term implications of nihilism. Indeed, these aspects of the topic have been so thoroughly charted that the simplest way to clarify the intent of this book is to explain what it does not do.

First and foremost, it does not treat nihilism as a disease, requiring diagnosis and the recommendation of an antidote. But neither does it extol the pathos of finitude as a bulwark against metaphysical hubris (Critchley 1997), or celebrate the indeterminacy of interpretation as a welcome liberation from the oppressive universalism of Enlightenment rationalism (Vattimo 1991 & 2004). Nor does it try to reassert the authority of reason in the face of scepticism and irrationalism, whether by defending Platonism from the depredations of Heideggerean existentialism (Rosen 2000), or Hegelianism against the slings and arrows of

French post-structuralism (Rose 1984). Lastly, it does not attempt to provide a conceptual genealogy of nihilism (Cunningham 2002), a critical pre-history of the problematic (Gillespie 1996), or a synoptic overview of its various ramifications in nineteenth- and twentieth-century philosophy and literature (Souche-Dagues 1996).

Two basic contentions underlie this book. First, that the disenchantment of the world understood as a consequence of the process whereby the Enlightenment shattered the 'great chain of being' and defaced the 'book of the world' is a necessary consequence of the coruscating potency of reason, and hence an invigorating vector of intellectual discovery, rather than a calamitous diminishment. Jonathan Israel's work provided a direct source of inspiration for this idea and his magisterial recounting of philosophy's crucial role in what was arguably the most far-reaching (and still ongoing) intellectual revolution of the past two thousand years furnishes a salutary and much-needed corrective to the tide of anti-Enlightenment revisionism with which so much twentieth-century philosophy has been complicit.[3] The disenchantment of the world deserves to be celebrated as an achievement of intellectual maturity, not bewailed as a debilitating impoverishment. The second fundamental contention of this book is that nihilism is not, as Jacobi and so many other philosophers since have insisted, a pathological exacerbation of subjectivism, which annuls the world and reduces reality to a correlate of the absolute ego, but on the contrary, the unavoidable corollary of the realist conviction that there is a mind-independent reality, which, despite the presumptions of human narcissism, is indifferent to our existence and oblivious to the 'values' and 'meanings' which we would drape over it in order to make it more hospitable. Nature is not our or anyone's 'home', nor a particularly beneficent progenitor. Philosophers would do well to desist from issuing any further injunctions about the need to re-establish the meaningfulness of existence, the purposefulness of life, or mend the shattered concord between man and nature. Philosophy should be more than a sop to the pathetic twinge of human self-esteem. Nihilism is not an existential quandary but a speculative opportunity. Thinking has interests that do not coincide with those of living; indeed, they can and have been pitted against the latter. It is this latter possibility that this book attempts to investigate. Its deficiencies are patent, and unfortunately the shortfall between ambition and ability means that it is neither as thorough nor as comprehensive as would be necessary to make its case convincingly. Much more needs to be demonstrated in order to field an argument robust enough to withstand the sceptical rejoinders which the book's principal contentions are sure to provoke. Nevertheless, the themes broached here, however unsatisfactorily, should be considered as preliminary forays in an investigation which I hope to develop more fully in subsequent work.

The book is divided into three parts. Chapter 1 introduces the theme which governs the first part of the book, 'Destroying the Manifest Image', by considering Wilfrid Sellars's distinction between the 'manifest' and 'scientific' images of 'man-in-the-world'. This opening chapter then goes on to examine the standoff between the normative pretensions of folk-psychological discourse, and an emerging science of cognition which would eliminate belief in 'belief' altogether in order to reintegrate mind into the scientific image. Chapter 2 analyses Adorno and Horkheimer's influential critique of scientific rationality in the name of an alternative conception of the relation between reason and nature inspired by Hegel and Freud. Chapter 3, the final chapter of Part I, lays out Quentin Meillassoux's critique of the 'correlationism' which underpins the Kantian–Hegelian account of the relationship between reason and nature, before pinpointing difficulties in Meillassoux's own attempt to rehabilitate mathematical intuition. The second part of the book charts the 'Anatomy of Negation' and begins with Chapter 4, which examines how Alain Badiou circumvents the difficulties attendant upon Meillassoux's appeal to intellectual intuition through a subtractive conception of being which avoids the idealism of intuition, but only at the cost of an equally problematic idealism of inscription. Chapter 5 attempts to find a way out of the deadlock between the idealism of correlation on one hand, and the idealism of mathematical intuition and inscription on the other, by drawing on the work of François Laruelle in order to elaborate a speculative realism operating according to a non-dialectical logic of negation. The third and final section of the book, 'The End of Time', tries to put this logic to work, beginning with Chapter 6's critical reconstruction of the ontological function allotted to the relationship between death and time in Heidegger's *Being and Time* and Deleuze's *Difference and Repetition*. Finally, Chapter 7 recapitulates Nietzsche's narrative of the overcoming of nihilism in light of critical insights developed over the preceding chapters, before proposing a speculative re-inscription of Freud's theory of the death-drive, wherein the sublimation of the latter is seen as the key to grasping the intimate link between the will to know and the will to nothingness.

Thanks to Dan Bunyard, Michael Carr, Mark Fisher, Graham Harman, Robin Mackay, Dustin McWherter, Nina Power, Dan Smith, Alberto Toscano, and my colleagues at the Centre for Research in Modern

European Philosophy: Eric Alliez, Peter Hallward, Christian Kerslake, Stewart Martin, Peter Osborne, Stella Sandford.

Special thanks to Damian Veal for help with the final preparation of the manuscript, and above all to Michelle Speidel.

Acknowledgements:

An early version of Chapter 2 appeared in *The Origins and Ends of the Mind* ed. R. Brassier and C. Kerslake, Leuven University Press, 2007; an abbreviated version of Chapter 3 appeared in *Collapse*, Vol. II, February 2007; an edited version of Chapter 4 provided the basis for the article 'Presentation as Anti-Phenomenon in Alain Badiou's Being and Event' in *Continental Philosophy Review*, Vol. 39, No. 1; finally, material from sections 3 and 4 of Chapter 7 originally appeared in an article entitled 'Solar Catastrophe' in *Philosophy Today*, Vol. 47, Winter 2003.

Part I Destroying the Manifest Image

1
The *Apoptosis* of Belief[1]

1.1   The manifest image and the myth of Jones: Wilfrid Sellars

In 'Philosophy and the Scientific Image of Man',[2] Wilfrid Sellars proposes a compelling diagnosis of the predicament of contemporary philosophy. The contemporary philosopher is confronted by two competing 'images' of man in the world: on the one hand, the *manifest* image of man as he has conceived of himself up until now with the aid of philosophical reflection; on the other, the relatively recent but continually expanding *scientific* image of man as a 'complex physical system' (Sellars 1963a: 25) – one which is conspicuously unlike the manifest image, but which can be distilled from various scientific discourses, including physics, neurophysiology, evolutionary biology, and, more recently, cognitive science. But for Sellars, the contrast between the manifest and the scientific image is not to be construed in terms of a conflict between naive common sense and sophisticated theoretical reason. The manifest image is not the domain of pre-theoretical immediacy. On the contrary, it is itself a subtle theoretical construct, a disciplined and critical 'refinement or sophistication' of the originary framework in terms of which man first encountered himself as a being capable of conceptual thought, in contradistinction to creatures who lack this capacity. To understand why Sellars describes the manifest image as a sophisticated theoretical achievement in its own right – one as significant as any scientific achievement since – it is necessary to recapitulate Sellars's now celebrated 'myth of Jones'.

In his seminal 'Empiricism and the Philosophy of Mind',[3] Sellars proposes a philosophical fable about what he calls 'our Rylean ancestors', who have acquired language but who lack any conception of the complex mental states and processes we take to be the precondition for any sophisticated cognitive behaviour. When these Ryleans attempt to explain a human behaviour such as anger, their resources are limited to a set of dispositional terms – e.g. 'bad-tempered' – which are operationally defined with regard to observable circumstances – such as 'ranting and raving' – these in turn being deemed sufficient to explain the observable behaviour – in this case, 'rage'. But these operationally defined dispositional concepts severely restrict the range of human activities which the Ryleans can explain. They lack the conceptual wherewithal for explaining more complicated behaviours. It is at this stage in the fable that Sellars introduces his 'myth of Jones'. Jones is a theoretical genius who postulates the existence of internal speech-like episodes called 'thoughts', closely modelled on publicly observable declarative utterances. These 'thought-episodes' are conceived as possessing the same semantic and logical properties as their publicly observable linguistic analogues, and as playing an internal role comparable to that of the discursive and argumentative role performed by overt speech. By postulating the existence of such internal processes even in the absence of any publicly observable speech-episodes, it becomes possible to explain hitherto inscrutable varieties of human behaviour as resulting from an appropriately structured sequence of these internal thought-episodes. Similarly, Jones postulates the existence of episodes of internal 'sensation' modelled on external perceptual objects. 'Sensations' are understood as instances of internal perception capable of causing cognition and action even in the absence of their externally observable counterparts. Following a similar pattern of reasoning, Jones goes on to postulate the existence of 'intentions', 'beliefs', and 'desires' as relatively lasting states of individuals which can be invoked as salient causal factors for explaining various kinds of behaviour: 'He pushed him because he *intended* to kill him', 'She left early because she *believed* they were waiting for her', 'He stole it because he *desired* it'. The nub of Jones's theory consists in establishing a relation between persons and the propositions which encapsulate their internal thought episodes: Jones teaches his peers to explain behaviour by attributing *propositional attitudes* to persons via the 'that' clauses in statements of the form: 'He believes that ...', 'She desires that ...', 'He intends that ...'. Though not yet recognized as such, these propositional attitudes have become the decisive causal factors in the new theory of human behaviour proposed by Jones; a theory which represents a vast increase in explanatory power relative to its behaviourist predecessor. All that remains is for individuals to learn to use this new theory not merely for the purposes of explaining others' behaviour, but also to describe their own: one *learns* to perceive qualitatively distinct episodes of inner sensation just as one *learns* to understand oneself by ascribing beliefs, desires, and intentions to oneself. The theory is internalized and appropriated as the indispensable medium for describing and articulating the structure of one's own first-person experience. The philosophical moral to this Sellarsian fable consists in Jones's philosophically minded descendants coming to realize that the propositional attitudes stand to one another in complex logical relations of entailment, implication, and inferential dependency, and that Jones's theory exhibits a structure remarkably akin to deductive-nomological models of scientific explanation. For these philosophers (and they include Sellars himself), Jones's theoretical breakthrough has provided the key to uncovering the rational infrastructure of human thought; one which is crystallized in the sentential articulation of propositional attitude ascription. 'Beliefs', 'desires', 'intentions', and similar entities now become the basic psychological kinds to be accounted for by any theory of cognition.

But what is the ontological status of these psychological entities? It is striking to note that though Sellars himself attributes a *functional* role to them, this is precisely in order to leave the question of their ontological status open. According to Sellars, '[Thought] episodes are "in" language-using animals as molecular impacts are "in" gases, not as "ghosts" are in "machines"'(1997: 104). Thus the point of the Jonesean myth is to suggest that the epistemological status of 'thoughts' (qua inner episodes) vis-à-vis candid public verbal performances is most usefully understood as analogous to the epistemological status of, e.g., molecules vis-à-vis the publicly observable behaviour of gases. However, unlike gas molecules, whose determinate empirical characteristics are specified according to the essentially Newtonian lawfulness of their dynamic interaction, 'thoughts' in Sellars's account are introduced as purely functional kinds whose ontological/empirical status is yet to be determined.

Accordingly, for Sellars, the fundamental import of the manifest image is not so much ontological as *normative*, in the sense that it provides the framework 'in which we think of one another as sharing the community intentions which provides the ambience of principles and standards (above all those which make meaningful discourse and rationality itself possible) within which we live our own individual lives'(Sellars 1963a: 40). Thus, the manifest image does not so much catalogue a set of indispensable ontological items which we should strive to preserve from scientific reduction; rather, it indexes the community of rational agents. In this regard, the primary component of the manifest image, Sellars suggests, is the notion of *persons* as loci of intentional agency. Consequently, although the manifest image is a 'disciplined and critical' theoretical framework, one which could also be said to constitute a certain kind of 'scientific image' – albeit one that is 'correlational' as opposed to 'postulational' (Sellars 1963a: 7) – it is not one which we are in a position simply to take or leave. For unlike other theoretical frameworks, Sellars maintains, the manifest image provides the ineluctable prerequisite for our capacity to identify our-selves as human, which is to say, *as persons*: '[M]an is that being which conceives of itself in terms of the manifest image. To the extent that the manifest image does not survive [...] to that extent man himself would not survive' (Sellars 1963a: 18). What is indispensable about our manifest self-image, Sellars concludes, is not its ontological commit-ments, in the sense of what it says *exists* in the world, but rather its normative valence as the framework which allows us to make sense of ourselves as rational agents engaged in pursuing various purposes in the world. Without it, we would simply not know what to do or how to make sense of ourselves – indeed, we would no longer be able to recog-nize ourselves as human. Accordingly, Sellars, echoing Kant, concludes that we have no option but to insist that the manifest image enjoys a *practical*, if not theoretical, priority over the scientific image, since it provides the source for the norm of rational purposiveness, which we cannot do without. In this regard, the genuine philosophical task, according to Sellars, would consist in achieving a properly *stereoscopic* integration of the manifest and scientific images, such that the language of rational intention would come to enrich scientific theory so as to allow the latter to be directly wedded to human purposes.

1.2   The instrumentalization of the scientific image

It should come as no surprise then that the manifest image continues to provide the fundamental framework within which much contempo-rary philosophizing is carried out. It encompasses not only 'the major schools of contemporary Continental thought' – by which Sellars, writing at the beginning of the 1960s, presumably meant phe-nomenology and existentialism, to which we should add critical theory, hermeneutics, and post-structuralism – but also 'the trends of contem-porary British and American philosophy which emphasize the analysis of "common sense" and "ordinary usage" [...] For all these philosophies can be fruitfully construed as more or less adequate accounts of the manifest image of man-in-the-world, which accounts are then taken to be an adequate and full description in general terms of what man and the world really are' (Sellars 1963a: 8). Despite their otherwise intractable differences, what all these philosophies share is a more or less profound hostility to the idea that the scientific image describes 'what there really is', that it has an ontological purchase capable of undermining man's manifest self-conception as a person or intentional agent. Ultimately, all the philosophies carried out under the aegis of the manifest image – whether they acknowledge its existence or not – are united by the common conviction that 'all the postulated entities of the scientific image [e.g., elementary particles, neurophysiological mechanisms, evolutionary processes, etc.] are symbolic tools which function (something like the distance-measuring devices which are rolled around on maps) to help us find our way around in the world, but do not themselves describe actual objects or processes' (Sellars 1963a: 32). This *instrumentalist* conception of science is the inevitable corollary of any philosophy that insists on the irrecusable primacy of man's manifest self-understanding. Thus, although they are the totems of two otherwise divergent philosophical traditions, the two 'canonical' twentieth-century philosophers, Heidegger and Wittgenstein, share the conviction that the manifest image enjoys a philosophical privilege vis-à-vis the scientific image, and that the sorts of entities and processes postulated by scientific theory are in some way founded upon, or derivative of, our more 'originary', pre-scientific understanding, whether this be construed in terms of our 'being-in-the-world', or our practical engagement in 'language-games'. From there, one may or may not decide to take the short additional step which consists in denouncing the scientific image as a cancerous excrescence of the manifest image (this is a theme to which we shall have occasion to return in chapters 2 and 3).

To his considerable credit, Sellars adamantly refused this instrumentalization of the scientific image. For as he pointed out, the fact that the manifest image enjoys a *methodological* primacy as the originary framework from which the scientific image developed in no way legitimates attempts to ascribe a substantive primacy to it. In other words, even if the scientific image remains methodologically dependent upon the manifest image, this in no way undermines its substantive autonomy vis-à-vis the latter. In this regard, it should be pointed out (although Sellars does not do so) that to construe scientific theory as an efflorescence from the more fundamental phenomenological and/or pragmatic substratum of our manifest being-in-the-world is to endorse a form of philosophical reductionism with regard to science. Yet unlike its oft-criticized scientific counterpart, the tenets of which are fairly explicit, even when it cannot carry out in fact the reductions it claims to be able to perform in principle, partisans of this philosophical reductionism about science conspicuously avoid delineating the conceptual criteria in accordance with which the structures of the scientific image might be reduced to the workings of the manifest image. Unsurprisingly, those who would instrumentalize the scientific image prefer to remain silent about the chasm that separates the trivial assertion that scientific theorizing supervenes on pre-scientific practice, from the far-from-trivial demonstration which would explain precisely how, for example, quantum mechanics is a function of our ability to wield hammers.

Sellars never succumbed to the lure of this crass philosophical reductionism with regard to the scientific image, insisting that philosophy should resist attempts to subsume the scientific image within the manifest image. At the same time, Sellars enjoined philosophers to abstain from the opposite temptation, which would consist in trying to supplant the manifest image with the scientific one. For Sellars, this cannot be an option, since it would entail depriving ourselves of what makes us human. However, it is important to note that the very terms in which Sellars formulated his hoped for synthesis between the manifest and scientific images continue to assume the incorrigibility of the characterization of rational purposiveness concomitant with the Jonesean theory of agency. Yet it is precisely this model of rational-purposive agency – along with the accompanying recommendation that the scientific image should be tethered to purposes commensurate with the workings of the manifest image – which some contemporary philosophers who refuse to sideline the scientific image are calling into question. These philosophers propose instead – obviously disregarding the Sellarsian edict – that the manifest image be integrated into the scientific image. While for Sellars it was precisely the manifest image's theoretical status which ensured its normative autonomy, and hence its ineliminability as an account of the nature of rational agency, for Paul Churchland, an ex-student of Sellars who has explicitly acknowledged the latter's influence,[4] the manifest image is revisable precisely because it is a corrigible speculative achievement that cannot be accepted as the definitive account of 'rational purposiveness'. Indeed, for Churchland, there is no guarantee that the latter notion indexes anything real independently of the particular theoretical framework embodied in the manifest image. Though the manifest image undeniably marked a significant cognitive achievement in the cultural development of humankind, it can no longer remain insulated from critical scrutiny. And while the adoption of the propositional attitude idiom in subjective reports seems to have endowed the manifest image with a quasi-sacrosanct status, lending it an aura of incorrigible authenticity, this merely obscures its inherently speculative status. Thus, Churchland invites us to envisage the following possibility:

> [A] spontaneous introspective judgement is just an instance of an acquired habit of conceptual response to one's internal states, and the integrity of any particular response is always contingent on the integrity of the acquired conceptual framework (theory) in which the response is framed. Accordingly, one's own *introspective* certainty that one's mind is the seat of beliefs and desires [or 'purposes'] may be as badly misplaced as was the classical man's *visual* certainty that the star-flecked sphere of the heavens turns daily.
>
> (P. M. Churchland 1989: 3)

Where Sellars believed stereoscopic integration of the two images could be achieved by wedding the mechanistic discourse of causation to the rational language of intention, Churchland proposes to supplant the latter altogether via a *neurocomputational* enhancement of the scientific image which would effectively allow it to annex the manifest image, thereby forcing us to revise our understanding of ourselves as autonomous rational agents or 'persons'. However, as we shall see below, Churchland's attempt to annex the manifest image to the scientific image is vitiated by a fundamental epistemological tension. Like Sellars, Churchland emphatically rejects the instrumentalist conception of science concomitant with the ontological prioritization of the manifest image: he claims to be a scientific realist. But as we shall see, his realism about science is mined at every turn by his pragmatist construal of representation.

1.3 Cognitive catastrophe: Paul Churchland

In his now-canonical 1981 paper 'Eliminative Materialism and the Propositional Attitudes',[5] Churchland summarizes eliminative materialism (EM) as:

> the thesis that our commonsense conception of psychological phenomena constitutes a radically false theory, a theory so fundamentally defective that both the principles and the ontology of that theory will eventually be displaced, rather than smoothly reduced, by completed neuroscience. Our mutual understanding and even our introspection may then be reconstituted within the conceptual framework

of completed neuroscience, a theory we may expect to be more powerful by far than the commonsense psychology it displaces, and more
substantially integrated within physical science generally.

(P. M. Churchland, 1989: 1)

Unsurprisingly, the claim that commonsense psychology may be false
has tended to provoke alarm, especially (though by no means exclusively) among philosophers who have devoted their entire careers to the
task of integrating it into the ambit of natural science. Thus Jerry Fodor
has remarked, 'If commonsense intentional psychology were really to
collapse that would be, beyond comparison, the greatest intellectual
catastrophe in the history of the species.'[6] Since professional philosophers of mind are not generally known for their apocalyptic proclivities,
the claim that one of their number might be harbouring the instrument
of 'the greatest intellectual catastrophe in the history of the species'
cannot but command our attention. Contemporary philosophy of mind
is a domain of often highly technical controversies between specialists
divided by allegiances to competing research programmes, but where
the truth or falsity of the eliminativist hypothesis is concerned, the
stakes would seem to transcend the bounds of this particular sub-
discipline and to have an immediate bearing upon human culture at
large. For what Churchland is proposing is nothing short of a cultural
revolution: the reconstruction of our manifest self-image in the light of
a new scientific discourse. What is at stake in EM is nothing less than
the future of human self-understanding.

Churchland's formulation of the eliminativist hypothesis[7] can be
boiled down to four claims:

1. Folk-psychology (FP) is a theory, hence susceptible to evaluation in
   terms of truth and falsity.
2. FP also encodes a set of practices, which can be evaluated in terms of
   their practical efficacy vis-à-vis the functions which FP is supposed
   to serve.
3. FP will prove irreducible to emerging neuroscience.
4. FP's neuroscientific replacement will exhibit practical as well as
   theoretical superiority over its predecessor.

Given these premises, Churchland cites three basic regards in which FP
has shown itself to be profoundly unsatisfactory:

1. There are a significant number of phenomena for which FP is
   incapable of providing either a coherent explanation or successful

prediction: e.g., the range of cognitive fractionation engendered by brain damage, the precise aetiology and typology of mental illness, the specific cognitive mechanisms involved in scientific discovery and artistic creativity.

2. FP is theoretically stagnant, it has conspicuously failed to develop in step with the rapidly accelerating rate of cultural evolution or evolve in accordance with the novel cognitive requirements imposed by advanced technological societies.

3. FP is increasingly isolated and anomalous with regard to the corpus of the natural sciences; specifically, it is conceptually irreducible to the emerging discourse of cognitive neuroscience.

Critics of EM have responded to each of these charges using a variety of argumentative strategies. They have denied that FP is a theory in the scientific sense and hence that it can be evaluated in terms of 'truth' or 'falsity', or indicted for its failure to explain anomalous psychological phenomena. They have denied that it is stagnant or anachronistic in the face of technological evolution or that it can be judged according to some superior standard of practical efficacy. Finally, they have challenged the claim that reduction is the only way of ensuring the integrity of natural science.[8]

Rather than recapitulate Churchland's premises and the objections to them individually, I shall consider the EM hypothesis from four different angles: (1) the nature of Churchland's neurocomputational alternative to FP; (2) the charge that EM is self-refuting; (3) the latent tension between Churchland's allegiance to scientific realism and his irrealism about the folk-psychological account of representation; (4) the accusation that EM, and reductionist science more generally, is incapable of acknowledging the reality of phenomenal consciousness.

1.4   The neurocomputational alternative

Churchland defines FP in the following way:

'Folk psychology' denotes the pre-scientific, commonsense conceptual framework that all normally socialized humans deploy in order to comprehend, predict, explain and manipulate the behavior of humans and the higher animals. This framework includes concepts such as belief, desire, pain, pleasure, love, hate, joy, fear, suspicion, memory, recognition, anger, sympathy, intention, and so forth. It embodies our baseline understanding of the cognitive, affective, and purposive nature of people. Considered as a whole, it constitutes our conception of what a person is.

(P. M. Churchland 1998b: 3)

As we saw above, it was Sellars who provided the basis for Churchland's characterization of FP as a quasi-scientific theory within which the notion of 'personhood' plays a central role. However, Sellars introduced propositional attitudes as *functional* kinds, leaving their ontological status deliberately indeterminate. But for Churchland, to attribute causal efficacy to functional kinds is already to have endowed them with an ontological status. What he considers problematic is not the functional role account of psychological kinds, but rather the premise that FP provides anything like a reliable catalogue of psychological functioning. Yet Churchland's antipathy to the characterization of propositional attitudes as functional kinds stems not so much from an antipathy to functionalism per se but rather from a deep suspicion about the reliability of FP as a guide to the individuation of the salient psychological types. Thus, his own neurocomputational alternative to FP proposes a different approach to the task of identifying psychological functions. By way of contrast to the 'top-down' approach to the study of cognition, for which linguistic behaviour is paradigmatic, Churchland champions a 'bottom-up' approach which seeks to ascend from neurobiologically realistic models of rudimentary sensory-motor behaviours to the more sophisticated varieties of linguistically mediated cognitive activity.

Consequently, Churchland proposes to replace FP, according to which cognition is conceived of as an intrinsically linguistic medium structured through the 'sentential dance' of propositional attitudes, with a new model drawing on the resources of connectionist neuroscience. According to this new paradigm, the internal kinematics of cognition find expression in activation patterns across populations of neurons, as opposed to sententially articulated structures, while its dynamics reside in vector-to-vector transformations driven by learned configurations of synaptic connection, as opposed to deductive inferences governed by relations of logical entailment from one sentence to another. Thus, while the brain's basic unit of representation is the activation vector, its fundamental computational operation is the vector-to-vector transformation, as performed on those configurations of neuronal activation. Crucially, according to this paradigm, a 'theory' is no longer to be understood as a linguaformal system of propositions connected to one another by relations of logical entailment; it consists rather in a determinate partitioning of vector space into a manifold of prototypical divisions and sub-divisions relative to typically reiterated inputs.

Nevertheless, it is important to emphasize how, for all its claims to greater biological plausibility, this new 'prototype vector activation' (PVA) model of cognition remains a computational idealization. In this regard, it perpetuates the functionalist distinction between psychological types and their material instantiation. But where traditional functionalism modelled this distinction in terms of the difference between an abstract computational state (characterized in terms of some Turing machine state) and its biophysical instantiation, it is configured here in terms of the distinction between weight space and vector space. While the weight configuration uniquely determines the partitioning of vector space, only the latter is to be identified with the theory or conceptual scheme in terms of which a network represents the world. Thus it is by acquiring a determinate configuration in synaptic weight space that a brain comes to achieve a specific prototypical partitioning of its vector activation space. And it is this partitioning of vector space, rather than that configuration of synaptic weights, which provides the functional index for the theory in terms of which the brain represents the world. As Churchland puts it:

> People react to the world in similar ways not because their underlying weight configurations are closely similar on a synapse-by-synapse comparison, but because their activation spaces are similarly partitioned. Like trees similar in their gross physical profile, brains can be similar in their gross functional profiles while being highly idiosyncratic in the myriad details of their fine-grained arborization.
>
> (P.M. Churchland 1989: 234)

It should be remarked at this juncture that Churchland's claims on behalf of this model's greater degree of biological realism have not gone unchallenged. Churchland invokes a relation of 'resemblance' between these so-called neural networks and brain-structure without specifying what the relation consists in or what the criterion for 'resemblance' might be. The putative 'analogy' between the units of a network and the neurons of a brain provide no guarantee that the network's instantiation of a vector prototype will be isomorphic with the brain's instantiation of a psychological type. Moreover, the unification of psychological categories remains autonomous with regard to the neurobiological level. John Marshall and Jennifer Gurd[9] have pointed out that pathology reveals fractionations of psychological functioning which provide constraints on the organization of cognitive function. Behavioural disorders index functional categories which are subject to different neurological instantiations – different physical aetiologies can engender identical cognitive disorders. So although cognitive function is undeniably related to neurological structure, it cannot be straightforwardly reduced to it. Thus while Churchland is undoubtedly right to emphasize the desirability of adopting a bottom-up approach to psychological research, he faces two difficulties.

First, the empirical 'resemblance' between brains and neural nets is no guarantee that the latter are inherently superior to other, less neurologically 'realistic' models of cognition. For it is the nature of the appropriate criterion for 'realism' that is in question here: should it be neurobiological? Or psychological? Churchland cannot simply assume that the two necessarily overlap.

Second, in the absence of any adequate understanding of the precise nature of the correlation between psychological function and neural structure, whatever putative resemblance might obtain between neural architecture and network architecture sheds no light whatsoever on the relation between the latter and the abstract functional architecture of cognition. Where network architecture is concerned, although some degree of biological plausibility is desirable, empirical data alone are not sufficient when it comes to identifying the salient functional characteristics of cognition.[10]

We will not pursue this issue further here. But we must now consider a still more damaging objection which is frequently raised against EM: that its very formulation is fundamentally incoherent.

1.5   The 'paradox' of eliminativism

Sellars was arguably the first philosopher to discern in the logical infrastructure of folk-psychological discourse, with its relations of inferential entailment, what has since been brandished as the emblem of FP's irreducibility to neurobiological or physical explanation: ascriptions of belief and desire inscribe the explananda within a normative (conceptual) space of reasons which cannot be reduced to or encompassed by the natural (material) space of causes. This supposed distinction between the putatively 'rational-normative' character of FP discourse and the merely 'causal-material' factors invoked in reductive explanation has tempted many philosophers to attribute some sort of quasi-transcendental, and hence necessarily ineliminable status to the

FP framework. Indeed, the notion that FP is necessarily ineliminable because it enjoys some sort of quasi-transcendental status motivates what is surely the most popular attempt at a knock-down 'refutation' of EM. Consider the following argument: the eliminative materialist claims to deny the existence of 'beliefs' (and of 'meaning' more generally). But to do so he must believe what he claims (or 'mean' what he says). Thus his belief that there are no beliefs is itself an instance of belief, just as the intelligibility of his claim that there is no such thing as meaning itself relies on the reality of the meaning which it claims to deny. Consequently, the proponent of EM is guilty of a performative contradiction.[11] It is important to see why this attempt to indict the eliminativist of self-contradiction is dubious from a purely logical point of view and otherwise suspect on broader philosophical grounds. From a purely formal point of view, the logic of the EM argument certainly appears to conform to the familiar structure of proof by reductio ad absurdum: it assumes Q (the framework of FP assumptions), then argues legitimately from Q and some supplementary empirical premises (which we shall describe below) to the conclusion that not-Q, and then concludes not-Q by the principle of reductio. There are no glaring or obvious anomalies here. Anyone wishing to denounce eliminativism as self-refuting using this stratagem should be wary lest they find themselves unwittingly indicting all arguments by reductio on the grounds that they too begin by assuming what they wish to deny. For the 'self-refuting' objection against EM to be sound, its scope would have to be such as to successfully invalidate all argument proceeding by reductio as necessarily incoherent. Although this may turn out to be possible (even if it is extremely doubtful), there is certainly nothing in the attempted refutation as it stands to even hint at how this could be done. Consequently there is every reason to suspect the fault lies in the 'self-refuting' argument against EM, rather than in EM's argumentation by reductio per se (cf. P.M. Churchland 1998b: 28–30).

In fact the crucial sleight of hand in this attempted 'refutation' of EM occurs in the second step, specifically the claim that 'the eliminativist's belief that there are no beliefs is itself an instance of belief, just as the intelligibility of his claim that there is no such thing as meaning itself relies on the reality of the meaning which it claims to deny'. But the intelligibility of EM does not in fact depend upon the reality of 'belief' and 'meaning' thus construed. For it is precisely the claim that 'beliefs' provide the necessary form of cognitive content, and that propositional 'meaning' is the necessary medium for semantic content, that the eliminativist denies. Thus Churchland's claim is not that there is no such thing as 'meaning' but rather that our spontaneous experience of 'understanding' what we mean in terms of propositional attitude FP does not provide a reliable guide for grasping what Churchland calls 'the underlying kinematics and dynamics' of meaning. According to Churchland's neurocomputational alternative to FP,

> [A]ny declarative sentence to which a speaker would give confident assent is merely a one-dimensional projection – through the compound lens of Wernicke's and Broca's areas onto the idiosyncratic surface of the speaker's language – of a four or five dimensional 'solid' that is an element in his true kinematical state. Being projections of that inner reality, such sentences do carry significant information regarding it and are thus fit to function as elements in a communication system. On the other hand, being subdimensional projections, they reflect but a narrow part of the reality projected. They are therefore unfit to represent the deeper reality in all its kinematically, dynamically, and even normatively relevant respects.
>
> (P. M. Churchland 1989: 18)

We shall see later just how troublesome this invocation of a 'normative' aspect to these multi-dimensional dynamics will prove to be for Churchland. Nevertheless, at this juncture, what should be retained from this particular passage is the following: Churchland is not simply claiming that there is no such thing as meaning *tout court* – a misleading impression admittedly encouraged by some of his more careless formulations – but rather that 'beliefs' (such as 'that FP is false') and 'propositions' (such as 'FP is false') are rendered possible by representations whose complex multi-dimensional structure is not adequately reflected in the structure of a propositional attitude such as a 'belief', and whose underlying semantics cannot be sentially encapsulated. The dispute between EM and FP concerns the nature of representations, not their existence. EM proposes an alternative account of the nature of representations; it is no part of its remit to deny that such representations occur.

Ultimately, the question-begging character of the 'self-refuting' objection to EM becomes readily apparent when we see how easily it could be adapted to block the displacement of any conceptual framework whatsoever by spuriously transcendentalizing whatever explanatory principle (or principles) happens to enjoy a monopoly in it at any given time. Patricia Churchland provides the following example, in which a proponent of vitalism attempts to refute anti-vitalism using similar tactics: 'The anti-vitalist claims there is no such thing as vital spirit. But if the claim is true the speaker cannot be animated by the vital spirit. Consequently he must be dead. But if he is dead then his claim is a meaningless string of noises, devoid of reason and truth.'[12] Here as before, the very criterion of intelligibility whose pertinence for understanding a given phenomenon – 'life' in this case, 'meaning' in the previous one – is being called into question, is evoked in order to dismiss the challenge to it. But just as anti-vitalism does not deny the existence of the various phenomena grouped together under the heading of 'life', but rather a particular way of explaining what they have in common, EM does not deny the reality of the phenomena subsumed under the heading of 'meaning' (or 'consciousness'), but rather a specific way of explaining their characteristic features.

Obviously, the key claim here is that the possibilities of 'intelligibility' (or 'cognitive comprehension') are not exhaustively or exclusively mapped by a specific conceptual register, and particularly not by that of supposedly intuitive, pre-theoretical commonsense. In this regard, Churchland's point, following Sellars, is that the register of intelligibility commensurate with what we take to be 'pre-theoretical common-sense', specifically in the case of our own self-understanding, is itself theoretically saturated, even if long familiarity has rendered its speculative character invisible to us. Though science has immeasurably enriched our understanding of phenomena by way of techniques and resources quite foreign to commonsense, as those resources begin to be deployed closer to home in the course of the investigation into the nature of mind, they begin to encroach on a realm of phenomena hitherto deemed to have lain beyond the purview of science, specifically, the phenomena grouped together under the heading of 'meaning', which for many philosophers harbour the key to grasping what makes us 'human'. The issue then is whether, as these philosophers insist, science is constitutively incapable of providing a satisfactory account of what we mean by 'meaning', or whether it is the authority of our pre-scientific intuitions about 'meaning' and 'meaningfulness' that needs to be called into question. In debates surrounding EM, it is important to dissociate these broader issues concerning the question of cognitive priority in the relation between the scope of scientific explanation and the authority of our pre-scientific self-understanding from the narrower issues pertaining to EM's own specific internal consistency. As we shall see, the vicissitudes of the latter do not necessarily vindicate those who would uphold the former.

1.6   From the superempirical to the metaphysical

The most serious problem confronting Churchland's version of EM resides in the latent tension between his commitment to scientific realism on one hand, and his adherence to a metaphysical naturalism on the other. To understand why this is the case, it is necessary to appreciate the two-tiered relation between Churchland's PVA paradigm and the linguaformal or folk-psychological accounts it is intended to displace. On the one hand, Churchland explicitly or empirically posits the explanatory excellence of the PVA model on the grounds of what he calls its 'superempirical virtues': conceptual simplicity, explanatory unity, and theoretical cohesiveness (P.M. Churchland 1989: 139–51). On the other hand, that excellence is implicitly or metaphysically presupposed as guaranteed a priori by an adaptationist rationale for the congruence between representation and reality.

Thus, although Churchland's PVA model of cognition remains explicitly representational – with propositional attitudes being supplanted by vector prototypes – it is one wherein representation no longer operates under the normative aegis of truth-as-correspondence. In lieu of truth, Churchland proposes to discriminate between theories on the basis of these super-empirical virtues of ontological simplicity, conceptual coherence, and explanatory power: 'As I see it then, values such as ontological simplicity, coherence and explanatory power are among the brain's most basic criteria for recognizing information, for distinguishing information from noise' (P. M. Churchland 1989: 147).[13] But as a result, Churchland is obliged to ascribe degrees of neurocomputational adequation between representation and represented without reintroducing a substantive difference between true and false kinds of representation. For by Churchland's own lights, there are no substantive, which is to say ontological, differences between theories: all theories, including FP, consist in a specific partitioning of a brain's vector activation space.[14] Yet there is a noticeable tension between Churchland's insistence that theories are to be discriminated between solely on the basis of differences in degree of superempirical virtue, rather than in representational kind, and his conviction that the PVA paradigm which reveals this underlying neurocomputational structure common to all representations exhibits such an elevated degree of superiority vis-à-vis FP in the realm of superempirical virtue as to necessitate the latter's elimination. As a result, Churchland's case for eliminativism oscillates between the claim that it is entirely a matter of empirical expediency,[15] and the argument that seems to point to the logical necessity of eliminating FP by invoking the PVA model's intrinsically metaphysical superiority. It is this tension between eliminativism's avowals of empirical humility and its unavowed metaphysical presumptions which we now propose to examine in greater detail.

On the one hand, since 'folk-semantical' notions as 'truth' and 'reference'[16] no longer function as guarantors of adequation between 'representation' and 'reality', as they did in the predominantly folk-psychological acceptation of theoretical adequation – which sees the latter as consisting in a set of word-world correspondences – there is an important sense in which all theoretical paradigms are neurocomputationally equal. They are equal insofar as there is nothing in a partitioning of vector space per se which could serve to explain why one theory is 'better' than another. All are to be gauged exclusively in terms of their superempirical virtues, viz., according to the greater or lesser degree of efficiency with which they enable the organism to adapt successfully to its environment. In other words, if all 'theories' are instances of vector activation, and if the PVA paradigm – to which all other theoretical paradigms reduce according to Churchland – dispenses with the notion of theoretical 'truth', then we are obliged to stipulate that theories be judged pragmatically in terms of the greater or lesser degree of adaptational efficiency with which they enable the organism to flourish:

> [I]f we are to reconsider truth as the aim or product of cognitive activity, I think we must reconsider its applicability right across the board [...] That is, if we are to move away from the more naïve formulations of scientific realism, we should move in the direction of pragmatism rather than positivistic instrumentalism [...] it is far from obvious that truth is either the primary or the principal product of [cognitive] activity. Rather, its function would appear to be the ever more finely tuned administration of the organism's behaviour.
>
> (P. M. Churchland 1989: 149–50)

Thus, Churchland is perfectly explicit in explaining why he considers the PVA paradigm of cognition to be 'better' than its folk-psychological rivals, and he proposes a precise formula for gauging theoretical excellence. Global excellence of theory is measured by straightforwardly pragmatic virtues: maximal explanatory cohesiveness vis-à-vis maximal empirical heterogeneity purchased via minimal conceptual expenditure. One theory is 'better' than another if it affords greater theoretical cohesiveness along with greater explanatory unity while using fewer conceptual means to synthesize a wider assortment of data.

But the problem for Churchland is that it remains deeply unclear in precisely what way the extent of an organism's adaptational efficiency, as revealed by the degree to which its representation of the world exhibits the superempirical virtues of simplicity, unity, and coherence, could ever be 'read off' its brain's neurocomputational microstructure. In what sense precisely are theoretical virtues such as simplicity, unity, and coherence necessarily concomitant at the neurological level with an organism's reproductively advantageous behaviour? Churchland simply stipulates that the aforementioned virtues are already a constitutive feature of the brain's functional architecture without offering anything in the way of argument regarding how and why it is that a neural network's learned configuration in synaptic weight space is necessarily constrained by the imperatives of unity, cohesion, and simplicity. Indeed, Churchland frequently adduces empirical data that would seem to imply the opposite: viz., his discussion of the ways in which a network can stop learning by becoming trapped within a merely local minimum in its global error gradient (P. M. Churchland 1989: 192–4) Perhaps Churchland's reticence in this regard is a matter of caution. For in order to make a case for the neurocomputational necessity of superempirical virtues, Churchland would need to demonstrate that the latter are indeed strictly information theoretic constraints intrinsic to the vector coding process, as opposed to extrinsic regulatory considerations contingently imposed on the network in the course of its ongoing interaction with the environment. However, in pursuing this particular line of argument, Churchland immediately finds himself confronted by a choice between two unappealing alternatives.

The first alternative follows inescapably from the fact that, by Churchland's own admission, the process of informational transduction via which the brain processes incoming stimuli is physically demarcated by the boundaries of the organism. Beyond those boundaries lies the world. Thus, if Churchland tries to integrate the superempirical virtues into the neurocomputational process by pushing the brain's coding activity out beyond the physical boundaries of the organism so that they become constitutive features of the world, he is forced into the uncomfortable position of having to claim that the physical world is neurocomputationally constituted. Since for Churchland perception and conception are neurocomputationally continuous, the result is a kind of empirical idealism: the brain represents the world but cannot be conditioned by the world in return because the latter will 'always already' have been neurocomputationally represented. We are left with a thoroughgoing idealism whereby the brain constitutes the physical world without it being possible to explain either how the brain comes to be part of the world, or indeed even how the world could have originally produced the brain.

Alternatively, instead of trying to achieve a neurocomputational reduction of the superempirical virtues by projecting the brain's coding activity out onto the environing world, Churchland can abjure the notion of an absolute physical boundary between world and information as already coded by the brain's prototypical vector partitions in order to allow the physical world to reach 'into' the brain, thereby allowing a pre-constituted physical reality to play an intrinsic role in neurological activity. But in widening the focus of his epistemological vision in this way, Churchland will be obliged to abandon the representationalist dualism of brain and world, and to forsake his deliberately neurocentric perspective in order to adopt a more global or meta-neurological – which is to say, meta-physical – perspective. Clearly, however, such a shift threatens to undermine the categorical distinction between processor and processed, network and world, which is fundamental to Churchland's account. Since this distinction underlies Churchland's commitment to neurobiological reductionism, and underwrites all his arguments for eliminativism, we cannot expect him to find this second alternative any more appealing than the first.

Thus, Churchland cannot effect a neurocomputational reduction of superempirical virtue without engendering a neurological idealism, and he cannot reintegrate the neurocomputational brain into the wider realm of superempirical virtue without abandoning eliminativism altogether. Nevertheless, let us, for the sake of argument, set the former of these two difficulties aside for the moment and suppose that Churchland were to manage a successful but non-idealizing reduction of superempirical virtue. The trouble then is that in arguing that simplicity, unity, and coherence are constitutive functional features of the brain's neuroanatomy, Churchland is but one slippery step away from claiming that brains represent the world correctly as a matter of evolutionary necessity, i.e. that they necessarily have 'true' representations. Unfortunately, this is precisely the sort of claim that Churchland had sworn to abjure: 'Natural selection does not care whether a brain has or tends towards true beliefs, so long as the organism reliably exhibits reproductively advantageous behavior' (P. M. Churchland 1989: 150).

Consequently, everything hinges on whether the superempirical virtues are a precondition or a by-product of the organism's 'reproductively advantageous behavior'. Churchland implies the former, on the basis of what appears to be a latent brand of neurocomputational idealism, whereas all available empirical (i.e. evolutionary) evidence seems to point to the latter, and hence towards a less neurocentric account of representation. From the perspective of the latter, that successful networks do indeed tend to exhibit these superempirical characteristics as a matter of empirical fact is uncontroversial, but it is a fact about cognitive ethology, which is to say, a fact which makes sense only within the macrophysical purview of evolutionary biology and in the context of the relation between organism and environment, rather than a fact obtaining within the microphysical or purely information-theoretic ambit of the brain's neurocomputational functioning. That the macrophysical fact has a microphysical analogue, that the ethological imperative is neurologically encoded, is precisely what we might expect having suspended the premise of an absolute representational cleavage between the micro and macrophysical dimensions, and accepted the extent to which these must remain not only physically conterminous, but bound together by reciprocal presupposition.

Thus, considered by itself, the neurocomputational encoding of superempirical virtue is not enough to vindicate Churchland. For Churchland's account is predicated on the idealist premise that neurocomputational representation is the necessary precondition for adaptational success, that neurocomputational function determines evolutionary ethology. Consequently, and in the absence of some non-question-begging account as to how macrophysical facts pertaining to evolutionary ethology ultimately supervene on microphysical facts about the brain's neurocomputational functioning, it seems that the superempirical virtues Churchland invokes in order to discriminate between theories must remain extra-neurological characteristics, characteristics which reveal themselves only in the course of an ethological analysis of the organism's cognitive behaviour within the world, rather than via a neurological analysis of the brain's microstructure.

Accordingly, the tension between eliminativism's avowals of empirical humility and its latent metaphysical pretensions reveals itself when it becomes apparent that the pragmatic or superempirical virtues in terms of which Churchland proposes to discriminate between theories cannot be accounted for exclusively in neurocomputational terms. The superempirical virtues seem to exceed the neurocentric remit of the neurocomputational economy. And it is in trying to accommodate them that Churchland begins unwittingly to drift away from the rigidly empirical premises that provide the naturalistic rationale for eliminativism towards a metaphysical stance wherein the PVA model begins to take on all the characteristics of a metaphysical a priori. As a result, the tenor of the argument for the elimination of FP shifts from that of empirical assessment to that of metaphysical imperative.

For presumably, were Churchland correct in maintaining that the superempirical virtues of ontological simplicity, conceptual coherence, and explanatory power are, as he puts it, 'among the brain's most basic criteria for recognizing information, for distinguishing information from noise', then a conceptual framework as baroque, as obfuscatory, and as allegedly incoherent as FP would have been eliminated as a matter of evolutionary routine, and Churchland would have been spared the trouble of militating so brilliantly for its displacement. If superempirical virtues were already endogenously specified and intrinsic to the brain's neurocomputational microstructure, then it would appear to be a matter of neurophysiological impossibility for an organism to embody any theory wholly lacking in these virtues. Paradoxically, it is the eliminativist's supposition that the former are intrinsically encoded in the brain's cognitive microstructure that ends up considerably narrowing the extent for the degree of superempirical distinction between theories, ultimately undermining the strength of the case against FP. Thus, although Churchland's trenchant critique of philosophies which insist on transcendentalizing FP as an epistemological sine qua non is well taken, it would seem that, whatever else is wrong with it, FP cannot be as chronically deficient in the superempirical virtues as Churchland requires in order to render the argument for its elimination incontrovertible – certainly not deficient enough to explain why Churchland insists on ascribing such a dramatic degree of superempirical superiority to the PVA paradigm.

Thus, even as the PVA paradigm continues to insist that all theories are neurocomputationally equal inasmuch as all display greater or lesser degrees of superempirical distinction, EM insinuates that the PVA paradigm is nevertheless more equal, more pragmatic, more superempirically virtuous than all previous folk-psychological paradigms of cognition. What underlies this claim to radical superiority? Given that Churchland seems to accept Quine's thesis that theories are underdetermined by empirical evidence (P. M. Churchland 1989: 139–51), the superiority of the PVA paradigm cannot be held to reside in any precisely quantifiable increase in the efficiency with which it enables the human organism to process information. For according to Churchland, there can be no absolute – which is to say, theory neutral – measure of superiority when we compare the degree of adaptational efficiency bestowed upon organisms by the theories they incorporate. By transforming the data it purports to explain, every theory shifts the empirical goalposts as far as adaptational efficiency is concerned.[17] Thus, it is perfectly possible to envisage the possibility of 'subtler' or more 'refined' versions of folk-psychological theory endowing organisms with all the additional discriminatory capacities, conceptual enhancements, and explanatory advantages of the PVA paradigm favoured by Churchland.[18]

But if this is the case, it suggests that, for Churchland, the putative superiority of the vector activation paradigm is 'meta-empirical' in a sense which is more than pragmatic and quite irreducible to those super-empirical virtues in terms of which Churchland discerns theoretical excellence: a sense which is meta-physical rather than merely super-empirical. This is to say that Churchland holds the PVA paradigm to be irrecusably superior to all available linguaformal alternatives simply because he implicitly supposes that it alone is capable of furnishing a genuinely universal explanation of cognition that encompasses all others. Thus, all theories are equally instances of vector activation, but the vector activation theory of vector activation is *more equal* because it is revealed as the precondition for all the others. Accordingly, the PVA paradigm is at once the latest in a historically embedded empirical sequence, and the latent precondition which explains the veritable character of the succession of paradigms encompassed in that sequence. The PVA paradigm is the universal prototype of which all other models of cognition are merely instantiations. In Hegelese, we might say that the latter are instances of vector coding in themselves, but not yet *in and for themselves*. For Churchland explicitly claims that he has found the veritable material instantiation of what Kuhn called a 'paradigm'[19]: this is precisely what a network's prototypical partitioning of vector activation space is. And we should also bear in mind that a paradigm in Kuhn's sense – just as in Churchland's meta-physically transformed sense – is as much a metaphysical 'factum' as an empirical 'datum'. Thus, a network's prototypical vector configuration is at once an empirical fact, and the precondition for anything's coming to count as an empirical fact, for it is what predefines the parameters for all perceptual judgement. In other words, Churchland's neurocomputational paradigm is at once empirically given as an intra-historical datum, but also, and in the very same gesture, posited as an a priori, supra-historical factum that furnishes us with the supposedly universal explanatory precondition for our ability to recognize and explain the historical sequence of paradigm shifts for what they were: changing configurations in vector space.[20]

Ultimately then, Churchland cannot provide a coherent account of the relation between network and world because he lacks any resources for establishing the correlation independently of his prototype vector paradigm. A model of representation cannot be at once a representation of the world and what establishes the possibility of that representation. It cannot represent the world and represent that representation. In Churchland's work, this dichotomy becomes inescapable in the tension between his determination to be a realist about scientific representation while remaining a pragmatist about the genesis of scientific representation in general. But this is not just a problem for Churchland; it vitiates the variety of philosophical naturalism which draws its account of the nature of science from one or other variety of evolutionary adaptationism. As Fodor rightly insists, the success of adaptationist rationales in explanations of organic functioning does not provide a legitimate warrant for co-opting the former in order to account for cognitive functioning.[21]

The trouble with Churchland's naturalism is not so much that it is metaphysical, but that it is an impoverished metaphysics, inadequate to the task of grounding the relation between representation and reality. Moreover, Churchland's difficulties in this regard are symptomatic of a wider problem concerning the way in which philosophical naturalism frames its own relation to science. While vague talk of rendering philosophy consistent with 'the findings of our best sciences' remains entirely commendable, it tends to distract attention away from the amount of philosophical work required in order to render these findings metaphysically coherent. The goal is surely to devise a metaphysics worthy of the sciences, and here neither empiricism nor pragmatism are likely to prove adequate to the task. Science need no more defer to empiricism's enthronement of 'experience' than to naturalism's hypostatization of 'nature'. Both remain entirely extraneous to science's *subtractive* modus operandi. From the perspective of the latter, both the invocation of 'experience' qua realm of 'originary intuitions' and the appeal to 'nature' qua domain of autonomous functions are irrelevant. We shall try to explain in subsequent chapters how science subtracts nature from experience, the better to uncover the objective void of being. But if, as we are contending here, the principal task of contemporary philosophy is to draw out the ultimate speculative implications of the logic of Enlightenment, then the former cannot allow itself to be seduced into contriving ever more sophistical proofs for the transcendental inviolability of the manifest image. Nor should it resign itself to espousing naturalism and taking up residence in the scientific image in the hope of winning promotion to the status of cognitive science. Above all, it should not waste time trying to effect some sort of synthesis or reconciliation between the manifest and scientific images. The philosophical consummation of Enlightenment consists in expediting science's demolition of the manifest image by kicking away whatever pseudo-transcendental props are being used to shore it up or otherwise inhibit the corrosive potency of science's metaphysical subtractions. In this regard, it is precisely Churchland's attempt to preserve a normative role for the 'superempirical virtues' that vitiates his version of EM.

1.7 The appearance of appearance

Unfortunately, Churchland is not the Antichrist, and EM's pragmatic accoutrements deprive it of the conceptual wherewithal required in order to precipitate cultural apocalypse. But this is not to lend succour to the defenders of FP, for even if the latter is neither as monolithic nor as maladaptive as Churchland makes out, and hence likely to survive as a set of pragmatic social strategies, all the indications seem to be that it will play an increasingly insignificant role in the future development of cognitive science.[22] Nevertheless, Churchland's estimable achievement (along with Daniel Dennett) consists in having driven an irrecusable philosophical wedge between our phenomenological self-conception and the material processes through which that conception is produced. Perhaps more than any other contemporary philosopher, Churchland's work gives the lie to phenomenology's 'principle of principles', which Husserl expressed as follows:

> No conceivable theory could make us err with respect to the principle of principles: that every originary presentive intuition is a legitimizing source of cognition, that everything originally (so to speak in its personal actuality) offered to us in intuition is to be accepted simply as what it is presented as being, but also only within the limits in which it is presented there.
>
> (Husserl 1982: 44)[23]

The critical force of Churchland's project is to show how the 'limits' which phenomenology would invoke in order to circumscribe the legitimacy of 'originary intuitions' cannot be phenomenologically transparent since they are themselves theoretically drawn. Moreover, whatever else may be wrong with it, EM is perfectly conceivable, yet this is precisely what phenomenology's transcendental pretensions cannot countenance. Consequently, this conceivability alone suffices to undermine the putative indubitability of our 'experience of meaning', along with the supposed incorrigibility of our 'originary presentive intuitions'. Regardless of the specific shortcomings of Churchland's own PVA paradigm, linguaformal 'meaning' is almost certainly generated through non-linguistic processes, just as our phenomenological intuitions are undoubtedly conditioned by mechanisms that cannot themselves be intuitively accessed. The upshot of Churchland's work, in a word, is simply that we are not as we experience ourselves to be.

In this regard, by drawing attention to the incommensurability between phenomenal consciousness and the neurobiological processes through which it is *produced*, Churchland casts doubt upon the transparency which many philosophers – and not just phenomenologists – claim must be granted to the phenomenon of consciousness construed as 'the appearance of appearance'. These philosophers insist that where phenomenal consciousness is concerned, the appearance– reality distinction cannot be invoked short of occluding the reality of the phenomenon of consciousness altogether, for 'the appearing is all there is'. As Searle puts it, '[C]onsciousness consists in the appearances themselves. Where appearance is concerned we cannot make the appearance–reality distinction because the appearance is the reality.'[24] But the notion of 'phenomenon' or 'appearance' in this strong phenomenological sense harbours an inbuilt circularity. This appeal to the self-evident transparency of appearance conveniently dispenses with the need for justification by insisting that we all already know 'what it's *like*' for something to appear to us, or for something 'to be like' something for us, or for other sentient entities capable of registering appearances in the way in which we do (indeed, this is precisely the force of Heidegger's *Dasein*, construed as the locus or *site* of phenomenological disclosure, which ostensibly avoids substantive metaphysical presuppositions pertaining to physical and/or biological differences between 'conscious' and 'non-conscious' entities). It is this seeming, and not its constitutive conditions, that has to be accounted for 'in its own terms'. Indeed, the founding axiom of phenomenology (Husserl's 'principle of principles') could be simply stated as: appearances can only be understood in their own terms. But what are 'their own terms'? Precisely the terms concomitant with the first-person phenomenological point of view. It is this assumption that leads many philosophers to insist that where appearance is concerned, any attempt to introduce an appearance – reality distinction is absurd, a misunderstanding of what is at stake: viz., the *appearing* of appearance *as such*, and not *as* something else. But if we enquire as to the source for the evidence that this absolute appearing occurs, the reply is invariably that it comes from 'our own conscious experience'. Thus we are invited to account for the autonomy of the appearing as such, and in order to do this, not only can we not invoke any appearance–reality distinction, we are obliged to stick to describing this phenomenal *seeming* strictly in its 'own' terms, without interpretative overlay or editorial amendment. But how exactly are we supposed to describe appearance strictly in its own terms, without smuggling in any extrinsic, objectifying factors? In actuality, the more closely we try to stick to describing the pure appearing and nothing but, the more we end up resorting to a descriptive register which becomes increasingly figurative and metaphorical; so much so, indeed, that it has encouraged many phenomenologists to conclude that only figurative and/or poetic language can be truly adequate to the non-propositional dimension of 'meaningfulness' harboured by 'appearing'. Accordingly, much post-Heideggerian phenomenology has been engaged in an ongoing attempt to deploy the figurative dimension of language in order to sound sub-representational experiential depths, which, it is claimed, are inherently refractory to any other variety of conceptualization, and particularly to scientific conceptualization. In this regard, the goal of phenomenology would consist in describing 'what it's like' to be conscious while bracketing off conceptual judgements about 'what it's like'. Yet as a result, an intimate link between phenomenology and literary hermeneutics has to be forged in order to stave off the obvious threat harboured by the phenomenological axiom: that the more we stick to describing pure appearing qua appearing, the more we realize that we invariably have to assume something *inapparent* within appearances in order to be able to describe them at all – we have to *excavate* some originary dimension of (non-propositional) 'meaning' or 'sense' (as Heidegger and his successors sought to) in order to describe the autonomy of appearances in their 'own' terms. Thus phenomenology invariably petitions figurative language in order to carry out its descriptive task. Yet it might be better to concede that the aims of phenomenological description *stricto sensu* are best served through the artifices of literature, instead of hijacking the conceptual resources of philosophy for no other reason than to preserve some inviolable inner sanctum of phenomenal experience. For the more attentively we try to scrutinize our originary phenomenal experiences independently of the resources of language, the more impoverished our descriptions become. This is not to say that there is no more to consciousness than what can be linguistically mediated and articulated, but on the contrary, to insist that consciousness harbours an underlying but sub-linguistic reality which is simply not accessible to first-person phenomenological description or linguistic articulation. Ironically, and contrary to phenomenology's guiding intuition, the *reality* of consciousness is independent of the subject of consciousness. Only the objective, third-person perspective is equipped with conceptual resources sensitive enough to map consciousness' opaque, sub-linguistic reality. For as Thomas Metzinger has pointed out, it is precisely the simplest, most rudimentary forms of phenomenal content that cannot be reliably individuated from the phenomenological perspective, since we lack any transtemporal identity criteria through which we could re-identify them. And in the absence of such criteria, we are incapable of forming logical identity criteria grounded in phenomenological experience, and consequently cannot form phenomenal concepts for these elementary experiential data. Though we can discriminate fine-grained differences in phenomenal content, we seem to be incapable of identifying those same contents individually. Once these phenomenal primitives have vanished from the conscious present, we cannot access them, whether through subjective phenomenological reflection, or through conceptual analysis operating within intersubjective space. Thus the primitive data of phenomenal consciousness are often epistemically and phenomenologically unavailable to the subject of consciousness. But this is precisely why the only hope for investigating the sub-symbolic reality of phenomenal consciousness lies in using the formal and mathematical resources available to the third-person perspective:

> The minimally sufficient neural and functional correlates of the corresponding phenomenal states can, at least in principle, if properly mathematically analyzed, provide us with the transtemporal, as well as the logical identity criteria we have been looking for. Neurophenomenology is possible; phenomenology is impossible.
>
> (Metzinger 2004: 83)

In his recent *Sweet Dreams*,[25] Dennett correctly identifies the fundamental quandary confronting those who would uphold the unconditional transparency of the phenomenal realm: if the constitutive features of 'appearing qua appearing' are non-relational and non-functional, and hence inherently resistant to conceptual articulation, then even the first-person phenomenological subject of experience lacks the resources to apprehend them; he or she will always be separated from his or her own immediate experience of the phenomenon per se by some mediating instance, for every description of a phenomenal *representatum* entails transforming the latter into the *representandum* of another phenomenal *representatum*, and so on. In this regard, Dennett's penetrating critique of some of the more extravagant superstitions entailed by philosophers' 'qualiaphilia' chimes with Derrida's critique of Husserl: the notion of an absolutely transparent but non-relational phenomenal appearance is incoherent much for the same reason as the idea of consciousness as locus of absolute self-presence is incoherent.[26] If one acknowledges that the conceit of a phenomenal appearing devoid of all relational and functional properties is nonsensical, then one must concede that phenomenological experience itself shows that we ourselves do not enjoy privileged access to all the properties intrinsic to appearance *qua* appearance. Accordingly, there is no reason to suppose that appearing is absolutely transparent to us, and therefore no reason not to accept the idea (long advocated by Dennett) that the phenomenon of consciousness itself invites a distinction between those features of appearance that are apprehended by us, and those that elude us. For if appearance is sufficient unto itself, the price of upholding the claim that our experience of appearance is entirely adequate to that appearance would seem to be a position perilously close to absolute solipsism (this is precisely the option embraced by some of Heidegger's phenomenological heirs, suh as Michel Henry).[27] Of course, having conceded that the notion of a non-manifest appearance is not entirely oxymoronic, the question remains whether to raise the stakes by insisting that this latent or non-manifest dimension of phenomenality transcends objective description altogether, as did the early Heidegger, who chose to see in it the unobjectifiable *being* of the phenomenon, which science is constitutively incapable of grasping; or whether to grant that this non-manifest dimension is perfectly amenable to description from the third-person point of view characteristic of the sciences, and hence something which falls under the remit of the scientific study of the phenomenon of consciousness. Obviously, such a choice depends on a prior decision about the scope and limits of scientific investigation, and about whether or not it is right to remove certain phenomena, specifically those associated with human consciousness, from the ambit of that investigation as a matter of principle. More abstractly, this can be characterized as a speculative decision about whether to characterize the latency of phenomena in terms of unobjectifiable transcendence, as Heidegger does with his invocation of 'being', or in terms of immanent objectivity, as Churchland and Metzinger do when invoking the un-conscious, sub-symbolic processes through which phenomenal consciousness is produced. Our contention here is that the latter option is clearly preferable, since it begs fewer questions; yet it remains compromised by an alliance with pragmatism which vitiates the commitment to scientific realism which should be among its enabling conditions. Naturalism may not be the best guarantor of realism, and in subsequent chapters we will try to define the rudiments of a speculative realism and elaborate on some of the conceptual ramifications entailed by a metaphysical radicalization of eliminativism. Our provisional conclusion at this stage however, is that far from being some incontrovertible datum blocking the integration of the first-person point of view into the third-person scientific viewpoint, the appearing of appearance can and should be understood as a phenomenon generated by sub-personal but perfectly objectifiable neurobiological processes. Indeed, as Metzinger persuasively argues, there are solid grounds for maintaining that the phenomenological subject of appearance is itself a phenomenal appearance generated by in-apparent neurobiological processes. Thus, for Metzinger, concomitant with this subversion of our phenomenological self-conception is a subversion of our understanding of ourselves as *selves*.[28] Yet faced with this unanticipated twist in the trajectory of Enlightenment, which seems to issue in a conception of consciousness utterly at odds with the image of the latter promoted by those philosophers who exalted consciousness above all other phenomena, philosophers committed to the canon of rationality defined by Kant and Hegel have vigorously denounced what they see as the barbaric consequences of untrammelled scientific rationalism. Ironically enough, it is precisely those philosophers who see the fundamental task of philosophy as critique who have proved to be among the staunchest defenders of the legitimacy of the manifest image. In the next chapter, we will examine one of the most sophisticated defences of the latter in the shape of the critique of Enlightenment rationality proposed by Theodor Adorno and Max Horkheimer.

2
The *Thanatosis* of Enlightenment

2.1 Myth and enlightenment: Adorno and Horkheimer

Myth is already enlightenment, and enlightenment's destruction of superstition merely reinstates myth: this is the speculative thesis proposed by Adorno and Horkheimer's *Dialectic of Enlightenment*.[1] Our contention in this chapter will be that this dialectic of myth and enlightenment is structured by an entwinement of mimicry, mimesis, and sacrifice which not only underlies the book's 'excursus' on Odysseus and its celebrated chapter on anti-Semitism, but arguably also furnishes it with its fundamental conceptual core. Though each of these concepts is undoubtedly complex, and mobilized for distinct purposes in different parts of Adorno's oeuvre in particular, their deployment in *Dialectic of Enlightenment* seems to harbour the key to Adorno and Horkheimer's speculative thesis. If, as Andreas Huyssen suggests, the concept of mimesis functions in five 'distinct but nevertheless overlapping' registers in Adorno's work,[2] three of these are fully operative in *Dialectic of Enlightenment*: the anthropological register, the biological-somatic register, and the psychoanalytic register. The argument of *Dialectic of Enlightenment* weaves these three registers together while distinguishing between mimicry, which ostensibly has a negative connotation in the book, and mimesis, whose speculatively positive sense may be glossed as 'similitude without conceptual subsumption'. At the same time, the concept of sacrifice assumes its decisive import for the book's speculative thesis as the paradigm of non-conceptual exchange. The entwinement of similitude without identity and exchange without subsumption provides the pulse of the dialectic of myth and enlightenment. Thus the book's thesis can be paraphrased as follows: the sacrificial logic of myth is repeated in reason's own compulsive attempt to overcome myth by sacrificing it. Enlightenment reiterates mythic sacrifice by striving to sacrifice it. But as a result, it unwittingly mimics the fatal compulsion which it intended to overcome. Only by 'working through' the sacrificial trauma that drives rationality – a working through which Adorno and Horkheimer characterize in terms of reason's reflexive commemoration of its own natural history – can reason renounce its pathological compulsion to sacrifice and thereby become reconciled to the part played by nature within it. True demythologization – the dialectical resolution of the opposition between myth and enlightenment – would then coincide with the relinquishment of the sacrificial drive to demythologize; or in Adorno and Horkheimer's own words: 'Demythologization always takes the form of the irresistible revelation of the futility and superfluity of sacrifices' (Adorno and Horkheimer 2002: 42). Reason becomes reconciled to nature by sublimating its compulsion to sacrifice myth. In this regard, *Dialectic of Enlightenment* is an attempt to fuse Hegel and Freud in what can only be described as a 'dialectical psychoanalysis' of Western rationality.

But everything hinges on the manner in which mimicry, mimesis, and sacrifice are dialectically entwined. More precisely put, the book's speculative coherence depends on the feasibility of maintaining a rigid demarcation between mimicry and mimesis, sacrificial repression and enlightened sublimation. If organic mimicry reduces to adaptation, then it falls under the aegis of identity, and anthropological mimesis can be confidently contrasted to it as a harbinger of non-identity: correspondence without a concept. But this neat distinction is far from assured. In the fragment entitled 'Toward a Theory of the Criminal', Adorno and Horkheimer explicitly identify mimicry with the death-drive: '[Criminals] represent a tendency deeply inherent in living things, the overcoming of which is the mark of all development: the tendency to lose oneself in one's surroundings instead of actively engaging with them, the inclination to let oneself go, to lapse back into nature. Freud called this the death-drive, Caillois *le mimétisme*' (Adorno and Horkheimer 2002: 189).[3] But how is this explicit identification of biological mimicry with the death-drive related to the following cryptic formulation from the excursus on Odysseus, which seems to identify the latter with mimesis rather than mimicry?: 'Only deliberate adaptation to it brings nature under the power of the physically weaker. The reason that represses mimesis is not merely its opposite. It is itself mimesis: of death' (Adorno and Horkheimer 2002: 44). This could be paraphrased as follows: by sacrificing the mimetic impulse (blind conformity to nature, the compulsion to repeat) in order to ensure human survival, instrumental reason fatally repeats its own submission to nature. It has to mimic death in order to stave it off. This would seem to encapsulate the nub of the dialectical critique of instrumental rationality; a critique which identifies the latter as the root cause of Occidental civilization's precipitation towards self-destruction. But there is another sense in which it also harbours the germ of this critique's non-dialectical reversal: mimesis may have distinguished itself from mimicry, but mimicry does not distinguish itself from mimesis. For the genitive 'of' in reason's mimesis of death may plausibly be taken to be objective as well as subjective. As we shall see, the fatal reversibility of mimicry and mimesis, though denounced by dialectical reflection, is latent in the enigma of mimicry's non-adaptive *thanatosis* – what Caillois called its 'assimilation to space', which transforms reflection itself into a purposeless instrument and signals the technological destruction of critique. *Thanatosis* marks the lethal equivalence whereby the logic of mimesis reverses into mimicry, and critical negativity into the annihilating positivity of reason which the reflexive dialectic of myth and enlightenment had sought to stave off.

2.2   The sacrifice of sacrifice

According to Adorno and Horkheimer, Enlightenment reason is driven by an inexorable drive to conceptual subsumption which subordinates particularity, heterogeneity, and multiplicity to universality, homogeneity, and unity, thereby rendering everything equivalent to everything else, but precisely in such a way that nothing can ever be identical to itself. Thus conceptual identification stipulates a form of differential commensurability which, in their own words, 'amputates the incommensurable' (Adorno and Horkheimer 2002: 9). 'Instrumental rationality' (which will later be called 'identity thinking') is an anthropological pathology expressing a materially indeterminate yet ubiquitous 'power' whose sole determination consists in its differentiation into dominating and dominated, rather than any historically determinate configuration between conditions and relations of production. In the speculative anthropology proposed by Adorno and Horkheimer, instrumental reason is the extension of tool-use and hence a function of adaptational constraints. The emergence of instrumental rationality is inseparable from the primordial confrontation between dominating and dominated powers which primitive humanity experienced in its powerlessness before all-powerful nature. Sacrifice is the attempt to effect a commensuration between these incommensurables – between the omnipotence of nature and the impotence of primitive humanity. Yet from the outset sacrificial magic presupposed the logic of mimesis: 'At the magical stage dream and image were not regarded as mere signs of things but were linked to them by resemblance or name. The relationship was not one of intention but of kinship. Magic like science is concerned with ends but it pursues them through mimesis, not through an increasing distance from the object' (Adorno and Horkheimer 2002: 7). Mimesis establishes the equivalence between dissimilars which provides the precondition for sacrifice. It provides a non-conceptual commensuration of particularity with generality, thereby allowing one to serve as a substitute for the other:

> Magic implies specific representation. What is done to the spear, the hair, the name of the enemy, is also to befall his person; the sacrificial animal is slain in place of the God. The substitution which takes place in sacrifice marks a step toward discursive logic. Even though the hind which was offered up for the daughter, the lamb for the firstborn, necessarily still had qualities of its own, it already represented the genus. It manifested the arbitrariness of the specimen. But the sanctity of the *hic et nunc*, the uniqueness of the chosen victim which coincides with its representative status, distinguishes it radically, makes it non-exchangeable even in the exchange.
>
> (Adorno and Horkheimer 2002: 7)

Sacrifice's magical power consists in establishing a correspondence between things for which no *ratio*, no proportion of conceptual equivalence yet exists. This is its quite literal *irrationality*. More importantly, mimetic sacrifice establishes the fundamental distinction whose rationality Adorno and Horkheimer believe enlightenment is in the process of eliding: the distinction between animate and inanimate: '*mana*, the moving spirit, is not a projection but the preponderance of nature in the weak psyches of primitive peoples. The split between animate and inanimate, the assigning of demons and deities to certain specific places arises from this pre-animism. Even the division of subject and object is prefigured in it' (Adorno and Horkheimer 2002: 11). Moreover, if as Adorno and Horkheimer argue, myth already exhibits the lineaments of explanatory classification which will be subsequently deployed in scientific rationality, then this distinction between animate and inanimate marks a fundamental cognitive accomplishment which science threatens to elide by converting all of nature into an undifferentiated material whose intelligibility requires a supplement of conceptual information. Scientific conceptualization mortifies the body: 'The transformation into dead matter, indicated by the affinity of *corpus* to corpse, was a part of the perennial process which turned nature into stuff, material' (Adorno and Horkheimer 2002: 194). Thus, Adorno and Horkheimer insist, 'the disenchantment of the world means the extirpation of animism' (2002: 2) – enlightenment 'equates the living with the non-living just as myth had equated the non-living with the living' (Adorno and Horkheimer 2002: 11). Yet animism harboured a form of non-conceptual rationality precisely insofar as its practice of sacrifice established a principle of reciprocity between inanimate power and animate powerlessness. The rationality of sacrifice consists in this power to commensurate incommensurables: power and impotence, life and death.

The speculative fusion of Hegel and Freud undertaken by Adorno and Horkheimer would seem to imply three successive strata of mimetic sacrifice and three distinct registers of exchange between life and death. The first strata, according to Freud's own excursus into speculative biology in *Beyond the Pleasure Principle*, would mark the emergence of the organism through the sacrifice which secures the relative independence of its interior milieu against the inorganic exterior.[4] Part of the organism has to die so that it may survive the onslaught of the inorganic: the organism sacrifices its outer layer to the inorganic as a 'shield against stimuli'.[5] The second strata would mark the emergence of mythic exchange as the stage at which humans learnt to sacrifice the animate in order to placate animating powers. According to Adorno and Horkheimer, this is the sacrifice that establishes a reciprocity between dominated and dominating, victim and gods, and hence represents a gain in human autonomy: 'If exchange represents the secularization of sacrifice, the sacrifice itself, like the magic schema of rational exchange, appears as a human contrivance intended to control the gods, who are overthrown precisely by the system created to honour them' (Adorno and Horkheimer 2002: 40). The third strata would be that of the emergence of the self and the definitive separation between culture and nature. The permanence of the ego is secured against the flux of fleeting impressions through the teleological subordination of present satisfaction to future purpose: thus, '[t]he ego [...] owes its existence to the sacrifice of the present moment to the future. [But] its substance is as illusory as the immortality of the slaughtered victim' (Adorno and Horkheimer 2002: 41). But where sacrifice had previously served as a means for mastering external nature, it now becomes introjected as the suppression of the power of internal nature. However, this sacrificial subordination of means to end in fact reverses itself into a subordination of ends to means, for in learning to repress the drives and desires whose satisfaction define it, the human organism effectively negates the ends for which it supposedly lives. For Adorno and Horkheimer, this marks the beginning of that dangerous substitution of means for ends, and of the reversibility between function and purpose, which they see as defining the reign of instrumental rationality, and which attains its pathological apogee in what they describe as the 'overt madness', 'the antireason', of technological capitalism. Yet the roots of this madness were already present at the origin of subjectivity:

> The human being's mastery of itself, on which the self is founded, practically always involves the annihilation of the subject in whose service that mastery is maintained, because the substance which is mastered, suppressed, and disintegrated by self-preservation is nothing other than the living entity, of which the achievements of self-preservation can only be defined as functions – in other words, self-preservation destroys the very thing which is supposed to be preserved [...] The history of civilization is the history of the introversion of sacrifice – in other words, the history of renunciation.
> (Adorno and Horkheimer 2002: 43)

Thus enlightenment becomes the sacrifice of sacrifice, its internalization. The separation between nature and culture, discipline and spontaneity, is secured by becoming internal to the subject. But in order to secure it, the subject must imitate the implacability of inanimate nature; it disenchants animate nature by miming the intractability of inanimate force: 'The subjective mind which disintegrates the spiritualization of nature masters spiritless nature only by imitating its rigidity, disintegrating itself as animistic' (Adorno and Horkheimer 2002: 44). For Adorno and Horkheimer, this furnishes the key to the fatal complicity between enchantment and disenchantment, myth and enlightenment. Enlightenment's pathological reiteration of the logic of mythic thought is exemplified in its exclusive regard for the immanence of the actual and its obsessive focus on the ineluctable necessity of the present:

> In the terseness of the mythical image as in the clarity of the scientific formula, the eternity of the actual is confirmed and mere existence is pronounced as the meaning it obstructs [...] The subsumption of the actual, whether under mythical prehistory or under mathematical formalism, the symbolic relating of the present to the mythical event

in the rite or abstract category in science, makes the new appear as something predetermined, which therefore is really the old. It is not existence that is without hope but the knowledge which appropriates and perpetuates existence as a schema in the pictorial or mathematical symbol.

(Adorno and Horkheimer 2002: 20–1)

Thus, according to Adorno and Horkheimer, the abyss that separates science's conceptual knowledge of the actual from 'existence' would be the abyss between the identical and the non-identical; an abyss of un-actual negativity whose inherently temporal structure only philosophical reflection is capable of recuperating. Reason can overcome its self-alienation from natural existence, suspend the oppressive immanence of absolute actuality, and redeem the possibility of hope, only through the commemorative reflection of its own historicity. Given its crucial role in Adorno and Horkheimer's account, this denouement of the dialectic of enlightenment warrants quoting at length:

Precisely by virtue of its irresistible logic, thought, in whose compulsive mechanism nature is reflected and perpetuated, also reflects itself as a nature oblivious to itself, as a mechanism of compulsion [...] In mind's self-recognition as nature divided from itself, nature, as in pre-history, is calling to itself, but no longer directly by its supposed name, which in the guise of *mana* means omnipotence, but as something blind and mutilated. In the mastery of nature, without which mind does not exist, enslavement of nature persists. By modestly confessing itself to be power and thus being taken back into nature, mind rids itself of the very claim to mastery which had enslaved it to nature [...] For not only does the concept as science distance human beings from nature, but, as the self-reflection of thought [...] it enables the distance which perpetuates injustice to be measured. Through this remembrance of nature within the subject, a remembrance which contains the unrecognized truth of all culture, enlightenment is opposed in principle to power, [it has] escaped the spell of nature by confessing itself to be nature's own dread of itself.

(Adorno and Horkheimer 2002: 32)

The reasoning here is impeccably Hegelian: mature reason achieves its independence from nature reflexively by remembering its own dependence upon it. But according to Adorno and Horkheimer, reflexivity is precisely that which science remains incapable of. If, as they maintain, 'all perception is projection' (Adorno and Horkheimer 2002: 154) – the mediation of sensible impressions by conceptual judgement – then an adequate cognitive reflection of things as they are necessitates bridging the abyss between sense data and actual objects, inner and outer. Thus '[t]o reflect the thing as it is, the subject must give back to it more than it receives from it' (Adorno and Horkheimer 2002: 155). But this is precisely what conceptual subsumption, whether positivistic or idealistic, is incapable of doing: 'Because the subject is unable to return to the object what it has received from it, it is not enriched but impoverished. It loses reflection in both directions: as it no longer reflects the object, it no longer reflects on itself and thereby loses the ability to differentiate' (Adorno and Horkheimer 2002: 156). Cognition becomes pathological when its projection excludes reflection. The privileging of reflection as the hallmark of rational sanity entails the pathologization of science's 'unreflecting naivety' as an instance of 'pathic projection' which merely differs in degree, rather than kind, from anti-Semitism: 'Objectifying thought, like its pathological counterpart, has the arbitrariness of a subjective purpose extraneous to the matter itself and, in forgetting the matter, does to it in thought the violence which will later will be done to it in practice' (Adorno and Horkheimer 2002: 159).[6]

2.3 Commemorating reflection

The upshot of this critique is clear: reason's reflexive mediation is contrasted to its irreflexive immediacy as health is to sickness: 'The subject which naively postulates absolutes, no matter how universally active it may be, is sick, passively succumbing to the dazzlement of false immediacy' (Adorno and Horkheimer 2002: 160). Adorno and Horkheimer counterpose the healthy mediation of reflexive negativity to the sick mediation of total subsumption, just as they contrast reflexive consciousness' 'living' incorporation of qualitative particularity to the latter's annihilating consumption through mathematical formalization. In the final analysis, 'only mediation can overcome the isolation which ails the whole of nature' (Adorno and Horkheimer 2002: 156). And this mediation must take the form of remembrance: 'What threatens the prevailing praxis and its inescapable alternatives is not nature, with which that praxis coincides, but the remembrance of nature' (Adorno and Horkheimer 2002: 212). Such remembrance would aim at inaugurating a 'second nature': a nature mediated by human history and reinvested with the full apparel of human socio-cultural significance. Second nature would be nature reflexively incorporated and internally memorized – or, in the words of Jay Bernstein, 'the nature whose appearing to us is conditioned by our belonging to it'.[7] As we shall see in the following chapter, Bernstein's formula perfectly encapsulates the fundamental tenet of what Quentin Meillassoux has called 'correlationism': viz., the claim that there is a necessary reciprocity between mind and nature. Correlationism hankers after second nature precisely insofar as the achievement of the latter would render material reality into a depository of sense fully commensurate with man's psychic needs. Moreover, if we accept Bernstein's suggestion that for Adorno 'the living/non-living distinction is the fundamental one' (Bernstein 2001: 194), then we begin to appreciate the extent to which the ultimate horizon of Adorno and Horkheimer's critique of scientific reason is the rehabilitation of a fully anthropomorphic 'living' nature – in other words, the resurrection of Aristotelianism: nature as repository of anthropomorphically accessible meaning, of essential purposefulness, with the indwelling, auratic *telos* of every entity providing an intelligible index of its moral worth. Underlying this philosophical infatuation with the lure of second nature is a yearning to obliterate the distinction between knowledge and value; a nostalgic longing to reconcile the 'is' and the 'ought', and thereby to 'heal' – since nature 'suffers' in its isolation from human contact – the modern rift between understanding what an entity is, and knowing how to behave towards it. Clearly then, this philosophical pining for second nature betrays nothing less than a desire to revoke spirit's estrangement from matter, to reforge the broken 'chain of being', and ultimately to repudiate the labour of disenchantment initiated by Galileo in the physical realm, continued by Darwin in the biological sphere, and currently being extended by cognitive science to the domain of mind.

The implicitly religious tenor of this reflexive commemoration of lost experience becomes explicit in its insistence on the redemptive value of memory. 'Reconciliation', Adorno and Horkheimer claim, 'is Judaism's highest concept and expectation its whole meaning' (2002: 165). Judaic monotheism is to be admired for managing to 'preserve [nature's] reconciling memory, without relapsing through symptoms into mythology', thereby prefiguring 'happiness without power, reward without work, a homeland without frontiers, religion without myth' (Adorno and Horkheimer 2002: 165). Judaism prefigures second nature precisely insofar as it provides a prototype of demythologized religion. But if the Judaic *Bilderverbot* (the prohibition of images) is the seal of rationally disenchanted religion, its reflexive rehabilitation as the prohibition of any positive conception of the absolute marks the apex of mystification – a mystification sanctified in the critical absolutization of the difference between the knowable and the unknowable, the finite and the infinite, immanence and transcendence – those very distinctions which science is deemed guilty of having disregarded. The critical interdiction of absolute immanence aims at the attainment of a second nature which would secure the reflexive redemption of the future on the basis of the present's commemoration of the past. Thus, the qualitative substance of experience, supposedly obliterated by abstract conceptual form, is retroactively projected as the irreducible material of socio-historical mediation.

But this substance of experience is itself a philosophical myth. For though the dialectic of myth and enlightenment may be formally plausible, it derives its substantive critical force from a conflation between dialectical form – exemplified in the analysis of the logic of sacrifice – and a positive content which is nothing but the retroactively posited residue of conceptual subsumption: the pre-conceptual experience of 'meaning' harboured in the perceptual apprehension of qualitative particularity. In this regard, Adorno and Horkheimer's thesis is vitiated by a constant slippage between two entirely distinct claims: viz., the claim that scientific reason has occluded a meaningful experience *of* nature, on the one hand; and the claim that it has obscured the experience of meaning *as* nature, on the other. To defend the first would involve a commitment to the primacy of some sort of pre-conceptual phenomenological understanding of nature – precisely the sort of stance precluded by Adorno and Horkheimer's Hegelian emphasis on the ineluctable socio-historical mediation of experience. To defend the second would be to relapse into the kind of reductive naturalism exemplified by contemporary evolutionary psychology, whose positivistic precursors Adorno and Horkheimer abhorred. Yet in spite of – or perhaps even because of – this emphasis on historical mediation, the meaningful particularity of forgotten experience, whether 'of' or 'as' nature, is evoked as the content which science has lost by abstracting from it. But this meaningful content is supposed to be at once qualitatively and positively substantive – 'experience' in the full-blooded phenomenological sense – and the negation of subsumptive abstraction. What is this dimension of meaningfulness which we have supposedly been deprived of if it is neither positively given as a transhistorical invariant nor some originary phenomenological datum, and if its determinate specificity is merely the shadow retroactively cast by its subsequent negation? Reflection provides the sole criterion of authentication for the memory that we used to experience more than we do now; and this memory is all that can substantiate the claim that we have been deprived of something. But *whose* memory is it? In light of the critical prohibition of absolute knowledge, and hence of the inaccessibility of absolute knowledge's self-commemoration, how are we to gauge the reliability of Adorno and Horkheimer's speculative remembrance of human history? Dialectical commemoration should never be taken on trust. The 'experience' whose attenuation Adorno and Horkheimer lament seems to have no other substance than the one which reflection retrospectively imparts to it.

In fact, the invocation of remembrance reveals how Adorno and Horkheimer's critique of enlightenment is carried out from the perspective of the commemorative consciousness which feels its own existence threatened by the scientific occlusion of 'meaningful particularity'. The critique proceeds from the viewpoint of reflection, which is to say, commemoration. It is nostalgic for an experience whose substance mirrors its own longing. It is fuelled by the yearning for the mythic form of history *as* experience, rather than for any specific or substantive historical experience. Thus it criticizes the sacrificial myth of disenchantment by rehabilitating a fantasy of rational enchantment which betrays its own pining for the reflexive redemption of experience. Accordingly, and by its own lights, it is incapable of operating as an immanent critique of actual experience, since reflection is precisely what the actuality of instrumental rationality already *lacks*. But this lack is imputed to it on the basis of an appeal to a reflexively recuperated and transcendent past. Thus critique is conservation; moreover, it is inherently conservative since its commemorative reflection wishes to postpone temporal rupture in the name of continuity. The expectation of reconciliation retroactively forecloses the future prospect of temporal caesura: for reconciliation and expectation are the theological guarantors of redeemed nature. But science *has* no concept of 'nature', and this is precisely what dissuades it from stipulating any limit between the natural and the extra-natural: nature is neither more nor less than the various discourses of physics, chemistry, biology, geology, ethology, cosmology ... The list remains necessarily open-ended. Where the sciences of nature are concerned, the irreconcilable is their highest concept and the irremediable their only meaning. Paradoxically, it is in the concept of mimetic reversibility that this irremediability finds expression.

2.4   The dispossession of space

For Adorno and Horkheimer, the primary sense of biological mimicry would be that of an expression of the compulsion to adapt: organisms must either habituate themselves to their environment or perish.

But mimicry in the biological sense spans a variety of different registers – from genetic replication, to behavioural compliance, to morphological imitation – none of which prove straightforwardly reducible to the logic of adaptation. It is this fundamentally non-adaptive character of mimicry which Roger Caillois draws attention to in his 1935 article 'Mimicry and Legendary Psychasthenia'.[8] In mimicking their own food, leaf insects such as the *Phyllium* frequently end up devouring each other. Their mimicry involves an uncanny teleplasty – a physical photography – which short-circuits any use-value the mimetic realism might have had by replicating the physical symptoms of corruption and decay. Mirroring the necrosis of its own food, the *Phyllium* identifies itself as a dying semblance of its own living sustenance. The exorbitant accuracy of this insect teleplasty initiates an autophagy which becomes part of the organic coding of the physical photograph itself. Thus the symbiosis between the information of one organism – *Phyllium* – and another – leaf – undergoes an involution which simultaneously engenders the collapse of their identity and the erasure of their difference in the paradoxical convergence of organic verisimilitude and living death.[9] Mimicking the death of that from which it draws nourishment, the *Phyllium* becomes the living index of its food's decay for its own vital appetite.

Far from being an instance of adaptation, this thanatropic mimicry marks the compulsion whereby the organism is driven to disintegrate into the inorganic. At the root of this thanatropism, Caillois suggests, is an attraction by space: organic individuation loses ground, 'blurring in its retreat the frontier between the organism and the milieu' (Caillois 1988: 121), and is thereby precipitated into a continuously expanding de-individuated space. Caillois proposes that this psychasthenic 'assimilation to space' is the common denominator underlying phenomena as apparently remote from one another as insect mimicry and schizophrenic depersonalization. Citing the work of Eugene Minkowski,[10] Caillois notes that the schizophrenic responds to the question, 'Where are you?' with the claim: 'I know where I am but I cannot feel myself in the place where I find myself' (Caillois 1988: 111) – they are dispossessed of their psychic individuality by space:

To these dispossessed souls space seems to be a devouring force. Space pursues them, encircles them, digests them in a gigantic *phagocytosis*.[11] It ends by replacing them. Then the body separates itself from thought, the individual breaks the boundary of his skin and occupies the other side of his senses. He tries to look at himself from any point whatever in space. He feels himself becoming space, *black*

space where things cannot be put. He is similar, not similar to something, but just *similar.* And he invents spaces of which he is 'the
convulsive possession'. All these expressions shed light on a single
process: depersonalization by assimilation to space, i.e., what mimicry
achieves morphologically in certain animal species.

(Caillois 1988: 111)[12]

Ultimately, the pathology of instrumental rationality diagnosed by
Adorno and Horkheimer would seem to be rooted in this psychasthenic
dispossession by space, through which reason abjures the dimension of
temporal transcendence which provided it with its capacity for reflexive
commemoration. Reason becomes schizophrenic, and hence self-
estranged, precisely insofar as it is evacuated of its temporal substance
and rendered immanent to space. The psychosis of instrumental reason
allows subjective reflexivity to be swallowed up in the brute opacity of
the object. Yet thanatropic mimicry is the symptom of a non-conceptual
negativity which is already at work among objects independently of their
relation to subjectivity; a non-dialectical negativity which is not only
independent of mind but realizes the indistinction of identity and non-
identity outside the concept. (We shall see in Chapter 5 how this is the
negativity of 'being-nothing' through which the object 'unilateralizes'
the constituting subject and becomes the subject of its own knowledge.)
In this regard, the *thanatosis* of enlightenment marks that point at which
the transcendental subject of cognition is expropriated and 'objective
knowledge' switches from expressing the subject's knowledge of the
object to the object's knowledge of itself *and* of the subject that thinks it
knows it. This intimate connection between thanatropic mimicry and
objective cognition is one which Caillois had already identified:

Accordingly, it is not only psychasthenia which resembles mimicry,
but the imperative of cognition as such, of which psychasthenia in
any case represents a perversion. As we know, cognition tends toward
the suppression of every distinction, toward the reduction of every
opposition, such that its goal seems to consist in presenting sensibility with the ideal solution to its conflict with the external world
and hence to satisfy sensibility's tendency toward the abandonment
of consciousness and life. In doing so, cognition immediately presents sensibility with a *calming image,* and one which is full of promise:
the scientific representation of the world, in which the picture of
molecules, atoms, electrons, etc., dissociates the vital unity of being.

(Caillois 1988: 119)

Yet Caillois's analysis continues to confine the thanatropism of cognition – and hence the dissociation of the 'vital unity of being' – to a subjective representation; as though the cleavage between representational image and represented world could remain immune to the dissociative virulence of this non-dialectical negativity. In fact, as we will see in subsequent chapters, in anatomizing consciousness and life, the *thanatosis* of enlightenment not only dismembers the vital unity of being; more fundamentally, it objectifies the subject in such a way as to sunder the putative reciprocity between mind and world. It dispossesses the subject of thought.

2.5   The mimesis of death

This thanatropic dispossession at the hands of what Hegel referred to as the 'concept-less exteriority' of space explains the horror which mimicry inspires not only in civilization, but also in the dialectical reflection which purports to be the latter's witness. It is not surprising then that reflection charts the progress of civilization in terms of successive sublimations of the mimetic impulse – first through magic, in which mimetic logic provided the condition for sacrificial exchange; then with organized work, which marked its definitive prohibition: 'Social and individual education reinforces the objectifying behaviour required by work and prevents people from submerging themselves once more in the ebb and flow of surrounding nature' (Adorno and Horkheimer 2002: 148). Civilization proscribes mimetic behaviour as a dangerous regression. This prohibition is at once social and conceptual: social, in that mimetic behaviour signals a weakening or loosening of egoic self-mastery and a regression to animal compulsion (which Adorno and Horkheimer see exemplified by the criminal); conceptual, in that mimetic semblance is an instance of similitude without a concept. It is this latter sense that bears a particularly significant philosophical import for Adorno and Horkheimer. When something mimes something else, it becomes like it, but without resembling it according to any criterion of conceptual equivalence. Thus mimesis is an index of non-identity: it marks a register of indifference or indistinction operating independently of any conceptual criterion for registering identity or difference. Consequently, mimetic phenomena threaten both social order and conceptual order, exchange and subsumption. Yet the identitarian fear of mimesis is mirrored by the terror which mimesis itself provokes. For Adorno and Horkheimer, both mimesis and subsumption are intimately connected to fear: a nexus of terror links civilization's fear of regression, the individual's fear of social disapprobation, the fear provoked by conceptual indistinction, and the prey's fear of its predator. Whether sameness is established conceptually through the synthetic subsumption of particularity, or organically via the imitation of the inorganic, it remains bound to terror. More precisely, the terror of mimetic regression engenders a compulsion to subsume, to conform, and to repress, which is itself the mimesis of primitive organic terror:

> Society perpetuates the threat from nature as the permanent, organized compulsion which, reproducing itself in individuals as systematic self-preservation, rebounds against nature as society's control over it [...] The mathematical formula is consciously manipulated regression, just as the magic ritual was; it is the most sublimated form of mimicry. In technology, the adaptation to lifelessness in the service of self-preservation is no longer accomplished, as in magic, by bodily imitation of external nature, but by automating mental processes, turning them into blind sequences. With its triumph human expressions become both controllable and compulsive. All that remains of the adaptation to nature is the hardening against it. The camouflage used to protect and strike terror today is the blind mastery of nature, which is identical to farsighted instrumentality.
>
> (Adorno and Horkheimer 2002: 149)

Thus mimetic phenomena are double-edged: mimicry is at once a defence mechanism and a weapon. It is exemplified not only by the prey's miming of the inorganic in order to evade the predator, but also by the predator's miming of its prey. But its ambiguity goes deeper: for it is the defence mechanism itself which converts into a weapon – the repression which served to preserve the organic individual against the threat of inorganic dissolution becomes its fundamental weapon against nature, whether organic or inorganic. Mimetic sacrifice effectuates a reversibility between the threatening power which is to be warded off, and the threatened entity which seeks to defend itself through sacrifice. It installs a reversible equivalence between dominating and dominated force, power and powerlessness, the organic and the inorganic. Ultimately, this reversibility renders the anthropomorphic vocabulary of fear and intimidation inappropriate: the organism's putatively defensive simulation of the inorganic – the horned lizard which simulates a rock – flips over into the inorganic's supposedly aggressive simulation of the organic – as in the case of viruses, which hijack their hosts' cellular machinery in order to replicate themselves. In disregarding this fundamental reversibility between mimic and mimicked, Adorno and Horkheimer ignore the return of mimicry within mimesis, and the possibility that anthropological mimesis itself may be a mask of mimicry. Though they recapitulate mimesis' anthropological and psychosocial aspects, they omit the first and arguably most fundamental strata of mimetic sacrifice: the biological level, in which Freud grounded the compulsion to repeat in his account of the organism's emergence from the inorganic (cf. Chapter 7). Freud's biological construal of the death-drive remains an ineliminable prerequisite of Adorno and Horkheimer's account for it explains the originary compulsion to repeat which is reiterated at the anthropological and psychosocial levels. Civilization's embrace of lifelessness in the service of self-preservation, its compulsive mimicry of organic compulsion in the repression of compulsion, reiterates the originary repression of the inorganic. Thus, if '[t]he reason that represses mimesis is not merely its opposite [but] is itself mimesis: of death' (Adorno and Horkheimer 2002: 44), this is because science's repression of mimesis not only mimes death, inorganic compulsion – it is death, the inorganic, that mimes reason. Mimesis is *of* death and *by* death. Life was only ever mimed by death, the animate a mask of the inanimate. The technological automation of intelligence which marks the consummation of self-destructive reason for Adorno and Horkheimer is nothing but the return of the repressed, not merely in thinking, but *as* thinking itself. Enlightenment consummates mimetic reversibility by converting thinking into algorithmic compulsion: the inorganic miming of organic reason. Thus the artificialization of intelligence, the conversion of organic ends into technical means and vice versa, heralds the veritable realization of second nature – no longer in the conciliatory aspect of a reflexive commemoration of reason's own natural history, but rather in the irremediable form wherein purposeless intelligence supplants all reasonable ends. Organic teleology is not abolished through reflection, but through synthetic intelligence's short-circuiting of instrumental rationality; a short-circuiting which overturns the sequential ordination of time and the future's subordination to the present by reinscribing time into space.

Dialectical thinking's horror at this prospect is intimately tied to its desire to expunge space from history. Space is dialectically deficient because it remains mere concept-less self-exteriority. Thus, for Adorno and Horkheimer, the sequential ordination of space via narrative is the necessary precondition for the irreversibility of historical time: 'Laboriously and irrevocably, in the image of the journey, historical time has detached itself from space, the irrevocable schema of all mythical time' (Adorno and Horkheimer 2002: 39). The topological reinscription of history appals reflection because it threatens to dissolve memory back into the concept-less exteriority of space. Moreover, if synthetic intelligence consummates thanatropic mimicry, then enlightenment's topological reinscription of history does not so much reinstate mythical temporality as the dynamic of a horror story: human reason is revealed to have been an insect's waking dream.[13] This negative consummation of enlightenment signals the end of the dream of reason as codified in Hegelianism – for which the reconciliation of mind and matter provided the *telos* of universal history – and the awakening of an intelligence which is in the process of sloughing off its human mask.

Yet one way of underlining the profound philosophical import of Darwin's achievement would be to characterize it precisely in terms of this re-inscription of history into space. As we shall see in the next chapter, natural history harbours temporal strata whose magnitude dwarfs that of the nature 'whose appearing to us is conditioned by our belonging to it' – for it proceeds regardless of whether anyone belongs to it or not. Even if it remains irreducible to it, cultural history is mediated by natural history, which includes both time and space, biology and geology. Disavowing the irreflexive immanence of natural history, Adorno and Horkheimer's speculative naturalism ends up reverting to natural theology. It is the failure to acknowledge the ways in which the socio-historical mediation of nature is itself mediated by natural history – which means not only evolutionary biology but also geology and cosmology – which allows philosophical discourses on 'nature' to become annexes of philosophical anthropology. In the next chapter, we shall see how natural history indexes a dimension of temporality which repudiates every claim concerning the putative reciprocity between man and nature.

3
The Enigma of Realism

> The virtue of the transcendental does not consist in rendering realism illusory but rather in rendering it astonishing, i.e. apparently unthinkable, yet true, and hence eminently problematic.
>
> (Quentin Meillassoux 2006)[1]

3.1   The arche-fossil: Quentin Meillassoux

The French philosopher Quentin Meillassoux has recently proposed a compelling diagnosis of what is most problematic in post-Kantian philosophy's relationship to the natural sciences. The former founders on the enigma of the 'arche-fossil'. A fossil is a material bearing the traces of pre-historic life, but an 'arche-fossil' is a material indicating traces of 'ancestral' phenomena anterior even to the emergence of life. It provides the material basis for experiments yielding estimates of ancestral phenomena – such as the radioactive isotope whose rate of decay provides an index of the age of rock samples, or the starlight whose luminescence provides an index of the age of distant stars. Natural science produces ancestral statements, such as that the universe is roughly 13.7 billion years old, that the earth formed roughly 4.5 billion years ago, that life developed on earth approximately 3.5 billion years ago, and that the earliest ancestors of the genus *Homo* emerged about 2 million years ago.[2] Yet it is also generating an ever-increasing number of 'descendent' statements, such as that the Milky Way will collide with the Andromeda galaxy in 3 billion years; that the earth will be incinerated by the sun 4 billions years hence; that all the stars in the universe will stop shining in 100 trillion years; and that eventually, one trillion, trillion, trillion years from now, all matter in the cosmos will disintegrate into unbound elementary particles. Philosophers should be more astonished by such statements than they seem to be, for they present a serious problem for post-Kantian philosophy. Yet strangely, the latter seems to remain entirely oblivious to it. The claim that these statements are philosophically enigmatic has nothing to do with qualms about the methods of measurement involved, or with issues of empirical accuracy, or any other misgivings about scientific methodology. They are enigmatic because of the startling philosophical implications harboured by their literal meaning. For the latter seems to point to something which violates the basic conditions of conceptual intelligibility stipulated by post-Kantian philosophy. In order to understand why this is so, we need to try to sketch the latter.

For all their various differences, post-Kantian philosophers can be said to share one fundamental conviction: that the idea of a world-in-itself, subsisting independently of our relation to it, is an absurdity. Objective reality must be transcendentally guaranteed, whether by pure consciousness, intersubjective consensus, or a community of rational agents; without such guarantors, it is a metaphysical chimera. Or for those who scorn what they mockingly dismiss as the 'antiquated' Cartesian vocabulary of 'representationalism', 'subject/object dualism', and epistemology more generally, it is our pre-theoretical relation to the world, whether characterized as *Dasein* or 'Life', which provides the ontological precondition for the intelligibility of the scientific claims listed above. No wonder, then, that post-Kantian philosophers routinely patronize these and other scientific assertions about the world as impoverished abstractions whose meaning supervenes on this more fundamental sub-representational or pre-theoretical relation to phenomena. For these philosophers, it is this relation to the world – *Dasein*, Existence, Life – which provides the originary condition of manifestation for all phenomena, including those ancestral phenomena featured in the statements above. Thus if the idea of a world-in-itself, of a realm of phenomena subsisting independently of our relation to it, is intelligible at all, it can only be intelligible as something in-itself or independent 'for-us'. This is the reigning *doxa* of post-metaphysical philosophy: what is fundamental is neither a hypostasized substance nor the reified subject, but rather the relation between un-objectifiable thinking and un-representable being, the primordial reciprocity or 'co-propriation' of *logos* and *physis* which at once unites and distinguishes the terms which it relates. This premium on relationality in post-metaphysical philosophy – whose telling symptom is the preoccupation with 'difference' – has become an orthodoxy which is all the more insidious for being constantly touted as a profound innovation.[3] Meillassoux has given it a name: 'correlationism'. Correlationism affirms the indissoluble primacy of the relation between thought and its correlate over the metaphysical hypostatization or representationalist reification of either term of the relation. Correlationism is subtle: it never denies that our thoughts or utterances *aim at* or *intend* mind-independent or language-independent realities; it merely stipulates that this apparently independent dimension remains internally related to thought and language. Thus contemporary correlationism dismisses the problematic of scepticism, and of epistemology more generally, as an antiquated Cartesian hang-up: there is supposedly no problem about how we are able to adequately represent reality, since we are 'always already' outside ourselves and immersed in or engaging with the world (and indeed, this particular platitude is constantly touted as the great Heideggerian–Wittgensteinian insight). Note that correlationism need not privilege 'thinking' or 'consciousness' as the key relation – it can just as easily replace it with 'being-in-the-world', 'perception', 'sensibility', 'intuition', 'affect', or even 'flesh'. Indeed, all of these terms have featured in the specifically phenomenological varieties of correlationism.[4]

But the arche-fossil presents a quandary for the correlationist. For how is the correlationist to make sense of science's ancestral claims? Correlationism insists that there can be no cognizable reality independently of our relation to reality; no phenomena without some transcendental operator – such as life or consciousness or *Dasein* – generating the conditions of manifestation through which phenomena manifest themselves. In the absence of this originary relation and these transcendental conditions of manifestation, nothing can be manifest, apprehended, thought, or known. Thus, the correlationist will continue, not even the phenomena described by the sciences are possible independently of the relation through which phenomena become manifest. Moreover, the correlationist will add, it is precisely the transcendental nature of the correlation as *sine qua non* for cognition that obviates the possibility of empirical idealism. Thus, contra Berkeley, Kant maintains that known things are not dependent upon being perceived precisely because known things are representations and representations are generated via transcendental syntheses of categorial form and sensible material. Synthesis is rooted in pure apperception, which yields the transcendental form of the object as its necessary correlate and guarantor of objectivity. The transcendental object is not cognizable, since it provides the form of objectivity which subsumes all cognizable objects; all of which must be linked to one another within the chains of causation encompassed by the unity of possible experience and circumscribed by the reciprocal poles of transcendental subject and transcendental object. Yet the arche-fossil indexes a reality which does not fall between these poles and which refuses to be integrated into the web of possible experience linking all cognizable objects to one another, because it occurred in a time *anterior to the possibility of experience*. Thus the arche-fossil points to a cognizable reality which is not given in the transcendental object of possible experience. This is a possibility which Kant explicitly denies:

> Thus we can say that the real things of past time are given in the transcendental object of experience; but they are objects for me and real in past time only in so far as I represent to myself (either by the light of history or by the guiding clues of a series of causes and effects) that a regressive series of possible perceptions in accordance with empirical laws, in a word, that the course of the world, conducts us to a past time-series as the condition of the present time – a series which, however, can be represented as actual not in itself but only in the connection of a possible experience. *Accordingly, all events which have taken place in the immense periods that have preceded my own existence really mean nothing but the possibility of extending the chain of experience from the present perception back to the conditions which determine this perception in respect of time.*
>
> (Kant 1929: A 495; emphasis added)

For Kant, then, the ancestral time of the arche-fossil cannot be represented as existing in itself but only as connected to a possible experience. But we cannot represent to ourselves any regressive series of possible perceptions in accordance with empirical laws capable of conducting us from our present perceptions to the ancestral time indexed by the arche-fossil. It is strictly impossible to prolong the chain of experience from our contemporary perception of the radioactive isotope to the time of the accretion of the earth indexed by its radiation, because the totality of the temporal series coextensive with possible experience itself emerged out of that geological time wherein there simply was no perception. We cannot extend the chain of possible perceptions back prior to the emergence of nervous systems, which provide the material conditions for the possibility of perceptual experience.

Thus it is precisely the necessity of an originary correlation, whether between knower and known, or *Sein* and *Dasein*, that science's ancestral statements flatly contradict. For in flagrant disregard of those transcendental conditions which are supposed to be necessary for every manifestation, they describe occurrences anterior to the emergence of life, and objects existing independently of any relation to thought. Similarly, science's descendent statements refer to events occurring after the extinction of life and the annihilation of thought. But how can such statements be true if correlationism is sound? For not only do they designate events occurring quite independently of the existence of life and thought, they also inscribe the transcendental conditions of manifestation themselves within a merely empirical timeline. How can the relation to reality embodied in life or thought be characterized as transcendentally necessary (*sine qua non*) for the possibility of spatiotemporal manifestation when science unequivocally states that life and thought, and hence this fundamental relation, have a determinate beginning and end in space-time? Don't science's ancestral and descendent statements strongly imply that those ontologically generative conditions of spatiotemporal manifestation privileged by correlationists – *Dasein*, life, consciousness, and so on – are themselves merely spatiotemporal occurrences like any other? If we begin to take these questions seriously, then the haughty condescension with which post-Kantian continental philosophy deigns to consider what the natural sciences say about the world begins to appear less like aristocratic detachment and more like infantile disavowal.

3.2 The correlationist response

Confronted by Meillassoux's argument from the arche-fossil, partisans of correlationism can be expected to mount a counter-offensive. In a supplement to the forthcoming English translation of *Après la finitude*,[5] Meillassoux recapitulates the two most frequently voiced objections elicited by the example of the arche-fossil and responds to both.[6] The correlationist rejoinder is two tiered. In the first stage, Meillassoux is accused of inflating an un-observed phenomenon into a negation of correlation, when in fact it is merely a lacuna in correlation. In the second stage, Meillassoux is deemed guilty of naively conflating the empirical and the transcendental. We will consider each of these objections, as well as Meillassoux's responses to them, in turn.

3.2.1 The lacuna of manifestation

In the first stage, the correlationist contends that, far from being novel and challenging, the argument from the arche-fossil is merely a restatement of a hackneyed and rather feeble objection to transcendental idealism. Thus, the correlationist continues, the arche-fossil is simply an example of a phenomenon which went un-perceived. But unperceived phenomena occur all the time and it is excessively naive to think they suffice to undermine the transcendental status of the correlation. In this regard, the temporal distance which separates us from the ancestral phenomenon is no different in kind from the spatial distance which separates us from contemporaneous but unobserved events occurring elsewhere in the universe. Thus the fact that there was no-one around 4.5 billion years ago to perceive the accretion of the earth is no more significant than the fact that there is currently no-one 25 million, million miles away perceiving events on the surface of Alpha Centauri. Moreover, the notion of 'distance' is an inherently ambiguous and unreliable indicator of the limits of perception: technology allows us to perceive objects extraordinarily far away in space and time, while myriad occurrences close at hand routinely go unperceived. In this regard, instances of spatiotemporal extremity are no different in kind from other banal instances of un-witnessed or un-perceived phenomena, such as the fact that we are never aware of everything going on inside our own bodies. Thus the arche-fossil is just another example of an un-perceived phenomenon and, as with all other examples of un-perceived phenomena, it merely exemplifies the inherently *lacunary* nature of manifestation – the fact that no phenomenon is ever exhaustively or absolutely apprehended by perception or consciousness. Far from denying this, both Kant and Husserl emphasized the intrinsically limited and finite nature of human cognition. Thus for Kant sensible intuition is incapable of exhaustively apprehending the infinite complexity of a datum of sensation. Similarly for Husserl, intentionality proceeds by adumbrations which never exhaust all the dimensions of the phenomenon. But the fact that every phenomenon harbours an un-apprehended remainder in no way undermines the constitutive status of transcendental consciousness. All that it shows is that manifestation is inherently lacunary and that the non-manifest inheres in every manifestation. A counterfactual suffices to establish the persistence of transcendental constitution even in cases of lacunary manifestation, such as the arche-fossil. Thus the contingent fact that no-one was there to witness the accretion of the earth is ultimately of no importance, for *had there been* a witness, they *would have* perceived the phenomenon of accretion unfolding in conformity with the laws of geology and physics which are transcendentally guaranteed by the correlation. Ultimately, the correlationist concludes, the argument from the arche-fossil fails to challenge correlationism because it has simply confused a contingent lacuna in manifestation with the necessary absence of manifestation.

Against this initial line of defence, Meillassoux insists that the arche-fossil cannot be reduced to an example of the un-perceived because the temporal anteriority involved in the notion of ancestrality remains irreducible to any notion of temporal 'distance' concomitant with correlational manifestation. To reduce the arche-fossil to an un-witnessed or un-perceived occurrence is to beg the question because it is to continue to assume that there is always a correlation in terms of which to measure gaps or lacunae within manifestation. But the arche-fossil is not merely a non-manifest gap or lacuna *in* manifestation; it is the lacuna *of* manifestation *tout court*. For the anteriority indexed by the ancestral phenomenon does not point to an earlier time *within* manifestation; it indexes a time *anterior to the time of manifestation in its entirety*; and it does so according to a sense of 'anteriority' which cannot be reduced to the past of manifestation because it indicates a time wherein manifestation – along with its past, present, and future dimensions – originally emerged. Thus, Meillassoux contends, the 'ancestral' cannot be reduced to the 'ancient'. There are always greater or lesser degrees of 'ancientness' depending on whatever temporal metric one happens to choose. 'Ancientness' remains a function of a relation between past and present which is entirely circumscribed by the conditions of manifestation and in this sense any past, no matter how 'ancient', remains synchronous with the correlational present. In equating temporal remove with spatial distance, the correlationist objection outlined above continues to assume this underlying synchronicity. But ancestrality indexes a radical 'diachronicity' which cannot be correlated with the present because it belongs to the time wherein the conditions of correlation between past, present, and future passed from inexistence into existence. Accordingly, ancestrality harbours a temporal diachronicity which remains incommensurable with any chronological measure that would ensure a reciprocity between the past, present, and future dimensions of the correlation.

Meillassoux detects in this initial correlationist response a subterfuge which consists in substituting a lacuna *in* and *for* manifestation – a lacuna that is contemporaneous with constituting consciousness, as is always the case with the un-perceived – for a lacuna *of* manifestation as such; one which cannot be synchronized with constituting consciousness (or whatever other transcendental operator happens to be invoked). The correlationist's sleight-of-hand here consists in reducing the arche-fossil – which is non-manifest insofar as it occurs prior to the emergence of conditions of manifestation – to the un-perceived, which is merely a measurable gap or absence within the extant conditions of manifestation. However, Meillassoux insists, the arche-fossil is neither a lacunary manifestation nor a temporal reality internal to manifestation (internal to the correlation), for it points to the temporal reality in which manifestation itself first came into existence, and wherein it will ultimately sink back into inexistence. Consequently, Meillassoux concludes, it is a serious misunderstanding to think that a counterfactual suffices to reintegrate the arche-fossil within the correlation, for the diachronicity it indexes cannot be synchronized with any correlational present.

3.2.2   Instantiating the transcendental

Having failed to rebuff the argument from the arche-fossil with this initial line of defence, the correlationist adopts a second strategy. This consists in contesting the claim that ancestrality indexes a temporal dimension within which correlational temporality itself passes into and out of being. For such an assertion betrays a fundamental confusion between the *transcendental* level at which the conditions of correlation obtain, and the *empirical* level at which the organisms and/or material entities which support those conditions exist. The latter are indeed spatiotemporal objects like any other, emerging and perishing within physical space-time; but the former provide the conditions of objectivation without which scientific knowledge of spatiotemporal objects – and hence of the arche-fossil itself – would not be possible. Though these conditions are physically instantiated by specific material objects – i.e. human organisms – they cannot be said to exist in the same manner, and hence they cannot be said to pass into or out of existence on pain of paralogism. Thus, the correlationist continues, the claim that the conditions of objectivation emerged in space-time is an absurd paralogism because it treats transcendental conditions as though they were objects alongside other objects. But the transcendental conditions of spatiotemporal objectivation do not exist spatiotemporally. This is not to say that they are eternal, for this would be to hypostatize them once again and to attribute another kind of objective existence to them, albeit in a transcendent or supernatural register. They are neither transcendent nor supernatural – they are the logical preconditions for ascriptions of existence, rather than objectively existing entities. As conditions for the scientific cognition of empirical reality – of which the arche-fossil is a prime example – they cannot themselves be scientifically objectified without engendering absurd paradoxes. The claim that ancestral time encompasses the birth and death of transcendental subjectivity is precisely such a paradox, but one which dissolves once the confusion from which it has arisen has been diagnosed.

Yet for Meillassoux, the initial plausibility of this response masks its underlying inadequacy, for it relies on an unacknowledged equivocation.

We are told that transcendental subjectivity cannot be objectified, and hence that it neither emerges nor perishes in space-time; but also that it is neither immortal nor eternal, in the manner of a transcendent metaphysical principle. Indeed, this is precisely what distinguishes transcendental subjectivity in its purported finitude from any metaphysical hypostatization of the principle of subjectivity which would render it equivalent to an infinitely enduring substance. But as finite, transcendental subjectivity is indissociable from the determinate set of material conditions which provide its empirical support. Thus Husserl insists on the necessary parallelism which renders the transcendental indissociable from the empirical. Indeed, it is this necessary parallelism which distinguishes the transcendental subject from its metaphysical predecessor. Accordingly, though transcendental subjectivity is merely instantiated in the minds of physical organisms, it cannot subsist independently of those minds and the organisms which support them. Although it does not exist in space and time, it has no other kind of existence apart from the spatiotemporal existence of the physical bodies in which it is instantiated. And it is precisely insofar as it is anchored in the finite minds of bounded physical organisms with limited sensory and intellectual capacities that human reason is not infinite. But if transcendental subjectivity is necessarily instantiated in the spatiotemporal existence of physical organisms, then it is not quite accurate to claim that it can be entirely divorced from objectively existing bodies. Indeed, in the wake of Heidegger's critique of the 'worldless' or disembodied subject of classical transcendentalism, post-Heideggerean philosophy can be said to have engaged in an increasing 'corporealization' of the transcendental. Merleau-Ponty is probably the most prominent (though certainly not the only) advocate of the quasi-transcendental status of embodiment. Accordingly, although transcendental subjectivity may not be reducible to objectively existing bodies, neither can it be divorced from them, for the existence of bodies provides the conditions of instantiation for the transcendental subject. Thus, Meillassoux concludes, while it is perfectly plausible to insist that the correlation provides the transcendental condition for knowledge of spatiotemporal existence, it is also necessary to point out that the time in which the bodies that provide the conditions of instantiation for the correlation emerge and perish is also the time which determines the conditions of instantiation of the transcendental. But the ancestral time which determines the conditions of instantiation of the transcendental cannot be encompassed within the time that is coextensive with the correlation because it is the time within which those corporeal conditions upon which the correlation depends pass into and out of existence. Where such conditions of instantiation are absent, so is the correlation. Thus the ancestral time indexed by the arche-fossil is simply the time of the inexistence of the correlation. This ancestral time is indexed by objective phenomena such as the arche-fossil; but its existence does not depend upon those conditions of objectivation upon which knowledge of the arche-fossil depends because it determines those conditions of instantiation which determine conditions of objectivation. (We shall see in Chapter 7 how this determining role which Meillassoux attributes to 'ancestral time' is better understood in terms of an 'objectivity' which provides the 'determinant-of-the-last-instance' for every variety of transcendental temporality.)

3.2.3   Ancestrality and chronology

Meillassoux's responses to his correlationist critics are as trenchant as they are resourceful, and they undoubtedly constitute a significant addition to his already weighty case against correlationism. However, they also invite a number of critical observations. First, it is not at all clear how Meillassoux's distinction between ancestrality and spatiotemporal distance can be squared with what twentieth-century physics has taught us concerning the fundamental indissociability of time and space, as enshrined in the Einstein–Minkowski conception of four-dimensional space-time. 'Anteriority' and 'posteriority' are inherently relational terms which can only be rendered intelligible from within a spatiotemporal frame of reference. In this regard, Meillassoux's insistence on the irreconcilable disjunction between a lacuna *in* manifestation and the lacuna *of* manifestation continues to rely on an appeal to the scalar incommensurability between the anthropomorphic time privileged by correlationism and the cosmological time within which the former is nested. This incommensurability is attributed to the fundamental asymmetry between cosmological and anthropomorphic time: whereas the former is presumed to encompass the beginning and end of the latter, the reverse is assumed not to be the case. However, Meillassoux conducts his case against correlationism in a logical rather than empirical register – indeed, we shall see below how this leads him to reiterate the Cartesian dualism of thought and extension – yet the asymmetry to which he appeals here is precisely a function of empirical fact, and as Meillassoux himself acknowledges (Meillassoux 2006: 161), there is no a priori reason why the existence of mind, and hence of the correlation, could not happen to be coextensive with the existence of the universe. Indeed, this is precisely the claim of Hegelianism, which construes mind or *Geist* as a self-relating negativity already inherent in material reality. Accordingly, the transcendence which Meillassoux ascribes to ancestral time as that which exists independently of correlation continues to rely upon an appeal to chronology: it is the (empirical) fact that cosmological time *preceded* anthropomorphic time and will presumably *succeed* it which is invoked in the account of the asymmetry between the two. In light of this implicit appeal to chronology in Meillassoux's claim that the arche-fossil indexes the absence of manifestation, rather than any hiatus within it, it is difficult to see how the temporal anteriority which he ascribes to the ancestral realm could ever be understood wholly independently of the spatiotemporal framework in terms of which cosmology coordinates relations between past, present, and future events. A simple change in the framework which determines chronology would suffice to dissolve the alleged incommensurability between ancestral and anthropomorphic time, thereby bridging the conceptual abyss which is supposed to separate anteriority from spatiotemporal distance.

The conclusion to be drawn is the following: as long as the autonomy of the in-itself is construed in terms of a merely chronological discrepancy between cosmological and anthropomorphic time, it will always be possible for the correlationist to convert the supposedly absolute anteriority attributed to the ancestral realm into an anteriority which is merely 'for us', not 'in itself'. By tethering his challenge to correlationism to the spatiotemporal framework favoured by contemporary cosmology, Meillassoux mortgages the autonomy of the in-itself to chronology. The only hope for securing the unequivocal independence of the '*an sich*' must lie in prizing it free from chronology as well as phenomenology. We shall see in Chapter 5 how this entails a conception of objectivity which excludes chronological relationality as much as phenomenological intentionality. Spatiotemporal relations should be construed as a function of objective reality, rather than objective reality construed as a function of spatiotemporal relations. By insisting on driving a wedge between ancestral time and spatiotemporal distance, Meillassoux inadvertently reiterates the privileging of time over space which is so symptomatic of idealism and unwittingly endorses his opponents' claim that all non-ancestral reality can be un-problematically accounted for by the correlation. Thus the trenchancy of Meillassoux's rejoinders above actually masks a significant concession to correlationism. For surely it is not just ancestral phenomena which challenge the latter, but simply the reality described by the modern natural sciences *tout court*. According to the latter, we are surrounded by processes going on quite independently of any relationship we may happen to have to them: thus plate tectonics, thermonuclear fusion, and galactic expansion (not to mention undiscovered oil reserves or unknown insect species) are as much autonomous, human-independent realities as the accretion of the earth. The fact that these processes are contemporaneous with the existence of consciousness, while the accretion of the earth preceded it, is quite irrelevant. To maintain the contrary, and insist that it is only the ancestral dimension that transcends correlational constitution, is to imply that the emergence of consciousness marks some sort of fundamental ontological rupture, shattering the autonomy and consistency of reality, such that once consciousness has emerged on the scene, nothing can pursue an independent existence any more.[7] The danger is that in privileging the arche-fossil as sole paradigm of a mind-independent reality, Meillassoux is ceding too much ground to the correlationism he wishes to destroy.[8]

3.3 The two regimes of sense

Notwithstanding these objections and counter-objections, there will undoubtedly be correlationists who simply refuse to acknowledge the pertinence of the argument from the arche-fossil. If so, then they have little choice but to deny the reality of the ancestral realm altogether. Thus, the obdurate correlationist will insist, though the arche-fossil seems to point to a non-correlational reality, this is an illusion, since the idea of a non-correlational reality is the idea of something's being manifest independently of the conditions of manifestation, which is absurd. For the unrepentant correlationist, the arche-fossil certainly exists here and now, in the correlational present, but as such its existence continues to depend upon the conditions of manifestation. However, the ancestral time which it seems to point to must be understood as a kind of cognitive hallucination. Since the meaning of the ancestral statement which designates the ancestral phenomenon as existing independently of the conditions of manifestation continues to depend upon the conditions which it seems to deny, the staunch correlationist will uphold the intelligibility of the ancestral statement, but only at the cost of denying the reality of the ancestral phenomenon. This is to convert the literal antecedence of the ancestral phenomenon indexed by the ancestral statement into something like a false memory-imprint generated within the human present but retroactively projected into the pre-human past. Accordingly, the correlationist will concede that the literal meaning of the ancestral statement does indeed refer to a non-correlational reality, but only before adding the decisive caveat: the ancestral statement certainly seems to designate a reality antecedent to the emergence of thought, but it can only designate it *in and for thinking*. For the correlationist, the literal meaning of the ancestral statement may well refer to a reality which predates the emergence of the conditions ensuring its conceptual intelligibility, but this literal meaning is merely superficial; it is rendered possible by a more profound regime of sense which anchors this empirical or ontic meaning in a more fundamental, i.e. transcendental or ontological dimension of sense, one which converts the independent reality designated by the ancestral statement into an independent reality *for us*. There are two regimes of meaning and truth for the correlationist: the ontic or empirical regime proper to the sciences; and the ontological or transcendental regime which is the privilege of philosophy. Scientists innocently assume the conceptual autonomy of the former, but the correlationist philosopher is always there to remind them that it is entirely dependent upon the latter. By the same token, the correlationist will insist that there are two temporalities at work here and that the scientist has 'naively' conflated them: there is the derivative, merely ontic temporality of physical-cosmological time, and the originary ontological temporality (or 'duration') which is the latter's precondition. The realist interpretation of the ancestral statement certainly seems to imply the inscription of ontological time within physical-cosmological time. But for the correlationist, this is to commit an elementary logical fallacy: for how could constituting ontological temporality ever be presumed to depend upon the ontic time which it constitutes? Thus the correlationist interpretation of the ancestral statement insists that we prioritize this 'logical' order over chronological succession: we should disregard the superficial chronology in which physical-cosmological time precedes and succeeds lived or conscious time, and look beyond it to the underlying logical order whereby the latter remains the precondition for the former. Indeed, for the correlationist, empirical chronology is merely an effect generated by the ontological temporality proper to the correlation.

Yet the correlationist's response continues to beg the question. For the logically conditioning function ascribed to lived or conscious time can only be maintained relative to those conditions which are taken to be constitutive of the experience of time commensurate with life or consciousness – it cannot be maintained independently of the possibility of any such experience. In fact, the correlationist defence already assumes from the outset the instrumentalist conception of science which should have been its result. Instrumentalism maintains that the entities postulated by scientific theory are merely heuristic fictions or calculating devices devoid of any mind-independent reality. Indeed, it is the un-stated assumption that scientific theorizing possesses a merely instrumental function within human experience, and is entirely encompassed within it, which underlies the claim that the preconditions for the human experience of reality are also the preconditions for the entities postulated by science.[9] The correlationist defence indulges in an illegitimate extrapolation from temporality as condition for experience to temporality as condition for the various non-experiential phenomena described by science, including physical-cosmological time itself. But this is already to assume precisely what the correlationist objection to the realist interpretation of the ancestral statement sought to demonstrate – namely, that scientific phenomena, ancestral or otherwise, are merely abstractions which derive whatever sense they have from some supposedly more primary dimension of experience. Though exposing this subreption does not suffice to establish the truth of scientific realism, it does reveal how, aside from pointing to its constitutive function vis-à-vis experience, correlationism is incapable of defending the claim that the temporality commensurate with life and consciousness is necessarily more fundamental than physical-cosmological time.

Of course, correlationism can simply obviate this difficulty by deciding to eternalize the correlation, which means eternalizing Life or Spirit as ontological absolutes – and the result is vitalism or absolute idealism. Alternatively, the correlationist can stop compromising with science altogether and simply deny the literal truth of science's ancestral statements *tout court*. This would mean insisting that the universe could not have existed prior to life or consciousness. In doing so however, they would find themselves endorsing a position which is remarkably close to that of creationists. And indeed, as Meillassoux acerbically remarks, the claim that the ancestral realm's chronological precedence vis-à-vis lived or conscious time is a lure distracting us from the latter's underlying logical primacy bears an uncomfortable resemblance to the creationist argument according to which fossils were planted by the Creator in order to test our faith in him.(Meillassoux 2006: 36) Perhaps cosmology was contrived by transcendental consciousness in order to test our faith in the perenniality of the latter?

Scientists have good reason to resist the correlationists' suggestion that the ultimate guarantor for the truth or falsity of ancestral statements resides in our present relation to the world rather than in a mind-independent reality billions of years in the past, for these are the blandishments of an urbane variety of creationism. In this regard, perhaps scientific realism towards the arche-fossil is less naive than the post-Kantian idealism which has become too coarse to be astonished by the latter. If the idea of a reality-in-itself has become philosophically unintelligible, then perhaps this is not so much symptomatic of a problem with 'reality' as with post-Kantian philosophy's criteria of intelligibility. For it is the literal intelligibility of the ancestral statement and the concomitant reality of the ancestral phenomenon which correlationism cannot countenance – for the good reason that the empirical inscription of the supposedly transcendental correlation would effectively pull the rug out from the correlationist edifice.

Ultimately, it is the Kantian dispensation of empirical and transcendental regimes of sense, and the concomitant division of labour between the ontic purview of the sciences and the ontological remit of philosophy, which needs to be called into question. For it has been turned into a pretext for evading the fundamental challenge posed to philosophy by modern science's unveiling of a reality which is as indifferent to life as it is to thought. Instead of cultivating a self-enclosed terrain from which to adjudicate transcendentally upon the claims of the natural sciences, philosophy should strive to rise to the challenge of the latter by providing an appropriate speculative armature for science's experimental exploration of a reality which need not conform to any of reason's putative interests or ends. Once we have discounted the claim that the empirical–transcendental division of labour presents a satisfactory resolution of the speculative problems put to philosophy by science, we can re-establish a level-playing field upon which it becomes incumbent for philosophy to rehabilitate the notion of a non-correlational reality the better to explicate the speculative implications of its scientific exploration – rather than continually reigning in the latter by tightening the correlationist leash. For once we have put science and philosophy on an equal footing before the real it becomes necessary to insist that there is no possible compromise between the claims of correlationism and the ancestral claims of science: if correlationism is true, science's ancestral claims are false; if the latter are true, correlationism is false. In point of fact, almost everything that the sciences teach us about the world seems to point to the falsity of correlationism: while the latter continues to insist on the uncircumventability of life and mind, the former patiently accumulates evidence of their peripheral and ephemeral status. The question then is: from its inception in Kant, how did correlationism ever come to seem like a plausible solution to the question about the possibility of scientific cognition?

3.4   The principle of factuality

To answer the above question we have to re-examine the remit of Kant's Copernican turn. Kant taught us to convert metaphysical questions about things-in-themselves into transcendental questions about our access to things. Thus, the post-Kantian philosophies of access[10] transform the metaphysical question 'What is X?' into the transcendental question 'Under what conditions do we come to be (experientially) related to X?' They convert the question about the possibility of knowledge into a question about the possibility of experience, encouraging us to translate questions about the nature of things into questions about our experience of things (whether cognitive/representational as in Kant or pre-cognitive/non-representational as in Heidegger). But post-Kantian correlationism has taught us to discard the distinction between phenomenal and noumenal realms, and as a result the very idea of a thinkable world subsisting in-itself, independently of our relation to it, is customarily dismissed as an unwarranted metaphysical leftover. Moreover, the ensuing priority of correlation over any metaphysical hypostatization of correlated terms entails either the reduction of the thing-in-itself to a regulative Idea of reason – i.e. to something which is wholly internal to thought – or its complete elimination. Yet what is the ancestral phenomenon if not a paradigmatic case of a thing-in-itself? The arche-fossil harbours a transcendental enigma about the possibility of rehabilitating the thing-in-itself. The transcendental question provoked by the ancestral phenomenon is: how is thought able to know an object whose existence does not depend upon some constituting relation to thought? In order to address this question, we need to be able to think terms independently of the primacy of relation, and hence to think the primacy of the object over any of its relations to things, whether they be thinking or non-thinking.[11] Only once we have confronted this transcendental quandary about the intelligibility of the thing-in-itself can we hope to address the attendant epistemological and semantic issues about the meaning of ancestral statements, realist versus instrumentalist conceptions of science, and so on. To believe that one can resolve these epistemological problems while suspending judgement about the transcendental issue is to continue to operate within the ambit of the correlationist circle and to leave its insidious ontological pretensions unquestioned. Science allows us to discover ancestral phenomena; it does not manufacture them. To claim the contrary is simply to have conceded everything to correlationism from the start. Thus what is at issue here is a re-interrogation of Kant's critical distinction between thinking and knowing.

Here again, Meillassoux's work proves indispensable. Following Meillassoux, we must distinguish between Kant's weak correlationism, which claims that we can *think* noumena even though we cannot *know* them, and strong correlationism, which claims that we *cannot even think them.* Weak correlationism insists on the finitude of reason and the conditional nature of our access to being. The conditions for knowledge (the categories and forms of intuition) apply only to the phenomenal realm, not to things in-themselves. Thus the cognitive structures governing the phenomenal realm are not necessary features of things-in-themselves. We cannot know why space and time are the only two forms of intuition, or why there are 12 rather than 11 or 13 categories. There is no sufficient reason capable of accounting for such a fact. In this sense, and this sense alone, these transcendental structures are contingent. But Hegel will point out that Kant has already overstepped the boundary between the knowable and the unknowable in presuming to know that the structure of things-in-themselves differs from the structure of phenomena. Accordingly, Hegel will proceed to re-inject that which is transcendentally constitutive of the 'for us' back into the 'in-itself'. Thus in Hegel's absolute idealism thinking grounds its own access to being once more and rediscovers its intrinsic infinitude. Where Kant's weak correlationism emphasizes the uncircumventable contingency inherent in the correlation between thinking and being, Hegelianism absolutizes the correlation and thereby insists on the necessary isomorphy between the structure of thinking and that of being. In this regard, strong correlationism can be understood as a critical rejoinder to the Hegelian absolutization of correlation. Though strong correlationism also jettisons the thing-in-itself, it retains the Kantian premium on the ineluctable contingency of the correlation, which Heidegger famously radicalizes in the notion of 'facticity' (*Faktizität*). Thus strong correlationism, as exemplified by figures such as Heidegger and Foucault, insists – contra Hegel – that the contingency of correlation cannot be rationalized or grounded in reason. This is the anti-metaphysical import of Heidegger's epochal 'history of being' or of Foucault's 'archaeology of knowledge'. Accordingly, if we are to break with correlationism, we must re-legitimate the possibility of thinking the thing-in-itself, yet do so without either absolutizing correlation or resorting to the principle of sufficient reason.

In a remarkable *tour de force*, Meillassoux shows how what is most powerful in strong correlationism can be used to overcome it from within. And what is most powerful in it is precisely its insistence on the facticity of correlation. For on what basis does strong correlationism reject the Hegelian rehabilitation of the principle of sufficient reason – the claim that contradiction is the ground of being[12] – and the ensuing isomorphy between thinking and being? It does so by insisting on the facticity or non-necessity of correlation against its Hegelian absolutization – thought's access to being is extrinsically conditioned by non-conceptual factors, which cannot be rationalized or reincorporated within the concept, not even in the form of dialectical contradiction. Thus, in order to emphasize the primacy of facticity against the speculative temptation to absolutize correlation, strong correlationism must insist that everything is without reason – even correlation itself. Against Hegel's speculative idealism, which seeks to show how the correlation can demonstrate its own necessity by grounding itself, thereby becoming absolutely necessary or *causa sui*, strong correlationism must maintain that such self-grounding is impossible by demonstrating that the correlation cannot know itself to be necessary. For though we can claim that an empirical phenomenon is necessary or contingent in conformity with the transcendental principles governing the possibility of knowledge, we cannot know whether these principles themselves are either necessary or contingent, for we have nothing to compare them to. This argument proceeds on the basis of a distinction between contingency, which is under the jurisdiction of knowledge, and facticity, which is not. Contingency is empirical and pertains to phenomena: a phenomenon is contingent if it can come into or out of existence without violating the principles of cognition that govern phenomena. Facticity is transcendental and pertains to our cognitive relation to phenomena, and hence to the principles of knowledge themselves, concerning which it makes no sense to say either that they are necessary or that they are contingent, since we have no other principles to compare them to. Against absolute idealism then, strong correlationism insists that to affirm the necessity of the correlation is to contravene the norms of knowledge. Yet in so doing, it violates its own stricture: for in order to claim that the correlation is not necessary, it has no choice but to affirm its contingency.

Accordingly, strong correlationism is obliged to contravene its own distinction between what is knowable and what is unknowable in order to protect it; it must assert the contingency of correlation in order to contradict the idealist's assertion of its necessity. But to affirm the contingency of correlation is also to assert the necessity of facticity and hence to overstep the boundary between what can be known – contingency – and what cannot be known – facticity – in the very movement that is supposed to reassert its inviolability. For in order to maintain the contingency of correlation and stave off absolute idealism, strong correlationism must insist on the necessity of its facticity – but it cannot do so without knowing something which, by its own lights, it is not supposed to know. Thus it finds itself confronted with the following dilemma: it cannot de-absolutize facticity without absolutizing the correlation; yet it cannot de-absolutize the correlation without absolutizing facticity.

But to absolutize facticity is to assert the unconditional necessity of its contingency, and hence to assert that it is possible to think something that exists independently of thought's relation to it: contingency as such. In absolutizing facticity, correlationism subverts the empirical–transcendental divide separating knowable contingency from unknowable facticity even as it strives to maintain it; but it is thereby forced to acknowledge that what it took to be a negative characteristic of our relation to things – viz., that we cannot know whether the principles of cognition are necessary or contingent – is in fact a positive characteristic of things-in-themselves.

It is worthwhile pausing here to underline the decisive distinction between the idealist and realist variants of the speculative overcoming of correlationism. Speculative idealism claims that the in-itself is not some transcendent object standing 'outside' the correlation, but is rather nothing other than the correlation as such. Thus it converts relationality per se into a thing-in-itself or absolute: the dialectician claims that we overcome the metaphysical reification of the in-itself when we realize that what we took to be merely for-us is in fact in-itself. Correlation is absolutized when it becomes *in itself for itself*. But this involves transforming correlation into a metaphysically necessary entity or *causa sui*. By way of contrast, Meillassoux's speculative materialism asserts that the only way to preserve the in-itself from its idealist incorporation into the for-us without reifying it metaphysically is by realizing that what is in-itself is the *contingency* of the for-us, not its necessity. Thus, when facticity is absolutized, it is the contingency or groundlessness of the for-us (the correlation) which becomes in-itself or necessary precisely insofar as its contingency is not something which is merely for-us. Speculative materialism asserts that, in order to maintain our ignorance of the necessity of correlation, we have to know that its contingency is necessary. In other words, if we can never know the necessity of anything, this is not because necessity is unknowable but because we know that only contingency necessarily exists. What is absolute is the fact that everything is necessarily contingent or 'without-reason'.

Consequently, when forced to pursue the ultimate consequences of its own premises, correlationism is obliged to turn our ignorance concerning the necessity or contingency of our knowledge of phenomena into a thinkable property of things-in-themselves. The result, as Meillassoux puts it, is that '[t]he absolute is the absolute impossibility of a necessary being' (Meillassoux 2006: 82). This is Meillassoux's 'principle of factuality' and though it might seem exceedingly slight, its implications are far from trivial. For it imposes significant constraints upon thought. If a necessary being is conceptually impossible then the only absolute is

the real possibility of the completely arbitrary and radically unpre-
dictable transformation of all things from one moment to the next. It is
important not to confuse this with familiar Heraclitean or Nietzschean
paeans to absolute becoming, for the latter merely substitutes the
metaphysical necessity of perpetual differentiation for the metaphysical
necessity of perpetual identity. To affirm the metaphysical primacy of
becoming is to claim that it is impossible for things not to change;
impossible for things to stay the same; and ergo to claim that it is necessary for things to keep changing. The flux of ceaseless becoming is
thereby conceived as ineluctable and as metaphysically necessary as
unchanging stasis. But metaphysical necessity, whether it be that of
perpetual flux or of permanent fixity, is precisely what the principle of
absolute contingency rules out. The necessity of contingency, Meillassoux
maintains, implies an absolute time which can interrupt the flux of
becoming with the same arbitrary capriciousness as it can scramble the
fixity of being. Absolute time is tantamount to a 'hyper-chaos' for which
nothing is impossible, unless it be the production of a necessary being.
It is a contingency which usurps every possible order, including the
order of disorder or the constancy of inconstancy. It is all-powerful; but
an absolute power which is 'without norms, blind, and devoid of all the
other divine perfections [...] It is a power possessing neither goodness
nor wisdom [...] a time capable of destroying becoming itself by bringing
forth, perhaps forever, fixity, stasis, and death' (Meillassoux 2006: 88).
Absolute time is omnipotent, but in the manner of a 'blind idiot god'
which is the ruin of every future-oriented faith, whether it be faith in
order, becoming, meaning, or redemption. Faith in the future, expectancy
of the *parousia* of sense, is among the principal tenets of Judaeo-Christian
monotheism. And lest we forget, it was precisely in order to make room
for faith that Kant set out to define the limits of scientific reason. For
however 'enlightened' or 'secular' its initial agenda might have been, the
critique of metaphysical rationalism has ended up providing a philosophical alibi for 'fideism': the claim that reason has no absolute jurisdiction
over reality, and hence cannot be invoked to disqualify the possibility
of religious faith. If reason's jurisdiction is confined to the phenomenal
realm, then reason is in no position to rule out the possibility that faith
might harbour a mode of non-conceptual access to the in-itself. Thus
post-Kantian philosophy has abjured rationalist atheism for a profoundly
equivocal species of agnosticism – something which is nowhere more
apparent than in the work of Heidegger and Wittgenstein, with their
thinly disguised exaltations of mystico-religious illumination over conceptual rationality.[13] But where the post-Kantian critique of reason seems to

license irrational and/or religious hypotheses about the ultimate nature of reality, Meillassoux's rationalist critique of the critique of reason aims to rehabilitate reason's claim to be able to access reality as it is in itself by purging rationalism of its metaphysical accoutrements. For it is reason itself that now prescribes the destitution of all rational necessity and the enthronement of absolute contingency as the only certainty.

3.5 The three figures of factuality

Meillassoux draws three unexpected consequences from this absolutization of contingency. First, that a contradictory entity is impossible. Second, that it is absolutely necessary that contingent entities exist. Third and lastly, that the laws of nature themselves are contingent. He refers to these speculative theses as 'figures' of factuality and the arguments through which they are established as 'derivations'. While the first two theses are derived directly from Meillassoux's principle of factuality, the third is established indirectly via an independent argument.[14] Where Kant assumes but never satisfactorily demonstrates that the in-itself exists, and that it is non-contradictory, Meillassoux's aim in establishing the first two theses is to progress from a Kantian to a Cartesian conception of the 'in-itself': one whose non-contradictoriness (or more precisely, logical consistency) ensures its mathematizability, and whose mind-independent existence can be directly demonstrated without resorting to God. For strange as it may seem, Meillassoux's project is essentially Cartesian: by rehabilitating thought's access to the absolute, he hopes to demonstrate mathematical science's direct purchase on things-in-themselves. Obviously, Meillassoux's is a non-metaphysical absolute of contingency, rather than the traditional absolute of necessity. Nevertheless, the claim is that mathematical thought enjoys direct access to noumena precisely insofar as the latter possess certain mathematically intuitable characteristics, to which all rational knowledge must conform: principally, that every entity is necessarily contingent, that contingent entities necessarily exist, and that even the regularities which mathematical science discerns in nature ('the laws of nature') are necessarily contingent. We shall recapitulate his arguments for each of these three theses in turn.

3.5.1 The impossibility of contradiction

Meillassoux's argument for the first thesis, as audacious as it is ingenious, runs as follows: Supposing a contradictory entity existed, it would be an entity capable of sustaining contradictory predicates; thus it would at once be what it is and what it is not. But if something is at once what it is and what it is not, then it cannot undergo transformation, for it is already what it is not. It is impossible to define a predicate or property which it does not now have but did possess in the past or could come to possess in the future, since, being contradictory, it is defined as that entity which is simultaneously A and not-A, B and not-B, and so on. Consequently, a contradictory entity could never become other than it is now, for it is already 'other than itself' as it exists now. But this is tantamount to saying that a contradictory entity has always been and will always remain as it is, for it is always already everything which it is not. Since it remains self-identical in being-other than itself, it cannot pass into or out of existence. Thus it exists necessarily, since it is impossible to conceive of it as not existing. And as Meillassoux points out, this necessary existence is in fact the hallmark of the Hegelian absolute, whose lifeblood is contradiction. Only the absolute is contradictory because only the contradictory necessarily exists. But as Hegel well knew, only absolute identity is capable of sustaining contradiction, since only the absolute can be identity of sameness and alterity. Moreover, it cannot be objected that the contradictory is not absolute since it excludes contingency – on the contrary, the Hegelian absolute is fully capable of embracing contingency as well as necessity. But the contingency which the Hegelian absolute incorporates within itself is merely the conceptless materiality of nature through which the Notion must pass in order to achieve and realize its own autonomy and independence, which is to say, its own necessity. The contingency which is predicated of its individual moments is subordinated to the superior necessity of the contradictory process as a whole. If Hegel affirms the necessity of material contingency, this is only insofar as it is determinately negated by the self-moving Notion.

Unlike Hegel, Meillassoux does not claim that contingency is necessary in the sense of being incorporated within the absolute, but that contingency and contingency alone is absolutely necessary. Where the speculative idealist affirms that 'contingency is necessary in the absolute' – as in Žižek's favoured example, where a contingent material determinant is retroactively posited by the subject as necessary for the realization of its own autonomy[15] – the speculative materialist affirms that 'contingency alone is absolute and hence necessary'. As we now know, this 'principle of un-reason', far from allowing anything and everything, actually imposes a hugely significant constraint on the chaos of absolute time: the latter can do anything, except bring forth a contradictory entity. For a contradictory entity – such as Hegel's absolute Spirit or the

Nietzschean–Heraclitean flux of absolute becoming – would be necessary and hence eternal. But this is precisely what the absolutization of contingency prohibits. Nothing is necessary, not even perpetual becoming; nothing is immutable, not even eternal flux.

Thus, far from licensing irrationalism, Meillassoux's principle of factuality effectively banishes it. It precludes the possibility of pantheism as much as of fideism. For just as the pathos of finitude can and indeed has left the door open for the claim that there are non-conceptual modes of access to infinite alterity – the 'Other to come', 'redemption', etc.; so Life's eternal becoming can and indeed has been divinized as the 'One-All' whose affirmation by vitalists so easily tips over into an imperative to mystical participation, perpetuating the pathos of reverence which remains the hallmark of religiosity. But the intelligible absurdity of absolute time stymies any temptation to revere it, whether as 'infinite Other' or as 'One-All' – and so the principle of un-reason precludes the temptation of vitalist pantheism as well as the fideism of finitude.

3.5.2 The necessary existence of contingency

The second consequence which Meillassoux derives from the principle of factuality is the claim that it is necessary that contingent entities exist. This claim is liable to a 'weak' and a 'strong' interpretation. The weak interpretation states that if and only if something exists, then it exists contingently. The strong interpretation claims that it is absolutely necessary that contingent entities exist. If one accepts the principle of factuality, then one is at least committed to the weak version of the claim. But as we know, this principle states that facticity is a property of things-in-themselves, not of our representation of things. Thus the weak interpretation is tantamount to the claim that there is a facticity of facticity or that contingent existence exists contingently. On this reading of the principle, not only is existence contingent; *that* contingent entities exist is itself nothing but a contingent fact. But the claim that it is not necessary that contingent things exist has to invoke a second-order facticity or contingency in order to deny the necessity of contingent existence at the level of fact. It has to absolutize this second-order facticity as something pertaining to existence 'in-itself' in order to relativize the first-order facticity of existing things to the status of a contingent fact 'for us'. Contingency is absolutized as something independent of the 'for us' even as it is deployed in order to relativize it to the latter. Thus the weak interpretation has to assert the necessity of contingently existing things at the transcendental level in order to deny it at the empirical level. Moreover, any attempt at cancelling this assertion by ascending to an even higher level which would render the facticity of facticity itself contingent would immediately entail an infinite regress. For at every level at which contingency is affirmed of itself it is also thereby absolutized. Thus the reaffirmation of facticity in the attempt to deny its necessity absolutizes it as something which is a necessary property of existence in-itself, rather than a contingent feature of our representation of existence. In so doing it unwittingly confirms the strong interpretation of the principle: it is not just a contingent fact that contingent entities exist; it is an absolute necessity.

Nevertheless, one could object to this as follows: Since the contingency of existence implies that existing things could not be as they are, and that inexistent things could exist, then all that the previous argument has established is the necessary contingency of the latter, i.e. the necessary contingency of inexistent things; not the necessary contingency of existing things. In other words, this objection maintains that, though it is absolutely necessary that inexistent things could exist, it is not absolutely necessary that existing things exist. The absolute necessity of facticity is merely a guarantor of the necessity of inexistent things; not a guarantor of the necessity of existing things. This objection may be countered as follows: To grant that facticity is thinkable as an absolute is to grant that it is thinkable *tout court*. If this is so then it cannot be divided up into the facticity of existence, on one hand, and the facticity of inexistence on the other. For the possible inexistence of existent things is as much an ineluctable feature of facticity as is the possible existence of inexistent things: both the possibility of existence and that of inexistence are necessary conditions for thinking facticity. And though we can conceive of the existence or inexistence of entities, we cannot conceive of the existence or inexistence of existence per se. A fortiori, though we can conceive of an existing entity as contingent, we cannot conceive of existence per se as contingent – for to do so would be to think its possible inexistence, and we are perfectly incapable of thinking nothingness.[16] Consequently, if one concedes the absoluteness of facticity (i.e. the absolute necessity of contingency), it is no more legitimate to restrict the necessity of contingency to inexistent things than it is feasible to think inexistence *tout court*. If the contingency of existence is absolutely necessary, then it is absolutely necessary that contingently existing things exist. Or as Meillassoux puts it: 'It is necessary rather than contingent that there is something rather than nothing because it is necessarily contingent that there is something rather than something else. The necessity of the contingency of the entity imposes the necessary existence of the contingent entity' (Meillassoux 2006: 103).

One of the more salutary effects of Meillassoux's approach here is its deliberate demystification of Leibniz's ultimate metaphysical quandary: 'Why is there something rather than nothing?' In this regard, it provides a telling contrast to Heidegger's treatment of the same question. For Heidegger's critique of metaphysics not only disqualifies traditional metaphysical responses to the question, appealing as they do to the principle of sufficient reason; it also rules out the possibility of any conceptual resolution of the problem, thereby engaging in an exorbitant inflation of the question which magnifies its difficulty to the point where it assumes the status of a supposedly abyssal challenge to conceptual rationality.[17] Contra Heidegger, Meillassoux proposes a deflationary resolution of the quandary which dispels the aura of fathomless profundity with which Heidegger and others have invested it. For it is precisely the disqualification of traditional metaphysical responses to the question evoking the transcendence of a supreme being or *causa sui* that leaves the door open for another, even more pernicious variety of transcendence: the unobjectifiable transcendence of the 'infinitely Other', or in the specific case of Heidegger's neo-pagan romanticism, of *Ereignis* as 'co-propriation' of gods, mortals, earth, and sky. Moreover, the positivist critique of metaphysics is no better at staving off this return of religious transcendence than its Heideggerean counterpart. For as the example of Wittgenstein's *Tractatus* makes clear, it is the claim that such metaphysical questions are meaningless, and hence unanswerable, which makes room for the mystical: 'It is not *how* things are in the world that is mystical, but *that* it exists' (Wittgenstein 1974: 6.4.4).[18] So long as the question remains unanswerable, the door is left open for every variety of religious mystification, and whether it is pagan, monotheistic, or pantheistic in tenor is beside the point. As Meillassoux puts it:

> The question must be resolved, since to claim that it is insoluble or devoid of meaning is still to legitimate its celebration; but its resolution should not elevate us to the eminence of a first cause – only to the reminder of the latter's eternal absence. We must free ourselves of the question – and this involves not just resolving it, but formulating an answer to it which is necessarily disappointing, so that this disappointment becomes the most instructive thing about it. The only appropriate attitude when faced with such a problem is to maintain that there is little at stake in it, and that the soul's *vibrato* when confronted with it, whether sardonic or profound, is inappropriate.
>
> (Meillassoux 2006: 98)

3.5.3   The inconstancy of nature

The third and final consequence of the principle of factuality is arguably the most provocative – no small feat given the controversial character of the first two. Meillassoux proposes a new perspective on Hume's 'problem of causality'. The latter is now commonly referred to as 'the problem of induction'. But Meillassoux considers this to be a misprision of the true character of Hume's problem, which concerns rather the principle of the uniformity of nature. Where many philosophers seem to identify the two problems, Meillassoux insists that they must be separated. To understand what is at stake in this separation, we must briefly recapitulate what is supposed to be at stake in the problem of induction.

In analysing our notion of causality, Hume breaks down the relationship between a cause A and an effect B into three fundamental components: spatiotemporal contiguity of A and B; temporal priority of A over B; and constant conjunction, such that A is invariably accompanied by B and vice versa.[19] But as Hume points out, there is nothing in contiguity, priority, and conjunction that accounts for the supposedly 'logical' necessity which we take to be an ineliminable feature of the causal relationship between A and B. Moreover, Hume insists, the only way of establishing something's existence or inexistence is either by reference to experience or to the principle of contradiction. Yet a posteriori, there is nothing in our experience of contiguity, priority, or conjunction to justify our assumption that the relationship between A and B is underwritten by logical necessity; and a priori, there is nothing logically contradictory about the idea of A or B occurring without any relationship of contiguity, succession, or conjunction between them. Hume concludes that even if all past occurrences of B have always been observed to follow occurrences of A, this does not justify the inference that B will follow A in the future. In other words, we cannot assume that any particular occurrence of AB – where A and B are bound together by contiguity, priority, and conjunction – instantiates a universal principle of causation. Inductive reasoning, which supposedly infers the truth of a universal principle from a particular instance, is invalid. Why then do we infer that a regularity which has always been observed until now will hold in the future? Hume's response is that our belief in causality, and inductive inference more generally, is merely a function of the association of ideas, and hence a psychological habit, nothing more. But habit does not provide a rational warrant for the inductive inference that the instance AB instantiates a universal law whereby B must follow A. Thus Hume's critical analysis of the concept of causality casts doubt upon the validity of the kind of inductive inference which is taken by many to be central to the scientific enterprise.

More specifically, Hume's critique of induction casts doubt upon the verifiability of scientific theory. For it is logically impossible to conclusively verify a universal proposition by reference to experience. And it is in response to Hume that Popper's falsificationist philosophy of science insists that science does not and need not resort to induction. Science's law-like generalizations are not inductively verified, but rather deductively falsified. Experiment can never verify a scientific law, since we cannot use inductive inference to confirm the truth of a generalization in the future; it can only falsify it, since a single counter-example to a scientific generalization allows us to deduce its falsity. Consequently, even our best-corroborated scientific theories could be falsified by new experiments and currently unforeseeable counter-instances. But note that Popper's anti-inductivism does not claim that the same experiments could falsify our theories in the future; rather, it claims that new experiments or new interpretations of old experiments could falsify currently corroborated theories. Thus even falsificationism seems to presuppose the uniformity of nature, for it requires a minimally stable reality such that identical experimental conditions yield identical results from one moment to the next. Were that stability to be lacking, so that the same experimental conditions which corroborated a theory at time t_1 falsified it at time t_2, then experimental science as we know it – whether inductivist or non-inductivist – would become impossible. Yet it is precisely this uniformity, and thus the very possibility of an experimental science of nature, which Hume's critique of causality undermines.[20]

The key moment in Hume's account which Meillassoux fastens upon is the point at which Hume underlines the striking discrepancy between the vast realm of logical possibility and the narrow domain of empirical actuality. When billiard ball A strikes billiard ball B, Hume reminds us, we can easily imagine any number of logically possible alternatives to the actual outcome which we invariably do observe:

> When I see, for instance, a Billiard-ball moving in a straight line towards another; even suppose motion in the second ball should by accident be suggested to me, as the result of their contact or impulse; may I not conceive, that a hundred different events might as well follow from that cause? May not both these balls remain at absolute rest? May not the first ball return in a straight line, or leap off from the second in any line or direction? All these suppositions are consistent

and conceivable. Why then should we give the preference to one, which is no more consistent or conceivable than the rest? All our reasonings a priori will never be able to shew us any foundation for this preference.

(Hume 1957: 44)

Though there is no good reason why we should find one outcome more inherently plausible than another, our belief in causality encourages us to assume that the actually observed outcome is somehow 'necessary', while all the other conceivable outcomes are merely contingent logical chimeras. And since neither experience nor reason provides grounds for this apparent necessity, Hume insists, we have to look elsewhere for it; specifically, to the psycho-physiological principle of association. Thus, finding no rationale for the putative necessity of causality in either logic or experience, Hume relocates it in our relation to phenomena. For as Meillassoux points out, Hume would rather root the uniformity of appearances in habit than give it up altogether. Having convincingly demonstrated that the uniformity of appearances cannot be legitimated by experience or reason, Hume refuses to opt for the obvious conclusion: viz., that appearances notwithstanding, causal necessity, and hence the uniformity of nature, is an illusion. Instead of endorsing reason's destruction of the consistency of appearances, Hume explains the appearance of uniformity by anchoring it in habit, which he characterizes as an unavoidable psycho-physiological disposition. In fact, Meillassoux continues, Hume's provision of a psycho-physiological basis for our irrational faith in uniformity, and his unwillingness to embrace its rational dissolution, reveals how, for all his anti-metaphysical scepticism, he remains in thrall to the principle of sufficient reason. Indeed, the principle of the uniformity of nature is merely an avatar of the latter, for to concede the undeniable albeit inexplicable existence of regularities in nature is to grant the implication that there is an underlying reason why one thing happens rather than another. Though Hume demonstrates that our belief that one outcome is more necessary than another is grounded in nothing more than habit, and though he insists that the existence of uniformity cannot be demonstrated by experience or reason, he nevertheless refuses to deny its existence altogether, since to do so would involve subordinating the authority of experience to that of reason. Since the appearance of uniformity is generated by habit, and since we are creatures of habit, Hume is effectively insisting that the appearance of uniformity is uncircumventable. Moreover, since Hume's empiricism rules out any appeal to noumena – sensibility providing our only access to reality – his claim that habit generates the appearance of uniformity is tantamount to claiming that uniformity inheres in the structure of phenomena, phenomena being the only reality there is. Accordingly, Hume never calls into question the reality of uniformity; he merely denies that we could ever know the reason for it – in other words, he denies that we could ever rationally demonstrate the necessity of uniformity. Hume continues to assume that there is a reason why one thing happens rather than another; that there is a reason why the world is thus and so rather than some other way. But, because he tethers reason to experience, he cannot avoid the sceptical conclusion that we will never be able to fathom the underlying reason for this uniformity. Where metaphysics provided a dogmatic warrant for the necessity of uniformity through the principle of reason, Hume's empiricism turns the constancy of appearances into a function of habit, while his scepticism confiscates insight into the ground of uniformity from reason and abandons it to faith. In this way, Hume's scepticism paves the way not only for Kant's transcendentalization of uniformity, but more profoundly, for Kant's critical legitimation of fideism.

By rooting uniformity in association and association in habit, Hume has already partly engaged the correlationist turn which it will fall to Kant to complete. Rather than denying the reality of uniformity, Hume denies the rationality of our belief in it and explains how that belief originates in habit. In so doing, he transforms the question of the uniformity of nature into a question about how our experience of constancy is possible. And this is precisely the question that Kant takes up in the *Critique of Pure Reason*. Kant transforms the metaphysical question about why uniformity should be a necessary feature of reality in-itself into a transcendental question about why constancy should be a necessary feature of our experience of phenomena. Kant's response is disarmingly straightforward: if there were no constancy whatsoever in appearances, then no representation of appearances (i.e. phenomena) would be possible. Hume's imaginary scenario in which the anomalous behaviour of billiard balls confounds our habitual expectations of causal necessity is only representable because it continues to assume the global stability of the context within which a local interruption of the causal order is envisaged. But if causality were suspended absolutely, it would also affect this global level and no such context would remain, for it would not just be the billiard balls which behaved unpredictably but the table, walls, floors, and everything else comprised in the scene, including we ourselves and our perceptual apparatus. Such a scenario is not even representable in imagination because representation itself would become impossible. But since representation manifestly occurs, this fact suffices to refute the sceptical hypothesis of a world without constancy. Without it, says Kant, '[I]t would be possible for appearances to crowd in upon the soul, and yet to be such as would never allow of experience. Since connection in accordance with universal and necessary laws would be lacking, all relation of knowledge to objects would fall away. The appearances might indeed constitute intuition without thought, but not knowledge, and consequently would be for us as good as nothing' (Kant 1929: A 111). Thus, Kant concludes, a world not subject to the rule of causality and to the principle of uniformity, is strictly inconceivable, for we cannot even represent to ourselves a reality totally devoid of constancy wherein all phenomena are subject to chaotic transformations. Kant's claim is not that uniformity is a necessary feature of things-in-themselves, but that the possibility of consciousness and representation require the constancy of phenomena, and this constancy itself presupposes the uniformity of phenomena, and hence of nature. Uniformity becomes a necessary feature of the representation of phenomena, and this necessity is underwritten by transcendental synthesis according to concepts and ultimately grounded in pure apperception. It is on this basis that the *Critique of Pure Reason* will go on to demonstrate why those law-like regularities which mathematical science discerns in nature are necessary features of phenomenal reality insofar as the very possibility of its representation presupposes them:

> Thus the concept of a cause is nothing but a synthesis (of that which follows in the time-series, with other appearances) *according to concepts*; and without such unity, which has its a priori rule, and which subjects the appearances to itself, no thoroughgoing, universal, and therefore necessary unity of consciousness would be met with in the manifold of perceptions. These perceptions would not then belong to any appearance, consequently would be without an object, merely a blind play of representations, less even than a dream.
>
> (Kant 1929: A 112)

In sum, Kant's solution to the riddle of induction is as follows: we do not illegitimately infer universal principles, such as the law of causality, from particular instances, since our representation of those instances is already conditioned by those universal principles. The necessity of causality is not inferred – it is presupposed.

But Meillassoux detects an unstated inference and an unavowed assumption in Kant's attempt to furnish a transcendental legitimation for the necessity of uniformity. The unstated inference is the one whereby Kant infers from the claim that science's representation of reality requires the uniformity of nature the quite distinct claim that this uniformity – and hence the laws of nature – is necessary. Yet the stability of the laws does not entail their necessity. For as Meillassoux points out, even if representation presupposes constancy, and constancy requires uniformity, one cannot conclude from this that uniformity is necessary. It simply does not follow unless one has already identified uniformity *with* necessity. But this is simply to beg Hume's question all over again. Moreover, Kant compounds this unwarranted inference with an unstated assumption, viz., that if phenomena were inconsistent, and the laws of nature contingent, they would transmogrify frequently, and it is the frequency of their transformation which would render representation impossible: 'If cinnabar were sometimes red, sometimes black, sometimes light, sometimes heavy, if a man changed sometimes into this and sometimes into that animal form, if the country on the longest day were sometimes covered with fruit, sometimes with ice and snow, my empirical imagination would never find opportunity when representing red colour to bring to mind heavy cinnabar' (Kant: A 100). The tempo of these alternating 'sometimes' implies a rate of transformation frequent enough to inhibit the act of synthesis whereby the mind reproduces the determinate properties of individuated appearances from one moment of consciousness to the next. Thus, Kant reasons, if appearances were not subject to necessary regularities, their rate of transformation would be such as to preclude the representation of objects, and this would not go unnoticed by consciousness. Just as the contingency of the laws of nature is taken to imply the inconsistency of appearances, conversely, their stability is taken to imply their necessity. In Kant's response to Hume's problem, it is the putative frequency of transformation, not the contingency of the laws, which entails the impossibility of representation. Meillassoux calls this 'the frequentialist implication'. Having identified it, he proceeds to elaborate an 'anti-frequentialist' argument to demonstrate why the contingency of the laws of nature need not entail their frequent transformation and hence the impossibility of representation. His ultimate purpose here, of course, is to show that the principle of un-reason is perfectly compatible with the stability of appearances and the scientific representation of nature.

The 'frequentialist argument' for the necessity of the laws of nature can be reconstructed in terms of a piece of probabilistic reasoning.[21] We noted above how, in Hume's example of the billiard-balls, there is a striking discrepancy between the vast realm of logical possibility and the relatively narrow domain of empirical actuality. Here, contrary to the familiar Kantian schema, it is the a priori realm of logical possibility which seems to be governed by contingency, and the a posteriori domain of empirical actuality which seems to be subject to necessity. Moreover, physics itself teaches us that it is perfectly possible to envisage universes in which different sets of physical constants obtain, and which would therefore be governed by alternative physical laws. If we imagine these alternative physical universes concomitant with the realm of logical possibility as the faces of a die and the structure of the physical universe uncovered by experimental science as one particular configuration of the die, then – bearing in mind that these dice are no longer just six sided but rather *n*-sided, and that the number of possible configurations is astronomical if not actually infinite – we can re-interpret Hume's problem thus: why is it that from among all the possible outcomes of throwing the die, every scientifically recorded throw so far has invariably registered the same configuration? On the basis of this analogy between possible universes and faces of the die, the frequentialist argument proceeds as follows: if the uniformity we discern in our universe were contingent, then the chance recurrence of those regularities which have been experimentally corroborated would be so unlikely as to be astronomically improbable. Indeed, the aleatory repetition of an identical outcome over billions of throws is so overwhelmingly unlikely as to indicate loaded dice. But this weighting of the dice cannot be understood in terms of logical possibility, since a priori every outcome is equally probable and hence equally contingent; therefore it must pertain to some set of physical factors inherent in the structure of the die as such, and it is these factors which make our universe, and by implication its physical structure, necessary rather than contingent – even if these factors and the reason for this necessity currently defy scientific explanation.

At the heart of this argument lies the contrast between the vast number of logically possible outcomes and the comparatively tiny number of actual outcomes. The argument assumes that it is possible to quantify the series of chance repetitions (causal regularities) and assign to them a determinate numerical value in order to then calculate the probability of the same regularities recurring time and time again throughout the series. In this regard, it does not matter whether the series is finite or infinite so long as it can be assigned a determinate numerical value, for infinities are no obstacle to probabilistic calculation. But this conclusion about the astronomical unlikelihood of observable regularities in a world in which uniformity is contingent relies on two assumptions: first, that it is possible to totalize chance as a whole, in the form of all logically possible outcomes; second, that the notion of probability which is applicable to occurrences *within* the world can be extended to the occurrence of the world *as such*. Meillassoux's counter-argument calls both assumptions into question.

First, he suggests, Cantor's work gives us good reason *not* to accept the assumption that it is possible to totalize chance as a numerically determinate 'whole'. In this regard, the dice analogy implicit in the frequentialist argument is misleading because it invites us to imagine that there could be a totality of possible universes – a 'multiverse', in effect – on a par with the totality of possible configurations of the dice. But whether the cardinality of the latter is said to be finite or transfinite, Cantor has shown that a bigger cardinality will always be possible. Though we may quantify one or several series of occurrences within the world, we cannot quantify 'all' possible series and take that totality to be equivalent to 'the world' itself. Yet this is precisely what the frequentialist argument would have to do in order to demonstrate the astronomical improbability of the experiential regularities we perceive occurring randomly from among a vastly greater number of logically conceivable possibilities. Thus, while the frequentialist assumes that these possibilities can be fixed as a numerical totality, Meillassoux insists that the concept of totality has no purchase in this context – not because we cannot quantify the infinite, since we clearly can, but because we cannot *totalize* it. Given any set of logically possible outcomes for any event in the world, regardless of whether the set is finite or infinite, there will always be possibilities not comprised within that set, and hence another 'bigger' set which comprises them. And this non-totalizable continuum of logically possible outcomes can never be hypostatized in the form of a 'world'. But if there is no set of 'all' logically possible outcomes, it makes no sense to call any one set of logically possible outcomes more or less 'probable' than any other; and hence there is no warrant for the claim that the configuration exhibited by our actual universe is somehow 'necessitated' by some as yet unknown set of physical factors, while alternative universes are merely contingent. Thus at the logical level, possibility is governed by *contingency*, not *probability*. The contingency of the laws of nature, and the possibility of their transformation, cannot be understood in terms of chance. Contingency is a logical characteristic obtaining at the level of global possibility, whereas chance is a mathematical feature obtaining at the level of intra-worldly occurrence. The frequentialist argument conflates intra-worldly probability, which is quantifiable, with global contingency, which is not. It mistakes chance for contingency. To say that the uniformity exhibited by phenomena is entirely contingent is not to say that it is governed by chance. Once this conflation between chance and contingency has been exposed, it becomes clear that it makes no sense to apply the notion of statistical likelihood to our universe, as though any logically possible universe could be said to be more or less likely than any other. Accordingly, there is no good reason to suppose, as Kant does, that the contingency of the laws of nature would imply a frequency of transformation which would render representation impossible. On the contrary, Meillassoux concludes, the absolute contingency of the world's physical structure is perfectly compatible with the stability of phenomena, the possibility of representation, and the regularities observed by science.

Yet note that, though Meillassoux has clearly diagnosed and called into question the frequentialist premise underlying Kant's transcendental argument for the necessity of uniformity, and demonstrated why the contingency of uniformity need not imply the ruin of representation, he has not explained why reality should exhibit the constancy it seems to, given its absolute contingency. He has shown that the frequentialist argument cannot assume that reality is totalizable, and that contingency is not necessarily incompatible with the appearance of stability, but he leaves the ontological status of stability entirely unclear. Is uniformity a real feature of things-in-themselves or merely a phenomenal illusion generated by our relation to things? The thesis of the impossibility of contradiction will not help us settle this issue, since non-contradictoriness need not conflict with instability: the sudden and unexpected transformation of phenomena would not render them contradictory so long as a minimal temporal diachrony separated one moment of determination from the next; for no matter how contradictory any two determinations may be, so long as they succeed one another at distinct times in the entity, the latter will not be contradictory. At most, Meillassoux's counter-frequentialist case suggests that the rate of transformation cannot be synchronized with the rhythm of human consciousness and that the temporal interval between discontinuities is too long to inhibit the possibility of experimental science. But since some degree of stability is, by Meillassoux's own admission (cf. Meillassoux 2006: 118), the condition of possibility for the experimental science whose ancestral claims Meillassoux wishes to account for, and since part of that account consists in maintaining that mathematical science has a direct purchase on things independently of our relation to them, the question of the ontological status of stability is of the utmost importance to his project.

Meillassoux is perfectly aware of this, since he himself points out that his anti-frequentialist argument does not suffice to establish the thesis which is most significant for his agenda, but which remains latent in his critique of the frequentialist implication – the thesis that reality in-itself is a non-totalizable multiplicity: 'We have not established the effectivity of this un-totalization – we have merely supposed it and drawn the consequences of the fact that such a supposition is possible' (Meillassoux 2006: 152). Meillassoux's speculative project requires that he absolutize the non-totalizability of the in-itself by deriving it directly from the principle of factuality, thereby turning it into an ontological property of reality in-itself, rather than a 'supposition' which we are free to take or leave: 'It would be a matter of establishing that the possibilities of which Chaos – which is the only in-itself – is effectively capable cannot be measured by any number, whether finite or transfinite, and that this super-immensity of the chaotic virtual is what allows the impeccable stability of the visible world' (Meillassoux 2006: 153). This is a clear indication that though Meillassoux has not yet unveiled it, there is a speculative argument which would found the stability of appearances upon the non-totalizability of absolute time. Obviously, we cannot hope to anticipate the details or appraise the merits of such an argument in advance of Meillassoux's elaboration of it. But the question of the status of stability and of the possibility of grounding the uniformity of appearances in the absolute contingency of noumenal chaos raises a question about the relation between these two realms, and specifically about the status of the relation between thinking and being in Meillassoux's speculative materialism. It is to this issue that we must now turn.

3.6 The diachronicity of thinking and being

In a move that effectively sidesteps the entire problematic of representation, Meillassoux boldly declares his intention to reinstate intellectual intuition:

[W]e must project unreason into the thing itself, and discover in our grasp of facticity the veritable *intellectual intuition* of the absolute. 'Intuition', since it is well and truly in [*à même*] *what is* that we discover a contingency with no bounds other than itself; 'intellectual', since this contingency is nothing visible, nothing perceptible in the thing: only thought can access it as it accesses the Chaos which underlies the apparent continuities of phenomena.

(Meillassoux 2006: 111)

The deployment of this presumably non-metaphysical variety of intellectual intuition circumvents Kant's critical distinction between knowable phenomena and unknowable things-in-themselves – between reality as we relate to it through representation and reality as it is independently of our representational relation to it – and rehabilitates the distinction between primary and secondary qualities; the former being mathematically intuitable features of things-in-themselves; the latter being phenomenological features of our relation to things (cf. Meillassoux 2006: 28).

This reinstatement of intellectual intuition is of a piece with Meillassoux's overturning of Kant's critical delimitation of the possibilities of reason. Intellectual intuition now provides us with direct access to a realm of pure possibility coextensive with absolute time. Kant displaced the metaphysical hypostatization of logical possibility by subordinating the latter to a domain of real possibility circumscribed by reason's relation to sensibility. Time qua form of transcendental synthesis grounds the structure of possibility.[22] But Meillassoux's absolutization of contingency effectively absolutizes the a priori realm of pure logical possibility and untethers the domain of mathematical intelligibility from sensibility. This severing of the possible from the sensible is underwritten by the chaotic structure of absolute time. Where the bounds of real possibility remain circumscribed by the correlational a priori, intellectual intuition uncovers a realm of absolute possibility whose only constraint is non-contradiction. Moreover, where real possibility is subsumed by time as form of transcendental subjectivity, absolute possibility indexes a time no longer anchored either in the coherence of a subjective relation to reality or in the correlation between thinking and being. Thus the intellectual intuition of absolute possibility underwrites the 'diachronicity' of thinking and being, a diachronicity which for Meillassoux is implicit in the ancestral dimension of being uncovered by modern science. However, in light of the problems attendant upon Meillassoux's distinction between ancestrality and (spatio-temporal) distance, and the idealism associated with attempts to privilege time over space, it would be better to characterize the autonomous reality discovered by modern science independently of any reference to time, whether transcendental or ancestral. In Chapter 5 we shall redefine the diachronicity which Meillassoux takes to be definitive of ancestral time in terms of a structure of 'unilateralization' which is the ultimate guarantor of the autonomy of the object. It is this unilateralization which ultimately accounts for diachronicity understood as the separability of thought and being, their non-correlation.

The speculative import of science's Copernican revolution consists in this ex-centring of thought relative to being. Ironically enough, as

Meillassoux caustically observes, philosophy has sought to account for science's Copernican turn by invoking a correlation which makes being orbit around thinking, in what effectively amounts to a Ptolemaic counter-revolution.[23] Yet it is precisely the dimension of diachronicity implicit in the arche-fossil but disregarded by correlationism which demands speculative 'explicitation'. For Meillassoux, the possibility of non-correlational reality – i.e. of an objective realm existing independently of any transcendental conditions of manifestation – finds its ontological guarantor in the structure of absolute possibility concomitant with absolute time. The difference between science and myth, Meillassoux suggests, is that while the latter inscribes this diachronic dimension of a time before and after humanity within the bounds of the human relation to the world in such a way as to render the premise of absolute time at once unverifiable and unfalsifiable, modern science transforms absolute time into a conjecture which, if not definitively verified, has at least successfully withstood successive attempts at falsification. It is not science's realism about the ancestral dimension of time which is unique, since this is also a characteristic of mythical thinking, but rather the fact that science deploys criteria through which it becomes possible to select between competing hypotheses about what was when we were not and what will be when we are no longer. The deployment of such criteria is intrinsically tied to the Galilean hypothesis that nature can be comprehensively mathematized. Where pre-Galilean science compartmentalized the mathematizable and the non-mathematizable in the distinction between the supra-lunar (celestial) and the sub-lunar (terrestrial) realms, the post-Galilean integration of both realms under the aegis of a unified physics provides a spectacular corroboration of the hypothesis that nature is exhaustively mathematizable. Thus, as Meillassoux sees it, the outstanding task yet to be accomplished by modern philosophy is a speculative explicitation of the dimension of diachronicity which subtends the Galilean hypothesis. It is philosophy's failure to recognize the speculative implications of science's Copernicanism which has resulted in the Ptolemaism of correlationism. In ratifying the diachronicity of thinking and being, modern science exposes thought's contingency for being: although thought needs being, being does not need thought.

3.7   The paradox of absolute contingency

The question, then, is whether or not Meillassoux's reinstatement of intellectual intuition compromises the very asymmetry which he takes to be science's speculative import. Similarly, it may be that the Galilean hypothesis harbours ramifications concerning the mathematization of thinking which also vitiate Meillassoux's appeal to intellectual intuition. To consider these questions, we must examine the distinction which Meillassoux invokes in order to stave off idealism. This is the distinction between the *reality* of the ancestral phenomenon and the *ideality* of the ancestral statement. It is on the basis of this distinction that Meillassoux, like Badiou, seeks to distance himself from the Pythagorean thesis according to which being is mathematical (we will examine the status of Badiou's mathematical ontology in the next chapter):

> [W]e will maintain that, for their part, the statements bearing on the ancestral phenomenon which can be mathematically formulated designate effective properties of the event in question (its date, its duration, its extension), even though no observer was present to experience it directly. Accordingly, we will maintain a Cartesian thesis about matter, but not, let us underline this, a Pythagorean one: we shall not claim that the being of the ancestral phenomenon is intrinsically mathematical, or that the numbers and equations deployed in ancestral statements exist in themselves. For it would then be necessary to maintain that the [ancestral phenomenon] is a reality every bit as ideal as that of a number or an equation. Generally speaking, statements are ideal insofar as they possess a signifying reality; but their eventual referents are not necessarily ideal (the cat on the mat is real, though the statement 'The cat is on the mat' is ideal.) In this regard, we will say that the referents of ancestral statements bearing on dates, volumes, etc. existed 4.56 billion years ago as described by these statements – but not these statements themselves, which are contemporaneous with us.
>
> (Meillassoux 2006: 28–9)[24]

This distinction between the reality of the ancestral phenomenon and the ideality of the ancestral statement is necessary in order to maintain the ontological disjunction between the correlational present and the ancestral past – precisely the diachronicity which correlationism cannot countenance. Although Meillassoux never elaborates upon it, it can be unpacked in terms of the familiar distinction between existence and essence; between the fact *that* something exists and *what* it is. Interestingly enough, Meillassoux's principle of factuality effectively implies that there is no more to the essence or 'whatness' of a thing than the fact that it exists contingently. Nevertheless, if Meillassoux evokes such a distinction, he cannot sequester it on the side of being alone, for it must pertain to thinking as well as to being. Thus this secondary disjunction between real and ideal subdivides both poles of the primary disjunction between thinking and being: thought possesses a real and an ideal aspect, just as being possesses real and ideal features. Clearly, the diachronicity harboured by the arche-fossil can only be indexed by a disjunction between the ideality of the ancestral statement and the reality of the ancestral phenomenon which promises to prove irreducible to the neighbouring distinctions between the real and ideal aspect of thought and the real and ideal features of being, for both of these remain entirely encompassed by the correlation between thinking and being. For the point of Meillassoux's distinction between physical reality and discursive ideality is to discount the idealist claim that the reality of the phenomenon is exhausted by its mathematical idealization in the statement. Although the reality of the ancestral phenomenon can be mathematically encoded, it must transcend this mathematical inscription, otherwise Meillassoux finds himself endorsing Pythagoreanism. And as Meillassoux well knows, the latter provides no bulwark against correlationism, since it effectively renders being isomorphic with mathematical ideality. The point seems to be that the reality of the ancestral phenomenon must be independent of its mathematical intellection – being does not depend upon the existence of mathematics. But Meillassoux's problem consists in identifying a speculative guarantor for this disjunction between reality and ideality which would be entirely independent of the evidence provided by the mathematical idealization of the ancestral phenomenon in the ancestral statement. To rely upon the latter would be to render this speculative disjunction supervenient upon the procedures of post-critical epistemology and thus to find oneself confronted by the injunction to verify or otherwise justify it within the ambit of the correlationist circle.

Thus the question confronting Meillassoux's speculative materialism is: under what conditions would this secondary disjunction between the real and the ideal be intellectually intuitable without reinstating a correlation at the level of the primary disjunction between thinking and being? To render the distinction between the reality of the phenomenon and the ideality of the statement dependent upon intellectual intuition is to leave it entirely encompassed by one pole of the primary disjunction, i.e. thought, and hence to recapitulate the correlationist circle. For just as we cannot maintain that this primary disjunction is intellectually intuitable without reinscribing being within the ideal pole of the secondary disjunction, similarly, we cannot maintain that the secondary disjunction is encoded in the ancestral statement without reincorporating the real within the noetic pole of the primary disjunction.

How, then, are we to guarantee the disjunction between real and ideal independently of the intelligible ideality of science's ancestral claims? For the ideality of the latter cannot be a guarantor of the reality of the former. Moreover, intellectual intuition subsumes both poles of the secondary disjunction within one pole of the primary disjunction.

Consequently, Meillassoux is forced into the difficult position of attempting to reconcile the claim that being is not inherently mathematical with the claim that being is intrinsically accessible to intellectual intuition. He cannot maintain that being is mathematical without lapsing into Pythagorean idealism; but this relapse into Pythagoreanism is precluded only at the cost of the idealism which renders being the correlate of intellectual intuition. The problem lies in trying to square the Galilean–Cartesian hypothesis that being is mathematizable with an insistence on the speculative disjunction whereby being is held to subsist independently of its mathematical intuitability. Part of the difficulty resides in the fact that although Meillassoux presumably discounts metaphysical and phenomenological conceptions of being, whether as necessary substance or eidetic presence, since both are encompassed within the correlationist circle, he has not provided us with a non-metaphysical and non-phenomenological alternative – such as we find, for example, in Badiou's subtractive conception of the void. Unlike Badiou, Meillassoux does not characterize ontology as a situation within which the presentation of being is subtractively inscribed in such a way as to obviate any straightforwardly metaphysical or phenomenological correlation between thought and being. As we will see in the next chapter, Badiou's subtractive conception of ontological presentation effectuates a scission in being as such which precludes its intuition in terms of presence, whether phenomenological or metaphysical. But just as Badiou's premium on subtraction subverts the idealism latent in his privileging of inscription, it may be that Meillassoux's premium on contingency subverts the idealism latent in his privileging of intellectual intuition. Like Badiou, Meillassoux recuses the Kantian formulation of the problematic of access while striving to uphold the authority of scientific rationality. But as a result he must explain why – given that science teaches us that intellection is in no way an ineliminable feature of reality but merely a contingent by-product of evolutionary history, and given that for Meillassoux himself reality can be neither inherently mathematical nor *necessarily* intelligible – being should be susceptible to intellectual intuition. In this regard, it is worth noting that one of the more significant ramifications of the Galilean–Cartesian hypothesis about the mathematizability of nature consists in the recent endeavour to deploy the resources of mathematical modelization in order to develop a science of cognition (some of whose claims we examined in Chapter 1). Admittedly, the latter is still in its infancy; nevertheless, its maturation promises to obviate the Cartesian dualism of thought and extension – and perhaps also the residues of the latter which subsist in Meillassoux's own brand of speculative materialism – while conceding nothing to correlationism. The diachronic disjunction between thinking and being is not the only speculative implication harboured by modern science; the development of a science of cognition implies that we, unlike Descartes and Kant, can no longer presume to exempt thought from the reality to which it provides access, or continue to attribute an exceptional status to it.

If thought can no longer be presumed to exempt itself from the reality which it thinks, and if the real can no longer be directly mapped onto being, or the ideal directly mapped onto thought, then thinking itself must be reintegrated into any speculative enquiry into the nature of reality. Thus the central question raised by Meillassoux's speculative materialism becomes: does the principle of factuality, which states that 'everything that exists is necessarily contingent', *include itself* in its designation of 'everything'? Meillassoux's appeal to Cantor in his anti-frequentialist argument suggests that he does not think that the concept of 'totality' has any ontological pertinence. But we do not have to assume a spurious totalization of existence in order to enquire whether the thought that everything is necessarily contingent is itself necessarily contingent. On the contrary, all that we assume is that thinking is just a contingent fact like any other. What we should refuse, however, is the claim that it is necessary to exempt the thought that 'everything is necessarily contingent' from the existential 'fact' that everything is contingent on the grounds that a transcendental abyss separates thinking from being. Once the recourse to this transcendental divide has been ruled out, we are obliged to consider what follows if the principle refers to itself. More precisely, we must consider whether the truth of the principle, and a fortiori Meillassoux's speculative overcoming of correlationism, *entails its self-reference*. Here we have to distinguish between the contingency of the existence of the thought, which does *not* generate paradox, and the contingency of the truth of the thought, which does. Two distinct possibilities can be envisaged depending on whether the thought does or does not refer to itself. First, let us consider what follows if it does refer to itself. Then if the thought exists, it must be contingent. But if it is contingent then its negation could equally exist: 'Not everything is necessarily contingent'. But in order for the thought to exclude the possibility of the truth of its negation, then its truth must be necessary, which means that the thought must exist necessarily. But if it exists necessarily, then not everything that exists is necessarily contingent; there is at least one thing which is not, i.e. the thought itself. Thus if the thought refers to itself it necessitates the existence of its own negation; but in order to deny the possible truth of its negation it has to affirm its own necessary truth, and hence contradict itself once more. What if the thought does not refer to itself? Then there is something which is necessary, but which is not included under the rubric of existence. Reality is 'not-all' because the thought that 'everything is necessarily contingent' is an ideality which exempts itself from the reality which it designates. But then not only does this very exemption become necessary for the intelligible ideality of the thought that 'everything is necessarily contingent', but the intelligibility of reality understood as the necessary existence of contingency becomes dependent upon the coherence of a thought whose exemption from reality is necessary in order for reality to be thought as necessarily contingent. Thus the attempt to exempt the ideal from the real threatens to re-instantiate the correlationist circle once more. Lastly, let us consider the possibility that the necessary contingency of existence does not depend on the truth of the thought 'everything is necessarily contingent'. If everything is necessarily contingent regardless of the truth of the thought 'everything is necessarily contingent', then everything could be necessarily contingent even if we had no way of thinking the truth of that thought coherently. But this is to re-introduce the possibility of a radical discrepancy between the coherence of thinking and the way the world is in-itself – any irrational hypothesis about the latter becomes possible, and strong correlationism looms once again.

Whatever the shortcomings attendant upon their lack of formal stringency, these conjectures seem to point to a fundamental dilemma confronting Meillassoux's project. If he accepts – as we believe he must – that thinking is part of being as the second fundamental speculative implication of scientific rationality after that of diachronicity, then the universal scope of the principle of factuality generates a paradox whereby it seems to contradict itself: the claim that everything is necessarily contingent is only true if this thought exists necessarily. Alternatively, if Meillassoux decides to uphold the exceptional status of thinking vis-à-vis being, then he seems to compromise his insistence on diachronicity, for the intelligible reality of contingent being is rendered dependent upon the ideal coherence of the principle of factuality. Indeed, the appeal to intellectual intuition in the formulation of the principle already seems to assume some sort of reciprocity between thinking and being.

As one might expect, both these criticisms – viz., that intellectual intuition re-establishes a correlation between thought and being, and that the principle of factuality engenders a paradox – have elicited typically acute responses from Meillassoux. In a personal communication, Meillassoux has explained why he believes he can parry both objections. For Meillassoux, the principle of factuality is designed to satisfy two requirements. First, the fundamental *rationalist* requirement that reality be perfectly amenable to conceptual comprehension. This is a rebuttal of the prototypical religious notion that existence harbours some sort of transcendent mystery forever refractory to intellection. Second, the basic *materialist* requirement that being, though perfectly intelligible, remains irreducible to thought. Meillassoux insists that the claim that everything that *is* is necessarily contingent satisfies both criteria. In his own words:

> Being is thought without-remainder insofar as it is without-reason; and the being that is thought in this way is conceived as exceeding thought on all sides because it shows itself to be capable of producing and destroying thought as well as every other sort of entity. As a factual act produced by an equally factual thinking being, the intellectual intuition of facticity is perfectly susceptible to destruction, but not that which, albeit only for an instant, it will have thought as the eternal truth which legitimates its name, viz., that it is itself perishable just like everything else that exists. [...] Thus, it is on account of its capacity for a-rational emergence that being exceeds on all sides whatever thought is able to describe of its factual production; nevertheless, it contains nothing unfathomable for thought because being's excess over thought just indicates that reason is forever absent from being, not some eternally enigmatic power.
>
> (Meillassoux, personal communication 8 September 2006)

These remarks already prefigure Meillassoux's recusal of the second objection, viz., that if applied to itself, the principle of factuality becomes contradictory. Meillassoux maintains that the paradox can be averted by carefully distinguishing the *referent* of the principle from its (factual) existence. Thus, though the latter is indeed contingent, and hence as liable to be as not to be, the former is strictly necessary, and indeed it is the eternal necessity of the principle's referent that guarantees the perpetual contingency of the principle's existence:

> One may then say that the principle as something that is *thought* in reality is factual, and hence contingent. But what is not contingent

is the referent of this principle; viz., facticity as such insofar as it is necessary. And it is because this facticity is necessary that the principle, insofar as it is – in fact – proffered and insofar as it will be or will have been thought by some singular entity – no matter when or under what circumstances – it is for this reason that the principle will always be true the moment it is posited or thought. What is contingent is that the principle, as a meaningful statement, is actually thought; but what is not contingent is that it is true insofar as it is – as a matter of fact – thought in a time and place – no matter when or where. Consequently there is no paradox so long as the principle's domain of application is precisely restricted to entities in their being.

(ibid.)

The crucial operative distinction here is that between the necessity of contingency qua referent of thought and the contingency of the (factual) existence of the thought that everything is necessarily contingent. The question then is: how does Meillassoux propose to account for this separation between the contingent existence of thought and the necessary existence of its referent? Clearly, this separation is intended to safeguard the coherence of the principle, as well as the materialist primacy of the real over the ideal, by ensuring a strict differentiation between thought and reality. But given that, for Meillassoux, thought's purchase on reality is guaranteed by intellectual intuition, it follows that it must also be the latter which accounts for this distinction between thought and referent. Accordingly, it would seem that it is in and through the intellectual intuition of absolute contingency that the contingency of the thought is separated from the necessity of its referent. Everything then hinges on how Meillassoux understands the term 'intellectual intuition'.

Clearly, he cannot be using the term in its Kantian acceptation, since, for Kant, intellectual intuition actively creates its object, unlike sensible intuition, which passively receives an independently existing object. According to Kant, only the intuitive understanding of an 'archetypical' intellect (*intellectus archetypus*) unburdened by sensibility – such as God's – possesses this power to produce its object; for our discursive understanding, mediated as it is by sensibility, it is the synthesis of concept and intuition which yields the cognitive relation between thought and its object. Meillassoux clearly rejects Kant's representationalist account of the relation between mind and world, just as he must refuse phenomenology's appeal to an intentional correlation between noesis and noema. Yet it is far from evident what plausible theory of intellectual intuition could simultaneously ensure the scission between the contingency of thought and the necessity of its referent – which Meillassoux takes to be sufficient to stave off contradiction – while circumventing representational and intentional correlation as well as abjuring the archetypical intellect's production of its object (since the claim that intellection creates its object is clearly incompatible with any commitment to materialism). Though Meillassoux insists that the paradox of absolute contingency can be obviated by restricting the principle's domain of reference to 'entities in their being', he does not explain how he proposes to enforce this rigid demarcation between the principle's contingently effectuated *intension* and what he deems to be its 'eternally' necessary *extension*.

'Reference', of course, is intimately related to 'truth', but though Meillassoux claims that the truth of the principle is guaranteed by its ontological referent, this connection is anything but semantically transparent, since the extension of the expression 'absolute contingency' is no more perspicuous than that of the term 'being'. The customary prerequisite for realist conceptions of truth is an extra-theoretical account of the relation between intension and extension, but Meillassoux's attempt to construe the latter in terms of intellectual intuition makes it exceedingly difficult to see how it could ever be anything other than intra-theoretical.[25] Indeed, it is unclear how the referent 'absolute contingency' could ever be rendered intelligible in anything other than a purely conceptual register. Consequently, Meillassoux presents us with a case in which the determination of extension, or 'truth', remains entirely dependent upon a conceptually stipulated intension, or 'sense' – the referent 'absolute contingency' is exclusively determined by the sense of the contingently existing thought 'everything that is, is absolutely contingent'. But if the only way to ensure the separation between the (contingently existing) ideality of meaning and the (necessarily existing) reality of the referent is by making conceptuality constitutive of objectivity, then the absolutization of the non-correlational referent is won at the price of an absolutization of conceptual sense which violates the materialist requirement that being not be reducible to thought. Far from reconciling rationalism with materialism, the principle of factuality, at least in this version, continues to subordinate extra-conceptual reality to a concept of absolute contingency.

Although Meillassoux's speculative overcoming of correlationism strives to deploy the latter's strongest weapons against it – as we saw with the principle of factuality itself – the distinction between the real and the ideal is part of the correlationist legacy which cannot be mobilized against it without first undergoing decontamination. For correlationism secures the transcendental divide between the real and the ideal only at the cost of turning being into the correlate of thought. Meillassoux is right to insist that it is necessary to pass through correlationism in order to overcome it, and in this regard we should follow his recommendation and find a way of deploying the distinction between real and ideal against correlationism itself. But precisely here a fundamental speculative problem reveals itself, namely, can we think the diachronic disjunction between real and ideal while obviating any recourse to a transcendental divide between thinking and being? The next two chapters will try to answer this question by critically appropriating conceptual resources from the works of Alain Badiou and François Laruelle.

Part II The Anatomy of Negation

4
Unbinding the Void

4.1 The unbinding of being: Alain Badiou

Like Meillassoux, Alain Badiou not only declares his fealty to the legacy of Cartesian rationalism; he openly endorses the Enlightenment project of disenchantment.[1] For Badiou, the denigration of mathematical rationality in much post-Kantian European philosophy is symptomatic of the sway which Romanticism continues to exert over philosophical sensibility. Where a belated philosophical Romanticism continues to bewail the 'nihilistic' consequences incurred by science's disenchantment of the world and capital's desecration of the earth, Badiou proposes that philosophy take up the challenge posed to it by the annihilating vectors of science and capital the better to accede to a register of universality capable not only of matching but of surpassing the abstractions of number and the value-form. Nihilism is not, as Heidegger would have it, the occlusion of being's unrepresentable presencing but rather the process of universal unbinding through which the twin vectors of science and capital together expose unbound multiplicity as the veritable figure of being:

> As far as nihilism is concerned, we shall grant that our era bears witness to it precisely insofar as nihilism is understood as *the rupturing of the traditional figure of the bond*; unbinding as the form of being of everything which acts as a semblance of the bond. [...] That everything that is bound testifies that it is unbound in its being; that the reign of the multiple is, without exception, the groundless ground of what is presented; that the One is merely the result of transitory operations; these are the ineluctable consequences of the universal placement of the terms of our situation within the circulatory

movement of the general monetary equivalent. [...] This is obviously the only thing that can and must be saluted in capital: it exposes the pure multiple as the ground of presentation; it denounces every effect of oneness as a merely precarious configuration; it deposes those symbolic representations in which the bond found a semblance of being. That this deposition operates according to the most complete barbarism should not distract us from its genuinely ontological virtue. To what do we owe our deliverance from the myths of presence, from the guarantee it provided for the substantiality of bonds and the perenniality of essential relations, if not to the errant automation of capital? [...] I propose the following paradox: only since very recently has philosophy become capable of a thinking worthy of capital, because even in its own domain, it had abandoned the terrain to the vain nostalgias for the sacred, to the spectre of presence, to the obscure domination of the poem, and to doubts as to its own legitimacy.
(Badiou 1989: 35–9, 1999: 55–8 translation modified – 'tm')

In order to be equal to the desecrating abstractions of modernity, philosophy must abjure any attempt to sanctify being in the figure of the bond. Thus it is not enough to denounce the hypostatization of being in the myth of presence; it is the phenomenological myth of presencing itself which must be deposed. The discourse of ontology must be disenchanted by being handed over to mathematical science. Accordingly, in the Introduction to *Being and Event*,[2] Badiou declares: 'The science of being-qua-being *has existed* since the Greeks for such is the status and meaning of mathematics, but only now do we possess the means to *recognize* this' (Badiou 1988: 9, 2006a: 3 tm). Since ontology is now the province of mathematical science, and since (contra Heidegger) being is neither inherently meaningful nor the harbinger of truth, meditative rumination upon being is no part of the philosophical remit. Informed by deconstructive critiques of the metaphysical ontologies of presence, Badiou establishes an anti-phenomenological conception of ontological presentation. Presentation's internal structure is that of an anti-phenomenon which is presence's necessarily empty and insubstantial contrary: 'For presence is the exact contrary of presentation' (Badiou 1988: 35, 2006: 27).

4.2　The a priority of ontological discourse

Badiou's identification of ontology with axiomatic set-theory is a claim about discourse, not about the world (Badiou 1988: 14, 2006: 8). Accepting the Aristotelian definition of ontology as the discourse on 'being qua being' (rather than qua something), Badiou's claim concerns the discursive intelligibility of being considered independently of any and every type of qualitative characteristic.[3] Ontology presents being as at once multiple and unitary: it is 'counted-as-one' and presented as a consistent multiplicity. Thus to be is to be multiple, but the intelligibility of being-multiple necessitates a distinction between consistent multiplicity insofar as multiplicity is counted-as-one, and inconsistent multiplicity as that upon which counting operates, and which is retroactively posited as being via the operation of the count. Anything that is must be counted-as-one, but unity is not an intrinsic characteristic of being; it is merely the result of an operation which produces consistent multiplicity from inconsistent multiplicity. Being qua being is neither one nor multiple – it is inconsistent multiplicity (Badiou 1988: 32, 2006: 24). Ontology is simply the discursive presentation of inconsistent multiplicity as such; which is to say, the presentation of inconsistent multiplicity considered independently of any predicative characteristic other than its sheer multiplicity (Badiou 1988: 36, 2006: 28).

It is important to emphasize from the outset two fundamental ways in which Badiou's account of the 'a priority' of ontological discourse differs from traditional metaphysical ontologies. First, for Badiou, ontology itself is a situation, which is to say, a locally circumscribed consistent multiplicity. For if presentation is necessarily multiple, and being is implicated in every presentation (Badiou 1988: 35, 2006: 27), then there is no single presentation of being capable of subsuming all others. Thus ontology is not a universal or 'all-encompassing' situation. It is a determinate situation alongside other determinate situations. But since, Badiou insists, all access to being is via presentation, and presentation is always the presentation of something, never of being itself (Badiou 1988: 35, 2006: 27) (we shall see why below), ontology distinguishes itself as that situation in which presentation as such is presented. The privilege of the ontological situation consists in its providing the site 'from which all possible access to being is grasped' (Badiou 1988: 36, 2006a: 28).

Second, the claim that ontology is mathematics is not a claim about the concept of being. It is not the claim that being must be conceptualized as multiple, and that the appropriate conceptual resources for thinking about multiplicity are to be found in mathematics. For Badiou, ontology cannot be coordinated around a 'concept of being' because the very idea of a 'concept of being' is incompatible with the claim that being is inconsistent multiplicity. The injunction that the One is not and the thesis that being is inconsistent multiplicity entail that ontological discourse operate without a concept of the multiple (or 'being'). Ontological discourse is coordinated around the prohibition of counting inconsistent multiplicity as one (as we shall see, *what* it is counted as is nothing), which is to say that it is forbidden from defining what it is that is consistently presented, or counted. To do so would entail subordinating inconsistent multiplicity to the consistency of a single concept, reintroducing a categorical difference between being and its concept, and thereby conceding the being of unity by acknowledging the existence of a relation between distinct terms (since such a distinction presupposes the ability to discriminate between individuated terms). Thus 'it is necessary that the operational structure of ontology be able to discern the multiple without having to make it one, and hence without relying on a definition of the multiple' (Badiou 1988: 37, 2006a: 29 tm). Set-theory satisfies this stricture by axiomatizing its discursive presentation, prescribing rules for the manipulation of terms which are compositionally rather than conceptually defined. Any composition violating the rules is prohibited; everything permitted by the rules is prescribed (Badiou 1988: 38, 2006a: 30). But at no point is *what* is presented explicitly (i.e. conceptually) defined; it is merely compositionally specified via the rules prescribing the legitimate deployment of the symbol of belonging. To be is to belong to a set, everything that belongs is itself a set, and every set is defined in terms of belonging, whose functioning is axiomatically specified. Thus the axiomatic form of ontological discourse is necessary in order to obviate any variety of conceptual definition which would re-objectify, and thereby unify inconsistent multiplicity. Although philosophy provides a 'metaontological' gloss on this axiomatic discourse through the use of such terms as 'being', 'presentation', 'situation', 'multiple', 'consistency', and 'inconsistency', it is imperative that its conceptual schematization of the rules governing ontological discourse not lapse into a re-presentation (in Badiou's technical sense) of ontological presentation by reintroducing a concept of being or of the multiple: 'For by putting being in the general position of an object, its re-presentation would immediately undermine the necessarily de-objectifying condition of ontological deployment' (Badiou 1988: 17–18, 2006a: 11 tm).

As we shall see, the peculiarly delicate status of the relation between ontological and metaontological discourse is not adequately resolved by Badiou. We will argue that the equivocal status of metaontological discourse vis-à-vis ontological discourse on one hand, and the world (or 'reality') on the other, is the rock upon which Badiou's philosophical edifice falters. Ultimately, we will suggest, a philosophy that chooses to relinquish worldly plenitude in favour of subtractive ascesis must be prepared to take the plunge into the black hole of subtraction. But in order to appreciate the prohibitive consequences of the logic of subtraction, it is necessary to consider the peculiar structure of Badiou's metaontological concept of presentation.

4.3   The law of presentation

The inaugural declaration of *Being and Event* is that 'the One is not' (Badiou 1988: 31, 2006a: 23). Ontological presentation is devoid of unity. Or rather, unity is only the result of an operation and 'it is because the one is an operation, that it is never a presentation' (Badiou 1988: 32, 2006a: 24 tm). Although presentation is necessarily structured, structure is not an intrinsic aspect of being. The necessity of structure is a nomological feature of discursive presentation, not an ontological characteristic of being itself. '[T]here is no structure of being', Badiou insists (Badiou 1988: 34, 2006a: 26). Thus it would appear that Badiou is merely reiterating a familiar transcendental distinction between the formal features of being as characterized relative to thought, or 'for us', and being as it is independently of thought, or 'in itself'; which would amount to the well-worn dualism of phenomenon and noumenon. But this is not the case. For in fact, the split between counted consistency and uncounted inconsistency, or structure and being, is an index of the underlying identity between the inexistence of structure (i.e. counting) and the inexistence of inconsistency (i.e. being itself). To grasp this identity is to grasp how the law of the count as condition for existence, which renders presentation possible by precluding the presentation of inconsistent multiplicity (i.e. being itself), is ultimately indiscernible from the ontological inconsistency whose presentation it forecloses. Thus the non-being (*non-être*) of the One, the merely nomological status of structure, converges asymptotically with the being-nothing (*être-rien*) of inconsistent multiplicity, whose necessary impossibility is retroactively attested to by the structure of the count. It is in this sense that, for Badiou, ontology complies with the Parmenidean injunction according to which 'thinking and being are the same' (Badiou 1988: 49, 2006a: 38 tm): the sense in which theirs is an identity without relation. Thinking and being are both nothing. Ontological discourse deploys their identity insofar as it operates through the coincidence of structured consistency and de-structured inconsistency, without stipulating any relation between them as distinct terms. It operates in complete disregard of any appeal to categorial distinctions between different types of being. Accordingly, subtractive ontology is impervious to attempts to hypostatize the difference between something called 'thinking' and something called 'being'. But, by the same token, it remains incapable of acknowledging any distinction between discourse and world, thought and reality, logical consequences and material causes.[4] The law of presentation is the guarantor of a literally vacuous isomorphy between thinking and being (all the more remarkable for being neither metaphysical nor transcendental); but the price is a peculiar variety of discursive idealism wherein even the supplement of inconsistency invoked as a real interruption of the ideal order of ontological discourse is itself merely an instance of unstructured thought: the event as aleatory *deciding* of the undecidable, wherein thinking itself comes to embody inconsistency.

4.4   Structure, metastructure, representation

The law of presentation is codified in the operation of the count, which is not, because it cannot count itself as one. By absolving itself from its own count, every count invites a 'count of the count', or what Badiou will usually refer to as a 'metastructure' in an ontological context, and as 're-presentation' in all other situations. Although Badiou himself has an unfortunate tendency to use them interchangeably, the distinction between these two intimately related terms is decisive for his entire project. For while the ontological metastructure provides the blueprint for non-ontological re-presentation, metastructure is foreclosed to re-presentation (we shall return to this point in section 4.7).

Badiou establishes the ontological necessity of the count of the count, or metastructure, on the basis of the power-set axiom and the theorem of the point of excess. The power-set axiom states that for every set α there is a set β comprising all the subsets of α. β counts-as-one everything that is included in α without belonging to α. The theorem of the point of excess demonstrates that the power-set β is invariably greater than α by at least one element. It is supplemented by the Cohen–Easton theorem, which shows that the excess of inclusion over belonging is ultimately immeasurable.[5] Since the counting of elements (sets) unwittingly includes uncounted parts (subsets), metastructure, or the count-of-the-count, is necessary because the consistency of presentation is compromised by the latent inconsistency of that which is included in it without belonging to it. The realm of inclusion implicit in presentation provides a potential haven for the inconsistency which the law of presentation prohibits. Thus 'the consistency of presentation requires that every structure be doubled by a metastructure' (Badiou 1988: 109, 2006a: 93–4 tm) which counts-as-one the inconsistency generated by the self-exemption of structuring. Ontological presentation is articulated around this metastructural doubling necessitated by the disjunction between belonging and inclusion. It is this reduplication of structure which furnishes the model for 're-presentation' in non-ontological situations and the distinction between situation and state of the situation: 'every situation is structured twice. Which means: there is always at once presentation and re-presentation' (Badiou 1988: 110, 2006a: 94 tm).

This 'at once' must be taken quite literally: there is a perfect indivisibility of structure and metastructure. But this indivisibility is precisely that of a radical division, albeit one that is neither spatial nor temporal in character.[6] Every presentation is split by this fissure between the count and the count-of-the-count, which is to say, between belonging and inclusion (the latter being only a variant of the former, rather than a second primitive relation), precisely insofar as the count itself is nothing:

> It comes to exactly the same thing whether one says that the operation of the count is nothing insofar as it is the source of the one, but is not itself counted, or whether one says that what is nothing is the pure multiple which is operated upon by the count, since it is distinct 'in itself', which is to say as un-counted, from itself as manifested by the count.
>
> (Badiou 1988: 68, 2006a: 55 tm)

Metastructure is required in order to stave off the threat posed to presentation by this underlying indiscernibility between the 'non-being' (*non-être*) of the One and the 'being-nothing' (*être-rien*) of inconsistency. It is necessary in order to preclude the presentation of nothing and 'the ruin of the One' (Badiou 1988: 109, 2006a: 93). For the 'being-nothing' of inconsistent multiplicity not only designates the gap between unified presentation and 'that on the basis of which' there is presentation; it is 'the nothing proper to the situation, the empty and un-localizable point which avers that the situation is sutured to being, and that *what* is presented roams in presentation as a subtraction from the count' (Badiou 1988: 68, 2006a: 55 tm). *What* is presented is nothing, sheer inconsistency; but this inconsistency is at once that of being and of structure: 'The nothing is as much that of structure, and thus of consistency, as that of pure multiplicity, and thus of inconsistency' (Badiou 1988: 68, 2006a: 55 tm). Ontological presentation grants us an 'unpresentable access' to inconsistency, to that which is not pre-sented and is nothing for it. This is 'the void' or being of the situation. It can never be presented as a term of the situation, since it is the inconsistency latent in its own structure. It is the name for that which in-consists within a situation; its subtractive suture to being.[7]

4.5   The suture to the unpresentable

Let us examine the argument whereby Badiou seeks to establish thought's suture to the unpresentable. The axiom of separation stipulates that every assertion of existence concerning a set necessarily presupposes a pre-existing set.[8] Thus there must be an originary set whose existence provides the precondition for every subsequent set. This is the empty-set: the set to which nothing belongs. Ontological discourse, which is the presentation of presentation, the presentation of counting-as-one qua belonging, affirms no existence, which is to say, no belonging prior to that to which nothing belongs. It affirms the being-nothing of belonging as that to which no belonging belongs. Consequently, it is not belonging (consistency) whose existence is originally declared, but non-belonging (inconsistency) as that which is already presupposed by every subsequent belonging. In fact, ontological discourse begins with a negation of belonging, rather than an affirmation of non-belonging; but a negation whose very act is equivalent to an affirmation, or as Badiou puts it, an 'existence which does not exist' (Badiou 1988: 81, 2006a: 68 tm). Thus the ontological axiomatic accomplishes what Badiou refers to as 'thought's subtractive suture to being' by declaring the existence of an inexistence. It asserts the being of the unpresentable through a negation of presentation.

François Wahl[9] raises a particularly interesting objection here: the argument that enjoins us to deduce the existence of non-belonging from the negation of belonging merely reiterates the ontological argu-ment. For even if, as Badiou claims, the axiom of the empty-set affirms an inexistence rather than an existence, since inexistence is no more of an 'index of existence' than was perfection in the classical version of the ontological argument, then why should the inexistence of belong-ing enjoy any more right to existence than any other inexistence – such as that of the One for instance? (Wahl 2002: 177) How does the negation of belonging which establishes the existence of the void's 'being-nothing' differ from the negation of unity through which Badiou asserts the 'non-being' of the One? However, Wahl's objection mis-represents Badiou's argument. The logical import of the axiom of the empty-set is neither that 'non-belonging exists', nor that 'the unpresentable' exists, nor even that 'inexistence exists'. It does not predicate existence of any concept, whether it be that of 'non-belonging' or 'inexistence'. Rather, the axiom asserts that 'there exists a set β such that no set α belongs to it'. The existential quantifier does not attribute a property to a concept. Its import is that, even in order to deny belonging, it is *at least* necessary to affirm the existence of a mark of belonging. It is this 'at least' that is singularized by the assertion of the existential quantifier. And it is by negating this mark of belonging that the axiom affirms the existence of a mark of non-belonging. This is also why the being-nothing of the void cannot be formally conflated with the non-being of the One. The former is an assertion of negation, while the latter is neither an assertion nor a negation since the unification of multiplicity carried out through the operation of belonging has no ontological status. Belonging is an operation, not an entity; an operation whose inexistence is converted into existence when it in turn is counted as belonging to another set. It is this operation whose negation is asserted by the axiom of the empty set, which is effectively the only belonging that exists. Set-theory begins by asserting the negation of belonging, a negation already presupposed by every subsequent operation of belonging through which multiplicity is counted-as-one. Thus the inexistence of the void, the assertion of the negation of belonging, is both the precondition for the operation of the One qua belonging, since all belonging presupposes the existence of (the name of) non-belonging; and that which ensures that the existence of belonging per se is never affirmed. Set-theory begins by declaring that non-belonging exists, a non-belonging which authorizes all subsequent belonging, but the theory neither asserts nor presupposes the existence of belonging.

The axiom of the empty-set asserts that the name of the unpresentable is presented; or that there exists a name of inexistence. This nuance is crucial: asserting the existence of a name in discourse is quite different from asserting the existence of an extra-discursive concept. For it is through this nomination that presentation is able to suture itself to the unpresentable without presenting it. Thus, Badiou writes, 'the inaugural advent' of the unpresentable consists in 'a pure act of nomination' (Badiou 1988: 72, 2006a: 59) which 'since it is a-specific [...] consumes itself, thereby indicating nothing but the unpresentable as such' (Badiou 1988: 72, 2006a: 59 tm). This nomination neither marks the return of the One, since it does not make anything consist, nor does it index a multiplicity, since what it presents is strictly nothing.

4.6 Presentation as anti-phenomenon

Presentation gives rise to an effect of unification, but is not itself unified because it is split between the consistency of multiple-entities (presented in terms of belonging) and its own inconsistent being, which is to say the non-being of the count insofar as it manifests a point of indiscernibility with the being-nothing of the void. This indiscernibility is at once the guarantor of the being of presentation (since the void of presentation is its suture to being) and what threatens to subvert its law. The law of presentation requires that this indiscernibility and the threat of structure's own latent inconsistency be forestalled through re-presentation insofar as it measures the gap between what belongs to presentation and what it includes. Thus re-presentation reinstates the law whereby the non-being of structure is separated from being-nothing. More precisely, it ensures that their point of convergence remains asymptotic by deferring it to the 'future anterior'. The inconsistent being or void of presentation (configured by the non-being of the count) 'will have been' presented through the re-presentation of everything which the count included without presenting:

> Consequently, since everything is counted, but since the one of the count, being merely a result, implies as its ghostly remainder the fact that multiplicity does not originally have the form of the one, it is necessary to acknowledge that, from within a situation, pure or inconsistent multiplicity is at once excluded from the whole, and hence excluded from presentation as such, but also included as what presentation itself or in itself 'would be', were that which the law forbids as inconceivable to be conceivable: that the one is not, and that the being of consistency is inconsistency.
>
> (Badiou 1988: 66, 2006a: 53 tm)

Thus presentation is internally fissured by the split between the consistency it presents and the inconsistency of its own being (i.e. the inconsistency of *what it presents* consistently). Every consistently presented situation harbours a latent reserve of inconsistency. But this inconsistency is only ever a retroactive effect of the count; an insubstantial shadow cast by the structure of substantiation. Consequently, the structuring operation whereby multiplicity is rendered consistent in presentation is also what prohibits the presentation of being or inconsistency as such. Being is foreclosed to presentation (Badiou 1988: 35, 2006a: 27); there is no conceivable 'experience' of presented being; it is ontologically intelligible precisely insofar as it remains 'inconceivable for every presence and every experience' (Badiou 1988: 35, 2006a: 27 tm). Moreover, since 'presence is the exact contrary of presentation' (Badiou 1988: 35, 2006a: 27), and since every phenomenon is definable in terms of presence to a subject of representation, or presence to consciousness, then presentation is not a phenomenon. But this is not, as mystics and negative theologians would have it, because being can only be presented as 'absolutely Other': ineffable, un-presentable, inaccessible via the structures of rational thought and therefore only approachable through some superior or initiatory form of non-conceptual experience. This is the 'Great Temptation' (Badiou 1988: 34, 2006a: 26) to which philosophers invariably succumb if the denial of the being of unity and the affirmation of being's inconsistency is not qualified by the proviso that there is no immediate, non-discursive access to being, and circumscribed by the insistence that ontology is a determinate situation; one in which the un-presentability of inconsistent multiplicity is rationally encoded in the compositional strictures of set-theoretical discourse. It is the axiomatic character of ontological presentation which guarantees that inconsistent multiplicity is inseparable from the operation of structuring. Consequently, the metaontological concept of presentation is that of an anti-phenomenon; a split noumenon which vitiates every form of intellectual intuition insofar as it embodies the unobjectifiable dehiscence whereby, in exempting itself from the consistency which it renders possible, structure unleashes the very inconsistency it is obliged to foreclose. The law of presentation conjoins the authorization of consistency and the prohibition of inconsistency in an unpresentable caesura wherein the deployment and subtraction of structure coincide. Thus the structure of presentation envelops a strictly 'non-phenomenologizable' scission which can only be *inscribed* in the formal ideography of set-theory. Ultimately, only an insignificant letter, Ø, indexes the originary fissure whereby presentation deposes presence and binds itself to the mark of the unpresentable. Ø is the initial incision that marks the hinge between consistency and inconsistency, non-being and being-nothing.

4.7   The metaontological exception

The question, then, is whether, given its anti-phenomenological structure, presentation obtains in any situation other than the ontological situation. In this regard, it is crucial to note that only the ontological situation, i.e. the set-theoretical axiomatic as presentation of presentation, is capable of remaining rigorously faithful to the injunction that the One is not:

> In non-ontological (i.e. non-mathematical) situations, multiplicity is only possible insofar as the law explicitly subordinates it to the law of the count [...] Ordinary situations, if one grasps them from their own immanent standpoint, invert the axiom which inaugurates our entire procedure. They state that the one is, and that pure multiplicity – i.e. inconsistency – is not. This is entirely natural, since not being the presentation of presentation, ordinary situations necessarily identify being with what is presentable, and hence with the possibility of the one [...] Thus it is veridical [...] from a standpoint internal to what a situation establishes as the form of knowledge, that to be is to be unifiable. Leibniz's thesis ('What is not *a* being, is not a *being*') governs the immanence of situations as their horizon of veridicality. It is a thesis of the law.
>
> (Badiou 1988: 65–6, 2006a: 52–3 tm)

But if metaontology is clearly not the presentation of presentation, since its discourse is entirely conceptual and since it has not sutured itself to the real of presentation (the empty set); and if it is not subject to the horizon of veridicality governing ordinary situations, since it has suspended the Leibnizian thesis, then what are its specific situational parameters? Where is Badiou speaking from in these decisive opening Meditations of *Being and Event*? Clearly, it is neither from the identity of thinking and being as effectuated in ontological discourse, nor from within a situation governed by knowledge and hence subject to the law of the One. But then how are we to situate Badiou's metaontological discourse, given that its stance is neither ontological *stricto sensu* nor that of ordinary knowledge? It is not ontological since the concepts it mobilizes – 'multiple', 'structure', 'counting-as-one', 'situation', 'state', and, most importantly, 'presentation' – are transcendent vis-à-vis the immanent resources of the set-theoretical axiomatic, whose defining characteristic is precisely not to recognize itself as the science of being qua being, and hence not to objectify being by reflecting upon it.[10] But it is not an ordinary form of knowledge, since it is not subordinated to the immanence of any particular situation – not even that of ontology – and thus does not seem to be entirely subject to the law of the One. Thus metaontological discourse seems to enjoy a condition of transcendent exception vis-à-vis the immanence of ontological and non-ontological situations.

Badiou maintains that it is the hallmark of philosophy to be conditioned by extra-philosophical truths, which remain irreducible to the immanent norms of knowledge, and which it must strive to 'compossibilize'.[11] But given that philosophy itself is not a truth procedure, there can be no subject of philosophy strictly speaking for Badiou, and thus he is at pains to explain how the metaontological discourse which conditions his entire philosophy (and from which he draws *all* the conceptual details for his theory of evental truth) is able to exempt itself from the immanent conditions of knowledge governed by the norm of the One. The question can be put another way: Is the relation between ontology and metaontology one of isomorphy or analogy? Badiou's metaontological stance in *Being and Event* perpetuates a dangerous equivocation between isomorphy and analogy; between the literal localization of ontological discourse as presentation of presentation and the de-localization of a metaontological discourse which seems to straddle the ontic (i.e. the ordinary situations in which the rule of the One ensures that being remains convertible with consistency) and the ontological (i.e. set-theory, in which what is presented is presentation's own latent inconsistency). The a-specificity of metaontological discourse in *Being and Event*, and the anomalous status of philosophical thought invite the impression that Badiou's metaontological theses float between a re-presentation of the mathematical presentation of being, and a presentation of the imaginary re-presentations of ordinary knowledge, which remain in thrall to the law of the One. Moreover, it is precisely the anti-phenomenological radicality of the concept of presentation which gives rise to the problem concerning the precise nature of the relations between the ontological situation, the metaontological (i.e. philosophical) situation, and ordinary situations; which is to say, between the set-theoretical axiomatic, subtractive metaontology, and the supposedly ubiquitous law of the One.

A cursory glance at the overarching structure of the argument of *Being and Event* reveals its complex character. On one hand, Badiou draws the consequences of the decision that mathematics is ontology. It would seem that this decision itself is ultimately 'evental' in nature. Thus it remains necessarily unverifiable within the conceptual apparatus which draws its consequences. But it is this apparatus which will explain how and why this unverifiability is not only possible, but valid, albeit illegitimizable in terms of the norms of knowledge.[12] Badiou proceeds by identifying the situation in which there is an authentic (albeit unexpected) 'self-grounding' of thought; the situation in which thinking sutures itself to being. This suturing, which authenticates the

Parmenidean thesis according to which 'thinking and being are the same', occurs within the set-theoretical axiomatic as presentation of presentation. And it is on the basis of the latter that Badiou will explain the possibility of evental decision in terms of a breakdown in the consistency of being; a breakdown which will give rise to the decision that being is not-all and that thought can find a foothold in ontological inconsistency.

Our aim here is not to denounce the putative 'circularity' of Badiou's argument, which may well be perfectly virtuous. Nevertheless, it is important to note that thought's suture to being – or to 'the real' (sheer inconsistency), since they are equivalent here – occurs within the set-theoretical axiomatic, rather than within Badiou's metaontological gloss on the latter; a gloss which he interposes between ontology and the reader via the use of concepts such as that of 'presentation'. In other words, we have no assurances that thinking has any purchase on being in situations other than the ontological situation. More importantly, there seems to be no reason to assume that the concept of 'presentation' indexes anything at all outside of ontological discourse, or that presentation has any extra-discursive existence. Citing so-called empirical evidence, according to which 'everyone can see that there is presentation' is out of the question here. A Platonist as intransigent as Badiou cannot appeal to the *doxas* of common sense as support for the existence of presentation. Moreover, to resort to the authority of consciousness – whether empirical or transcendental – would be to capitulate completely to the norm of the One insofar as its inviolability is encoded in the putative incorrigibility of phenomenological intuition. Why, then, does Badiou speak of the 'presentation' of multiple-being from the very opening of *Being and Event*? Of what variety of manifestation is subtractive being capable, given that, as Badiou himself emphasizes 'being does not present *itself*' ('l'être ne *se* présente pas') (Badiou 1988: 35, 2006a: 27) and 'it is pointless to seek out anything in a situation that would bolster an intuition of being-as-being' (Badiou 1988: 67, 2006a: 54 tm). If subtractive being is never *given*, what is the link between the presentation of presentation and the so-called ordinary or non-ontological regime of presentation? For despite the putative 'a priority' of ontological discourse as 'condition for the apprehension of every possible access to being', it is far from clear whether the argument of *Being and Event* proceeds a priori from the void of being to the multiplicity of presentation, or on the contrary, and a posteriori, from the multiplicity of presentation to the void of being. In other words, how is it that the unpresentable can give rise to anything but subtractive – ontological – presentation?

Ultimately, *Being and Event* establishes a necessary link between the void of being and the ontological situation only at the cost of severing any intelligible connection between being and the multiplicity of presentation. The discrepancy between Badiou's claims about the a priority of the ontological and his surreptitious appeal to the a posteriori is revealed in the fundamental tension between certain of his more uncompromisingly anti-phenomenological declarations, such as 'there is no structure of being' (Badiou 1988: 34, 2006a: 26), and other more equivocal claims, such as 'presentation is never chaotic, even though its being is that of inconsistent multiplicity' (Badiou 1988: 110, 2006a: 94 tm). The multiplicity of presentation implies that there must be presentational situations other than the ontological. But since the set-theoretical axiomatic guarantees the consistency of presentation through the operation of counting-as-one, the aforementioned tension obtains only insofar as presentation occurs in non-ontological contexts. What, then, are we supposed to understand by the term 'chaotic' in non-ontological situations? If Badiou means disordered, then the claim is at least empirically contestable, if not downright false. But if 'chaotic' simply means 'inconsistent' then Badiou is merely reiterating an empty tautology: 'what is consistently presented does not in-consist'. It is precisely the failure to clarify the connection between ontological inconsistency and ontical consistency that obliges Badiou to resort to hollow tautologies such as 'consistency must be consistent'. If unity is only ever the result of an inexistent operation, then what non-tautological instance accounts for the necessary ubiquity of consistency?

4.8 The two regimes of presentation

The key to the nature of the articulation between the a priori and the a posteriori (or ontology and 'world') in Badiou lies in grasping the difference between the two regimes of presentation, ontological and non-ontological. Both, their distinction and their relation are rooted in the difference between metastructure and re-presentation. Ontology as the site for 'the apprehension of every possible access to being' cannot be re-presented. Thus, although the metastructural doubling of presentation provides the ontological paradigm for the distinction between situation and state of the situation, and thereby for the gap between presentation and re-presentation – the yawning chasm wherein the possibility of the eventual break with ontological consistency takes root – it is precisely ontology as presentation of presentation, presentation of sheer inconsistent multiplicity, which precludes the possibility of interruption insofar as it remains exempt from re-presentation:

> [O]ntology is simultaneously obliged to [...] draw all the consequences of the gap between belonging and inclusion while not being governed by this gap [...] Thus the state of the ontological situation is insepara-ble, i.e. non-existent [...] Ontology's integral effectuation of the non-being of the one, implies the inexistence of the state of the situation which it is, and infects inclusion with the void, having already stipu-lated that belonging is woven solely from the void. The unpresentable void here sutures the situation to the inseparability of its state.
>
> (Badiou 1988: 117–18, 2006a: 101)

This is a particularly gnomic passage, even by the standards of *Being and Event*. But in fact it provides a decisive clue as to the underlying connection between the ontological situation and non-ontological situations, that is, between subtractive discourse and presented reality. The ontological presentation of presentation presents nothing; every consistent presentation is drawn from the originary mark of unpre-sentable inconsistency. It is because ontology is the 'consummate effec-tuation' of the non-being of the One, the unique situation wherein consistency is only ever derived from inconsistency, that it only ever presents nothing, and can never encounter something – it can never count the inclusion of anything other than the void. But recall that in non-ontological situations, consistency prevails over inconsistency, the One is and inconsistency is not: thus what is presented is convert-ible with unity. It is precisely in such non-ontological situations that the immeasurable excess of inconsistent inclusion over consistent belong-ing allows for singularities, i.e. elements that are presented by the situation but none of whose elements are re-presented by the state of the situation (Badiou 1988: 116, 2006a: 99). And it is such singularities that provide a point of leverage for the event (they can become 'even-tal sites').[13] The ontological situation only ever harbours the latent inconsistency of the void, whereas non-ontological situations harbour the latent inconsistency of unity. It is the inconsistency latent in the units of ordinary presentation that provides the resource for a tran-scendent break with the immanent form of ontological presentation. The event is the transcendent intervention that splits the immanent ontological disjunction between belonging and inclusion into an unde-cidable duality or 'two', the better to transform the state of the situa-tion. This intervention is of course the operation of the subject, whose transcendence the immanent objectivity of ontological discourse forecloses. The transcendence of the subject can be given a precise definition in contradistinction to the objective immanence of ontological discourse: whereas the latter is the consistent presentation of the inconsistency latent in the void, the subject is the consistent presentation of the inconsistency latent in unity (it effectuates the generic).[14]

Ontological discourse precludes the possibility of the subject because it can only draw the consequences of the gap between belonging and inclusion up to the 'point of impasse' where their hiatus becomes strictly measureless and undergoes a phase-transition from immanence to transcendence.[15] The axiomatic consistency of ontological discourse encounters its own 'impossibility', that is, its own extra-discursive 'real', at the point at which the immanent disjunction between structure and metastructure turns into the transcendent excess of re-presentation over presentation. In other words, the ontological a priori (mathematical discourse) intersects with the a posteriori (the 'world') at the point where its effectuation of the inconsistency of consistency (the being-nothing of non-being) flips over into an effectuation of the consistency of inconsistency (the non-being of being-nothing, or subjective 'truth') through the mediation of the event. Badiou generates the distinction between discursive and extra-discursive presentation, presentation of presentation and presentation of 'something', by extrapolating from an immanent disjunction between structure and metastructure in ontological discourse and converting it into that measureless transcendence of re-presentation over presentation which he claims characterizes non-ontolological situations.[16] The result is that Badiou can only delimit the sovereignty of symbolic law – the authority of ontological structure or the count – or acknowledge the domain of extra-discursive reality by invoking a surplus of transcendence – incalculable, unverifiable, unobjectifiable, and necessarily subjective – whose ontological schematization fails to mask its inherent gratuitousness. Badiou bridges the gap between ontological discourse and mundane reality by surreptitiously converting an immanent hiatus in ontological presentation into a transcendent interruption of ontological consistency. As a result, his philosophy simply stipulates an isomorphy between discourse and reality, logical consequences and material causes, thinking and being. Thinking is sufficient to change the world: such is the ultimate import of Badiou's idealism. The exorbitant inflation of the eventual exception follows directly from this idealist sublation of the distinction between thinking and being: the only events are events in and as thinking, where the modalities of thinking are articulated according to generic cultural

forms: politics, science, art, and love. Ultimately, Badiou is only inter-
ested in thinking as event and vice versa. Accordingly, the Big Bang, the
Cambrian explosion, and the death of the sun remain mere hiccups in
the way of the world, in which he has little or no interest. Nevertheless,
it would be inaccurate to accuse him of anthropocentrism, since he
does not privilege human existence so much as a capacity for thinking
which he only sees exemplified by the human animal. The problem lies
in Badiou's 'noocentrism' rather than in any alleged anthropocentrism.

Ultimately, the role of subtractive ontology in Badiou's philosophy is
merely auxiliary: it is essentially a de-mystificatory screen designed to
prevent us from becoming fascinated by the luxuriant plenitude of what
there is, by the actuality of the world as it is now, so that we may be
prepared to seize the possibility of its radical transformation. Hence
its essentially propaedeutic function vis-à-vis the theory of the event.
But Badiou's problem is this: if ontology is a discursive situation, if there
is no non-discursive access to being, and if being is neither a concept
nor a datum of 'experience', then all that mediates between ontolologi-
cal presentation *stricto sensu*, in which neither 'being' nor 'presentation'
play any conceptual role, and non-ontological presentation, is Badiou's
own metaontological discourse. Its relationship to ontological discourse
on one hand, and non-ontological 'reality' on the other, consists in
schematizing the immanent disjunction between belonging and inclusion in the former so as to convert it into a locus of radical transcendence in the latter. The goal of this schematization is to synthesize the
a priori regime of ontological presentation with the a posteriori regime
of ordinary presentation. But ontology cannot be the guarantor of
'the apprehension of every possible access to being' if its paradigm of
presentation undermines the very possibility of access to being outside
the confines of the ontological situation. In fact, it is not ontology, but
metaontology that is the secret guarantor of the ubiquity of presentation for Badiou: it simply stipulates the impossibility of denying the
existence of presentation in non-ontological situations. Nevertheless, the
structure of presentation is such as to render the idea of translating it
from the ontological situation to ordinary situations absurd. There is
only ontological presentation. Either Badiou denies that ontology is a
situation, in which case he is obliged to choose between mysticism,
phenomenology, or metaphysics; or he accepts that the subtractive
nature of presentation is such as to undermine all the non-ontological
consequences he wishes to draw from it; specifically, his theory of the
event.

4.9 Consequences of subtraction

The claim that ontology is mathematics, then, generates the following quandary: If mathematical ontology stands to reality as conceptual scheme to empirical content, then Badiou finds himself resurrecting the empiricist dualism of formal scheme and material content which he himself had already castigated in his first book, *The Concept of Model*.[17] But in order to avoid such scheme–content dualism, Badiou must show that presentation occurs in non-ontological (i.e. non-discursive) contexts. This remains an insuperable difficulty, not only because the claim that the One is not effectively undermines any attempt to privilege the ontological situation as the transcendental ground of access to all other situations; but also because Badiou's attempt to distinguish between ontological and non-ontological situations in terms of the primacy of inconsistency over consistency or vice versa renders it very difficult to understand how non-discursive presentation could ever 'occur'. Consequently, Badiou finds himself confronted by two equally unappetizing alternatives. On the one hand, he faces a relapse into the empiricist dualism of formal scheme and material content, which he himself had previously sworn to abjure, and one wherein the only available criteria for legitimating the identification of ontology with set-theory are pragmatic since – as Quine and others have convincingly argued – empirical content underdetermines the choice of conceptual scheme. Or, on the other hand, there is the prospect of a discursive variety of absolute idealism – or crypto-Hegelianism – in which the difference between the conceptual and the extra-conceptual, or discourse and world, is reduced to the distinction between consistent and inconsistent multiplicity, and for which, ultimately, thinking is all that matters.

At this juncture, Badiou can respond in two ways: he can either choose to correct the anti-phenomenological bias of the concept of presentation by supplementing the subtractive ontology of being qua being with a doctrine of appearance and of the ontical consistency of worlds[18] – albeit at the risk of lapsing back into some variant of the ontologies of presence. Or he can accept the stringency of his concept of presentation and embrace the prohibitive consequences of the logic of subtraction. The recently published *Logiques des mondes*[19] (*Logics of Worlds*) suggests that he has – perhaps reasonably, albeit somewhat disappointingly from our point of view – opted for the former. Yet in our eyes, the veritable worth of Badiou's work lies not in his theory of the event but rather in the subtractive ontology which was merely intended as its propaedeutic.

Badiou's inestimable merit is to have disenchanted ontology: 'being' is insignificant, it means, quite literally, nothing. The question of the meaning of being must be abandoned as an antiquated superstition. This is the profound import of Badiou's anti-phenomenological but post-metaphysical rationalism, and one which, despite Badiou's own fierce antipathy towards empiricism and naturalism, is perfectly consonant with that variant of naturalized epistemology we considered in Chapter 1 and which proposes that nothing has ever meant anything. As we saw in Part I, this is one of the principal consequences of the disenchantment of sapience which cognitive science is currently undertaking. Accordingly, rather than pursuing any sort of qualitative supplement to subtractive ontology, we believe it is necessary to sharpen and deepen the letter's disqualification of phenomenological donation (and of its dyadic structures such as temporalization/spatialization, continuity/discontinuity, quantity/quality). This sharpening and deepening entails abandoning the discursive idealism which vitiates Badiou's conception of subtractive presentation and which betrays itself in the fact that the sole real presupposition for the latter is that of the existence of the *name* of the void. As we have seen, any attempt to deduce this ultimate presupposition by assuming the consistency of multiplicity involves an illegitimate recourse to phenomenological donation and/or empirical experience. But as we shall see in our discussion of the work of Laruelle in the following chapter, it is possible to presuppose the existence of the void qua being-nothing independently of the discursive structure of mathematical science, without positing the primacy of the signifier, invoking phenomenological donation, or resorting to empirical experience.

As it stands, however, subtractive ontology is compromised by the idealism of the discursive a priori on one hand, and by the dualism of scheme and content on the other, both of which severely undermine Badiou's avowed commitment to materialism. The discursive structure of presentation seems to stipulate an isomorphy between nomological and ontological structure which conflicts with the realist postulates of the physical sciences, which assume that objects exhibit causal properties rooted in real physical structures that obtain quite independently of the ideal laws of presentation. At the same time, the dualism of ontological form and ontic content generates a dichotomy which also seems to contradict the requirements of scientific realism: either discursively structured presentation or unstructured chaos. But can one maintain that being is mathematically inscribed without implying that nothing exists independently of mathematical inscription? This would be one of the more nefarious consequences of the Parmenidean thesis, which would seem to stipulate a pre-established harmony between thinking and being. Accordingly, the question must be whether it is possible to demonstrate thought's purchase on 'the real' without invoking the idealism of a priori intuition or inscription on the one hand, yet without relapsing into a pragmatic naturalism wherein the correspondence between scientific representation and reality is evolutionarily guaranteed (cf. Chapter 1) on the other. The next chapter shall pursue this question via an examination of the work of François Laruelle.

5
Being Nothing

5.1 Realism, constructivism, deconstruction: François Laruelle

If realism has become philosophically unintelligible for post-Kantian European philosophy, then the singular virtue of François Laruelle's work consists in showing how the resources of transcendental philosophy can be turned against idealism in order to render transcendental realism thinkable. Where the speculative materialisms proposed by Badiou and Meillassoux circumvent the forced choice between metaphysics and critique at the cost of privileging discursive inscription or rehabilitating intellectual intuition, Laruelle provides us with some of the resources required for a version of transcendental realism that would not be vitiated by the idealism of inscription or intuition. But it will be necessary to criticize Laruelle's own concessions to transcendental *doxa* in order to wrest a viable conception of realism from his work. More precisely, we shall try to extract from his writings a de-phenomenologized conception of the real as 'being-nothing'. This process of extraction will necessarily conflict with much of what Laruelle says about his own enterprise; indeed, in what follows, we will contest Laruelle's characterization of his project as 'non-philosophy'. Nevertheless, our aim is not to denigrate Laruelle's achievement, which strikes us as nothing short of extraordinary, but on the contrary to dislodge a rebarbative carapace which, far from warding off misinterpretation, seems to have succeeded only in barring appreciation of his thought's significance. Thus, after 36 years and 18 books,[1] Laruelle's writings have yet to inspire anything beyond uncritical emulation or exasperated dismissal. It is the preponderance of the latter in reaction to his work that needs to be squarely confronted. In this regard, there is no doubt that it is possible to perceive in Laruelle's voluminous writings little more than an unfortunate conjunction between two deplorable tendencies in recent French philosophy: a tiresome preoccupation with non-philosophical alterity coupled with an indulgent penchant for terminological obscurantism. From the former point of view, Laruelle's work would merely represent an aggravation of Derrida's: a largely negative characterization of philosophy provides the impetus for unearthing an absolute alterity which would resist philosophical conceptualization even as the latter is shown to depend upon it. But where Derridian deconstruction (following Heidegger) tends to identify philosophy with 'metaphysics' and the latter with 'ontotheology', Laruelle's 'non-philosophy' ups the ante by including the deconstruction of metaphysics in an even more nebulously expansive 'definition' of philosophy, now simply equated with 'decision'. Similarly, where Derrida proposed *différance* as one of many names for the non-conceptual transcendence which simultaneously conditions and subverts metaphysics, Laruelle proposes *l'Un* ('the One') as one among a series of names for the non-conceptual immanence which simultaneously determines and suspends philosophy. Conversely, from the latter point of view, Laruelle's terminological eccentricities and his baroque conceptual constructions would almost amount to a parody of Deleuze's philosophical constructivism. An unsympathetic critic glancing at the unseemly bulk of the Laruellean corpus might be forgiven for dismissing it as combining the worst of Derrida and Deleuze, deconstructionist sterility with constructivist extravagance.

This would be a particularly brutal caricature, yet it nevertheless contains a grain of truth: there is indeed an undeniable respect in which Derrida (along with Heidegger) and to a lesser extent Deleuze (along with Nietzsche) provide the most immediate reference points for understanding Laruelle's thought, in which the negative characterization of philosophy provides the precondition for the positive creation of 'non-philosophical' concepts. Nevertheless, such a caricature would elide one of the most valuable aspects of Laruelle's work, for although he recommends abstaining from decision, which he views as a quasi-spontaneous philosophical compulsion, it is precisely insofar as his thought seeks to define a precarious point of equilibrium between the competing claims of transcendental critique and metaphysical construction that it can be said to harbour a decisive – which is to say, *philosophical* – import that transcends the sum of its influences. Thus we will try to show why Laruelle's non-philosophy is not just a curious but ultimately bootless exercise in extravagant sterility by arguing – against Laruelle himself – that its conceptual import can and should be philosophically interpreted. The nub of this philosophical re-interpretation will be that Laruelle has not achieved a non-philosophical suspension of philosophy but rather uncovered a non-dialectical logic of philosophical negation: viz., 'unilateralization'.

It is difficult, when trying to summarize and appraise Laruelle's thought, to know which texts to privilege from among his vast and ever-expanding corpus, in which key theses and formulations are continuously revised or qualified, and previous claims often abandoned or retracted. Thus any presentation of his thought is bound to involve a certain amount of distortion and caricature. Nevertheless, we shall privilege six texts which we take to represent significant crystallizations of crucial aspects of his thinking and which contain particularly emphatic formulations and detailed analyses not reproduced elsewhere in his work. These are *The Philosophies of Difference* (1986), *Philosophy and Non-Philosophy* (1989a), 'The Transcendental Method' (1989b),[2] *The Principles of Non-Philosophy* (1996), *Introduction to Non-Marxism* (2000a), and 'What Can Non-Philosophy Do?' (2003).[3]

5.2   The essence of philosophy

According to Laruelle, 'non-philosophy' is not a negation of philosophy but rather an autonomous theoretical practice (or 'science', as Laruelle once liked to call it)[4] which seeks not to supplant or eliminate philosophy but rather to *use* it as a material and object of study. The ostensible rationale for this non-philosophical usage of philosophy proposed by Laruelle is a theory and practice of philosophy which would expose the latter's innermost workings and explain its fundamental operations while opening up a realm of conceptual possibility hitherto un-envisaged within philosophy. Thus, Laruelle maintains, non-philosophical practice entails a suspension of the practicing philosopher's own spontaneous acceptance of the legitimacy of the characteristic problems, methods, and strategies of philosophy. But for Laruelle, this suspension of the authority of philosophy (which Laruelle refers to as 'the principle of sufficient philosophy') is the precondition for the exploration of an entirely novel theoretical domain, which – so it is claimed – cannot be reduced to, or interpreted in terms of, any of the concepts, structures, or tropes which govern philosophical thinking. Thus Laruelle identifies what he takes to be the constrictive essence of philosophical thinking – which he calls 'decision' – the better to propose a more inventive theoretical and practical alternative; i.e. a non-philosophical use of decision, which lets the non-philosopher generate new concepts even as it illuminates the functioning of philosophical thinking. This contrast between the inventive and (intellectually) emancipatory potency of non-philosophical thought and the essentially inhibitory and repetitive nature of philosophy is a recurring motif throughout Laruelle's work.[5]

It is this more or less 'standard' characterization of non-philosophy according to Laruelle, whose coherence and viability we intend to interrogate in what follows. However, at the outset, our basic critical contention can be simply stated: Laruelle has conflated the critique of a certain kind of philosophizing with a critique of philosophy *tout court*. And it is Laruelle's own self-avowed preoccupation with identifying the essence of philosophizing (which he prefers to call its 'identity'), his attempt to uncover a trans-historical invariant governing the possibilities of philosophy, which lies at the root of this conflation.[6] Although Laruelle firmly disavows any such filiation, this need to identify the essence of philosophy is arguably inherited from Heidegger: where the latter discerned the essence of metaphysics in something like *Vorhandenheit*'s occlusion of *Zuhandenheit* – the representational erasure of being's withdrawal from presence – Laruelle sees something like the essential structure of philosophical thinking delineated in this very distinction between *Vorhandenheit* and *Zuhandenheit*, or representation and its un-representable condition.[7] Thus Laruelle explicitly reinscribes Heideggerian *Destruktion* and Derridian deconstruction within the perennial logic of philosophy: they are supposedly manifestations of the same invariant which has governed philosophizing since Parmenides and Heraclitus.[8] But he is driven to do so because he uncritically accepts the Heideggerian premise that the entire history of philosophy can be reduced to a single structure. More egregiously, and unlike his deconstructionist predecessors, Laruelle does not even attempt to legitimate his identification of the essence of philosophy by way of evidence gathered during a prolonged engagement with the tradition, but does so largely on the basis of a protracted negotiation with the legacies of Heidegger and Derrida themselves.[9] According to Laruelle, the aporias of deconstruction merely mark the fated consummation of philosophy's perennial Greek essence. The twentieth century's deconstruction of metaphysics provides the datum on the basis of which the essence of philosophy is retroactively identified as that which has 'always already' delimited in advance the range of conceptual possibilities open to philosophy. But where Heidegger sought to provide an account of this essence's historical unfolding by periodizing the epochal dispensations of being (however unconvincingly), Laruelle attempts to deflect the question of the interplay between essence and history on the grounds that it is still beholden to the philosophical structure he is call-ing into question; a move which simply evades the vexed issue of the relation between non-philosophy and its own determinate historical preconditions.

By way of mitigation, it could be pointed out that the speciousness of Heidegger's *Seinsgeschichte* betrays the absurdity inherent in any attempt to uncover philosophy's essence inductively using textual exegesis. If the history of philosophical texts is the history of contingency, an arbi-trary tissue of elisions, distortions, and misrepresentations enmeshed in the vagaries of socio-political circumstance, then no amount of archival evidence will be sufficient to legitimate claims about philosophy's essential nature – which are invariably claims about its current respon-sibilities made on the basis of a historically circumscribed understand-ing of its present. Heidegger sought to turn this hermeneutic circularity inherent in historical self-understanding into a virtue, yet the fanciful-ness of his 'history of Being' only evinces the inadequacy of the former when it comes to underwriting claims about philosophy's essence. Only from the perspective of a putative absolute could the fixed essence sup-posedly underlying philosophy's historico-empirical variation be grasped. Unsurprisingly, if challenged to defend his own account of phi-losophy's essence, Laruelle can lay claim to the perspective of his own non-philosophical 'absolute' (a term he explicitly disavows because of its philosophical connotations), which is the viewpoint of what he calls 'radical immanence'. This perspective and the definition of philosophy concomitant with it are precisely what, for Laruelle, remain withdrawn from the ambit of philosophical legitimation. But once we have dis-counted the gratuitous assumption that philosophy per se possesses an invariant structure, we will see that what 'radical immanence' suspends is a certain type of philosophical argumentation and the demand for a specific kind of philosophical validation, rather than 'philosophy' or the requirement of philosophical legitimation as such. Moreover, we shall also see why Laruelle's own characterization of the suspending instance, i.e. radical immanence, can be called into question inde-pendently of the governing assumptions proper to the suspended structure.

5.3   Philosophical decision as transcendental deduction

Laruelle's identification of the essence of philosophy as 'decision', and his characterization of the perspective from which this identification occurs as that of 'radical immanence', conjoins three basic terms: immanence, transcendence, and the transcendental. For Laruelle, a philosophical decision is a dyad of immanence and transcendence, but one wherein immanence features twice, its internal structure subdivided between an empirical and a transcendental function. It is at once internal to the dyad as the empirical immanence of the datum coupled to the transcendence of the a priori factum, but also external as that supplement of transcendental immanence required for gluing empirical immanence and a priori transcendence together. Every decision divides immanence between an empirical datum which it supposes as given through the a priori factum, and a transcendental immanence which it has to invoke as already given in order to guarantee the unity of a presupposed factum and a posited datum. It is as a result of this decisional splitting of immanence that philosophy requires the latter to intervene both as the empirical corollary of transcendence and as the transcendental guarantor for the unity of a priori condition and empirically conditioned – a unity which yields what philosophers call 'experience'.

Thus, Laruelle maintains, every philosophical decision recapitulates the formal structure of a transcendental deduction. In 'The Transcendental Method', he proposes an account in which the latter represents a methodological invariant for philosophy both before and after Kant – one whose functional features can be described independently of any determinate set of ontological or even epistemological premises – and proceeds to identify the three distinct structural moments which he takes to be constitutive of this method and hence of philosophizing as such:

1. The analytical inventory of a manifold of categorial a prioris on the basis of the empirical reality or experience whose conditions of possibility one seeks. In Kant, this is the moment of the metaphysical exposition of space and time as a priori forms of intuition and of the metaphysical deduction of the categories as pure, a priori forms of judgement.[10] It corresponds to the moment of metaphysical distinction between conditioned and condition, empirical and a priori, datum and factum.

2. The 'gathering-together' or unification of this manifold of local or regional (i.e. categorial) a prioris into a form of universal unity by means of a single, unifying, transcendental a priori. Whereas the form of every categorial a priori remains a function of the a posteriori, that of the transcendental is no longer tied to any form of regional experience because it functions as that superior or absolute condition which makes experience itself possible. It is no longer the result of synthesis, but rather the pre-synthetic unity that makes all

a priori forms of synthesis themselves possible. This unity is said to be 'transcendental' then because it is supposed to exceed experience absolutely, rather than merely relatively, in the manner of the meta-physical or categorial a prioris, which are always local, multiple, and tied to a specific region or form of experience. It transcends absolutely beyond the specific generic distinctions of the relatively transcendent categorial a prioris which it ultimately grounds and unifies. Kant will famously locate this transcendental ground of the synthetic a priori in the indivisible unity of pure apperception. Crucially, Laruelle points out, it is this very absoluteness required of the transcendental a priori which is compromised insofar as it remains tied in varying degrees, depending on the philosopher in question, to one or other form of metaphysically transcendent empirical entity: Laruelle gives as examples the 'I think' and the fac-ultative apparatus in Kant, and the Ego of pure phenomenological consciousness in Husserl. Thus, the supposedly unconditional tran-scendence demanded of the transcendental remains compromised precisely because the structure of transcendence invariably binds it to some reified, transcendent entity.

3. The third and final moment is that of the unification of these modes of categorial synthesis with this transcendental unity, but now understood in terms of their constitutive relation to experience through the offices of the latter. It is the binding of the metaphysical a priori to the empirical experience that it conditions via the tran-scendental unity conditioning the possibility of the a priori itself. This is the stage corresponding to Kant's transcendental deduction of the categories.[11] It is the moment of transcendental synthesis, of reciprocal co-belonging, guaranteeing the immanence to one another of conditioning and conditioned, whether it be in terms of the unity of possible experience (Kant), or of intersubjectivity (Husserl), or of being-in-the-world as 'care' (Heidegger). The divisive moment of transcendental analysis functions only as the enabling preliminary for this binding moment of transcendental synthesis.[12]

Laruelle's account of transcendental deduction here seems to deliber-ately invoke a Heideggerian resonance: deduction constitutes the move-ment whereby the transcendent metaphysical scission of analytic division 'pivots back' (*Kehre*)[13] towards empirical immanence via the binding function of transcendental unity and its indivisible synthesis. Through deduction, the movement from the metaphysically transcen-dent categorial manifold to the transcendental unity which makes that a priori manifold possible is turned back towards empirical experience in the form of a transcendental synthesis binding the a priori to the a posteriori, the logical syntax of the ideal to the contingent empirical congruencies of the real. In this way, deduction simultaneously circumscribes the empirical insofar as it is concerned with its a priori condition, and delimits the transcendent by folding the a priori back within the bounds of empirical sense and forbidding metaphysical attempts to loose it from its moorings as defined according to the limits of possible experience.

Yet not only does deduction explain the empirical reality of cognition, but also the transcendental reality of its a priori possibility. Thus Laruelle seems to concur with Kant's immediate successors in ascribing an unparalleled philosophical importance to the discovery of the synthetic a priori.[14] But only if – as Schelling and Hegel perceived – the function of the latter is at once de-subjectivized and de-objectivized, or generalized beyond its Kantian reification in pure apperception. Laruelle sees in the synthetic a priori an abstract philosophical mechanism which is at once the means and the end of transcendental deduction; so much so that he detects one or other version of the synthetic a priori qua synthesis of ideal and real, *logos* and *physis*, at the heart of every philosophical decision. It is this indivisible synthesis operated through the offices of the transcendental a priori in deduction; this an-objective, pre-subjective and thereby superior (which is to say, transcendental) reality proper to the unity-in-difference of real and ideal, which Laruelle identifies as the consummating moment of philosophical decision. It constitutes the transcendental indivision (= One) which is simultaneously intrinsic and extrinsic, immanent and transcendent to the fundamental dyadic scission between metaphysical factum and empirical datum, condition and conditioned. Thus, for Laruelle:

> The telos of the transcendental is fulfilled by deduction and this constitutes the real: not in any empirical or contingent sense, but in the superior or specifically philosophical sense which is that of the concrete synthetic unity of the empirically real and of a priori or ideal possibility.
>
> (Laruelle 1989b: 697)

Only now does it become possible to make sense of Laruelle's provocative claim that decision presumes to 'co-constitute' the real. For the 'reality' in question at the level of decision is neither that of the empirically immanent 'thing' or *res*, nor that of the metaphysically transcendent and ideal a priori – as in Kant, where 'reality' is defined as coextensive with the bounds of real possibility through the objective validity of the a priori conditioning of possible experience – but rather that which conditions both. It is the reality peculiar to transcendental synthesis as what unifies and constitutes the possibilities of thought and experience at a level which remains both pre-subjective and an-objective, so that, for Laruelle, it is not only operative in Kant and Husserl, but also in Nietzsche and Deleuze. This higher unity of decision is not only indissociable from the unity of experience; it yields it, so that the latter is always structurally isomorphic with the former. Through the operation of deduction, philosophical decision as indivisible division or One-of-the-dyad is always coextensive with the a priori categorial manifold of experience.

Moreover, the philosopher reinscribes his or her own philosophical activity within the transcendental structure which renders the experience of that thought possible as a part of the real at a level that is simultaneously ontic-empirical and ontological-transcendental (this is the 'decisional hybrid' or 'composite' once again). More exactly, the syntax of decision enacts or performs its own transcendental reality in what effectively amounts to an operation of auto-deduction possessing a tripartite structure: decision is at once an empirical event of thought, some immanent being or some thing; but also a transcendent, ontological-metaphysical thought of being as event; and finally that which transcendentally enunciates the being of thought as event of being. This is the complex internal architecture proper to decision as self-positing/self-donating circle or doublet.

Once again, Heidegger exemplifies the decisional structure Laruelle has in mind here. Heidegger reinscribes the conditions for the genesis of the project of fundamental ontology within the structure of fundamental ontology itself. Thus, the philosophical project delineated in *Being and Time* incorporates its own conditions of possibility, as explicated in *Dasein*'s shift from dispersion in average everydayness to the properly meta-physical appropriation of being-unto-death as its ownmost potentiality for being. Since it is via the latter that *Dasein*'s own being comes into question for it, fundamental ontology as theoretical project ultimately supervenes on the existential *Ur*-project delineated in being-unto-death. For Laruelle, Heidegger's account of finite transcendence radicalizes Kantian finitude, and hence the critique of metaphysics, by uncovering the real or ontic condition which determines ideal or metaphysical conditioning. Thus, in *The Philosophies of Difference*, Laruelle credits Heidegger with going some way towards delimiting the autonomy of philosophical decision by identifying a real determinant for ideal conditioning – a project whose realization, according to Laruelle, necessitates the shift from philosophy to non-philosophy and the suspension of decisional thinking altogether. But perhaps it would be more apt to characterize Laruelle's non-philosophy as the *terminus ad quem* of Heidegger's delimitation of metaphysics through his identification of the thing-in-itself with *Dasein*'s unobjectifiable transcendence. Laruelle intends to radicalize deconstruction by redefining the thing-in-itself as unobjectifiable immanence rather than transcendence – a move partially indebted to Michel Henry's phenomenological critique of Heidegger[15] – so that it can be used to delimit philosophy as such by including it within the ambit of transcendence. Where Heideggerian deconstruction sought to circumscribe the *topos* of metaphysics by exposing its determination at the hands of unobjectifiable transcendence (first that of *Dasein*, then that of *Ereignis*), non-philosophy puts philosophy as such (deconstruction included) to one side – puts it in its place or objectifies it, so to speak (as we shall see, this is partly what Laruelle means by 'unilateralization') – by showing how the decisional complex of transcendence, immanence, and the transcendental is ultimately determined by the unobjectifiable immanence which Laruelle identifies with 'the real'.

5.4 Naming the real

Yet even as he denounces the fundamental idealism of philosophical decision, Laruelle insists on identifying the unobjectifiable immanence of the real with 'man' or 'the human' in person: 'Man is precisely that real which is foreclosed to philosophy' (Laruelle 1998: 86). Elsewhere he writes: 'The essence of man resides in the One, i.e. in a non-positional inherence (to) self, in something which is nothing-but-subject or an absolute-as-subject, i.e. a *finitude*'(Laruelle 1985: 15). In so doing, Laruelle reveals the extent to which, despite his claims to non-philosophical radicality, his critique of the pretensions of philosophical decision remains all too beholden to Heidegger's phenomenological radicalization of the post-Kantian pathos of finitude. As with Heidegger's *Dasein* or Henry's 'Life', and notwithstanding the now familiar claim that subject–object dualism has been left behind, the unobjectifiable immanence of Laruelle's 'One' seems to be situated squarely on the side of the subject rather than on the side of the object.

To see why this identification is problematic, it is first necessary to understand to what extent it remains gratuitous by the lights of Laruelle's own axiomatic definitions of radical immanence. Rather than being posited and presupposed via an act of decisional synthesis, radical immanence is axiomatically determined using the vocabulary of transcendental philosophy as a real instance which does not require constitution. In other words, the real is axiomatically defined – to use the language of transcendental constitution – as 'already-constituted'. More precisely, it is axiomatically defined as that which is 'always already' given as the precondition for every operation of transcendental synthesis. Here are six such definitions which we have adapted from Laruelle's *Philosophy and Non-Philosophy*:

1. The real is the phenomenon-in-itself, the phenomenon as *already*-given or given-*without*-givenness, rather than constituted as given via the transcendental synthesis of empirical and a priori, given and givenness.
2. The real is the phenomenon as *already*-manifest or manifest-*without*-manifestation, the phenomenon-without-phenomenality, rather than the phenomenon which is posited and presupposed as manifest in accordance with the transcendental synthesis of manifest and manifestation.
3. The real is that in and through which we have been *already*-gripped rather than any originary factum or datum by which we suppose ourselves to be gripped.
4. The real is *already*-acquired prior to all cognitive or intuitive acquisition, rather than that which is merely posited and presupposed as acquired through the a priori forms of cognition or intuition.
5. The real is *already*-inherent prior to all the substantialist forcings of inherence, conditioning all those supposedly inherent models of identity, be they analytic, synthetic, or differential.
6. The real is *already*-undivided rather than the transcendent unity which is posited and presupposed as undivided and deployed in order to effect the transcendental synthesis of the empirical and the metaphysical. (Laruelle 1989a: 41–5)

The reiteration of the modifiers 'already' and 'without' here functions as a marker for an instance which is axiomatically defined – again, to use the vocabulary of transcendental constitution – as unconditionally sufficient, autonomous, and necessary. Where the circular movement of decision ascends from empirical to metaphysical to transcendental, only to descend again from transcendental to metaphysical to empirical, Laruelle suggests that, rather than seeking to break out of the circle from within, thought should refuse to be bullied into accepting that it is 'always already' within it and adopt a non-decisional posture from the outset. It is not so much a question of breaking out of the circle as realizing that you were never inside it in the first place. Indeed, the claim that thought is always already inside the circle of decision, and that it can only negotiate an opening onto its outside from within, by deploying some form of non-conceptual alterity, is symptomatic of the spontaneous idealism of post-critical philosophy: the very idea of being outside the circle is dismissed as the apex of 'naïve', pre-critical realism. Thus for much of twentieth-century continental philosophy, from Heidegger and Derrida to Levinas and Adorno, the only conceivable alternative to the Scylla of idealism on one hand, whether transcendental or absolute, and the Charybdis of realism – which it seems is only ever 'naïve' – on the other, lies in using the resources of conceptualization against themselves in the hope of glimpsing some transcendent, non-conceptual exteriority. Yet as we have already tried to suggest in Chapter 3, it is no longer realism which is naive, but rather the compulsive idealism inherent in the post-critical assumption that all access to reality is necessarily circumscribed by the circle of transcendental synthesis. It is this spontaneous supposition, this transcendental reflex so characteristic of post-critical philosophy, which Laruelle proposes to call into question by exposing the underlying structure of transcendental synthesis. By suspending the premise that decision co-constitutes the real, thought comes to realize that it can have a relation to a real instance which is neither empirically presupposed nor transcendentally posited as determining, but defined by thought as already-determined and determining for it – a 'real of the last instance' in accordance with which thought can approach the circle of transcendental synthesis from a place which is 'always-already' outside it:

> Determination is not an auto-positional act, a Kantian-Critical operation involving the primacy of determination over the determinate [...] It is the determinate, the real as matter-without-determination, which effects the determination. If radical immanence has the character of the given, it is not in any specifically empirical sense – as is the case with *Bestand* [standing reserve]. Rather, it entails the primacy of the given over givenness, of the determined over determination.
>
> (Laruelle 2000a: 45)

Yet at the same time, this real of the last-instance is not simply material, for 'materiality', whether ontico-empirical or ontological-metaphysical, continues to be posited and presupposed within the ambit of decision. Thus the real as last-instance cannot be ontologically specified:

> [R]adical immanence cannot assume an ontological form which would be specifying, restrictive and transcendent as matter continues to be. It is by right inalienable, unequal to its most distant effects – it is the 'last instance', universal by right (through which all forms of ontic and ontological causation must 'pass'), but only in the last instance (it maintains the relative autonomy of these secondary forms of causation).
>
> (Laruelle 2000a: 46)

Accordingly, the agency of the last-instance can only be effectuated if thinking adopts a posture in which the ultimate synthesizing instance is neither posited nor presupposed as binding for the purposes of transcendental synthesis, but already-given as the undivided real which is the precondition for transcendental binding. The modifier 'already' points to a real which subsists prior to any constituting process of transcendental realisation, just as the modifier 'without' indicates that it is given non-synthetically, independently of any phenomenological conditions of 'givenness', or transcendental operator of manifestation. These modifiers amend the apparatus of transcendental constitution in order to describe a real which is un-synthesizable and hence not constituted by its description. They index a non-synthetic disjunction between the real and its intellection. Accordingly, though each of the descriptions listed above is *adequate*, none of them can be presumed to be *sufficient to* or *constitutive of* the real which they describe. Hence Laruelle's insistence that non-philosophy represents a specific use of philosophical discourse, rather than its negation: it suspends the binding power of transcendental synthesis as something which presumes to constitute the real and subjects synthesis to an operation of unbinding in order to describe a real which cannot be described as 'being', so long as the latter is understood, following Heidegger, as a function of transcendence.

In the final analysis, the use of the modifiers 'already' and 'without' in describing the real of the last-instance is effectively shorthand for 'non-decisional'. Moreover, we have already identified the defining characteristic of decision in terms of the structure of reciprocal articulation whereby the metaphysical posits its own empirical presupposition, while the empirical presupposes its own metaphysical position – via the mutual and complementary auto-position and donation of condition and conditioned. Consequently, the 'non-' in the expression 'non-decisional' must itself be understood as an abbreviation for 'non-auto positional/-donational', where the prefix 'auto-' is now seen as condensing the essence of decisional synthesis.

Once again, Heidegger is the key reference for Laruelle here. For if, as Heidegger's own conception of 'the turning' (*die Kehre*) in thought would seem to suggest,[16] every philosophical decision carries an implicit ontological charge as a 'de-scission' (*Unter-schied*) wherein being operates as the One-of-the-dyad – the indivisible division which discloses and withholds, or joins as it disjoins – then the self-positing, self-presupposing transcendence articulated in the decisional 'auto-' will also express the essence of all ontological transcendence insofar as it is decisionally deployed. Thus, Laruelle concludes:

> To the extent that philosophy exploits 'transcendence' or 'being' in a privileged and dominant manner [...] the essence of transcendence or being according to their philosophical usage [...] is the 'auto', that is to say, the idea of philosophy's absolute autonomy in the form of a circle, of a self-reference such as becomes apparent in the dimensions of auto-donation and auto-position.
>
> (Laruelle 1996: 284)

5.5   Ventriloquizing philosophy

Yet the one philosophy which explicitly avows the power of absolute self-positing which Laruelle takes to be characteristic of philosophy per se is not Heidegger's but Hegel's. Despite his penetrating critical analyses of Heidegger,[17] Laruelle's denunciation of the putative 'sufficiency' of conceptual synthesis amplifies the former's critique of philosophical rationalism to the point where Hegelianism is no longer just one philosophical position among others, but rather the limit-tendency of all philosophizing; at once its ideal type and its hubristic apex. In his most recent work,[18] Laruelle goes so far as to claim that 'philosophy gathers itself in a *cogito* enlarged to the form of the world and the *cogito* is a distillation of philosophy' (Laruelle 2004: 30). Thus philosophy's 'I think' formalizes the world, rendering everything 'philosophizable'. This is not so much to totalize philosophy as to identify philosophy *with* totalization. Philosophy becomes an auto-affecting whole. Anticipating the charge that this is a gratuitously Hegelian characterization of philosophy, Laruelle writes:

> [P]hilosophy itself tells us what it is, it exists in the best of cases as a system which posits and thinks itself: Plato, Leibniz, Kant, and obviously above all Hegel and Nietzsche have delineated, projected,

delimited, and sometimes effectuated this Idea of philosophy as the system of a universal *cogito*. The definite article '*la*' when one speaks of '*la philosophie*' can first be interpreted as an auto-affecting whole, which is the concern of philosophy itself, before being understood as identity (of) that whole, which is the concern of non-philosophy.

(Laruelle 2004: 160)

It is because the putative 'identity' of this whole is non-totalizable that it is 'non-philosophical'; but it is so only because the essence of philosophy qua logic of totalization has already been identified with the logic of auto-positional transcendence. Moreover, since the essence of a thing can only either be intuited or deduced from its functioning, there can be no question of Laruelle proving his claim that philosophy is totalization. He simply stipulates it and then draws the consequences, while we are invited to admire his powers of intuition and his deductive acumen, and to appreciate the ingenuity of his non-philosophical alternative. The trouble is that this alternative is at once over-determined by the negative characterization of philosophy as decision, upon which it entirely depends, and – as evinced by Laruelle's own non-philosophical treatments of philosophical themes – significantly insensitive to the vagaries of concrete specificity which, for all its faults, philosophical conceptualization is acute enough to register. Lacking the capacity for conceptual specificity, the non-philosophical theory which Laruelle elaborates as a consequence of his negative characterization of the essence of philosophy is undermined not so much by its abstraction as by its sheer generality: it is too loose-cut to fit its object; too coarse-grained to provide useful conceptual traction upon the material for which it is supposedly designed.

Thus, when Laruelle turns from his elaborate descriptions of the mechanisms of non-philosophical theory to put the latter into practice in the treatment of philosophical themes – as he does in the wake of 1996's *Principles of Non-Philosophy* in his three subsequent books on ethics, Marxism, and mysticism – one cannot but be struck by the formalism and the paucity of detail in his handling of these topics, which seems cursory even in comparison with orthodox philosophical treatments of the same themes. Indeed, the brunt of the conceptual labour in these confrontations with ethics, Marxism, and mysticism is devoted to refining or fine-tuning his own non-philosophical machinery, while actual engagement with the specifics of the subject matter is confined to discussions of more or less arbitrarily selected philosophemes on the topic in question.[19] The results are texts in which descriptions of the workings of Laruelle's non-philosophical apparatus continue to occupy centre-stage while the philosophical material which is ostensibly the focus of analysis is relegated to a perfunctory supporting role. Moreover, this increasingly formulaic modus operandi has tended to recur whenever Laruelle has sought to subject a philosophical material to non-philosophical processing. Ultimately, the sheer generality of Laruelle's account of the essence of philosophy, coupled with the fact that the latter is all he has to work with, encourages him to disregard all those aspects of philosophical thought that cannot be subsumed within this rigid schema. Thus Laruelle's overly exiguous analysis of philosophy leaves him no option but to squeeze every conceptual material into the straightjacket of decision. Only then can it be processed and made to yield non-philosophical theses. Yet the latter invariably exhibit a structural uniformity (that of the 'unilateral duality') which betrays their excessively attenuated relationship to the different philosophical source materials which they are supposed to illuminate.

Given these comparatively meagre results, why insist on identifying the essence of philosophy in the first place? In the passage quoted above, as elsewhere, Laruelle's all too Heideggerian preoccupation with uncovering the essence of philosophy is bolstered by an appeal to the fact that the French noun '*philosophie*' must be prefixed by the definite article '*la*'. But in English, no such prefix is necessary when referring to 'philosophy'. Thus Laruelle's insistence on identifying the essence of *la philosophie* over and above any listing of all those things which are named 'philosophy' seems as misguided as would be the attempt to define the essence of *le sport* over and above a list of all those activities which we happen to call 'sport'. What we call 'philosophy' is an intellectual practice with a complex material history, and even though its register of abstraction distinguishes it from others, only idealists like Heidegger have sought to exalt it above all other activities by imbuing it with a perennial and abyssal 'essence' whose epochal unfolding is deemed capable of determining the course of history. Thus Laruelle conflates the defensible claim that Plato, Leibniz, Kant, Hegel, and Nietzsche exemplify what is most profound in philosophy with the indefensible idealist claim that they embody its essence. This is like claiming that great sportsmen not only exemplify certain physical and mental prowesses, but also embody the essence of sport. So when Laruelle declares that 'philosophy itself' has told him that it is an auto-affecting whole, one can only respond that 'philosophy itself' never speaks, since it is a figment; only philosophers speak – even and especially those philosophers who claim philosophy itself speaks through them. Far from unmasking philosophy's totalitarian propensities, the assertion that the contingent collection of texts and practices called 'philosophy' instantiates an auto-affecting whole, and that those individuals designated as 'philosophers' effectuate the system of a universal *cogito* which ventriloquizes its practitioners, actually reiterates the Hegelian idolatry of philosophy which Laruelle claims to subvert. Laruelle ventriloquizes philosophy and then expresses distaste for the authoritarian pretensions which he has put in its mouth.

Ultimately, the claim that decisional auto-position embodies the essence of philosophy saddles Laruelle with an intolerable burden. Either he continues to insist that all philosophers are Hegelians, whether they know it or not – a claim which is exceedingly difficult, if not impossible to defend; or he maintains that those who are not are not really philosophers; in which case vast swathes of the philosophical tradition, from Hume to Churchland, must be excised from the discipline since their work no longer qualifies as philosophy. Alternatively, and more sensibly, Laruelle can simply drop the exorbitant claim that his account of decision is a description of philosophy *tout court*; in which case it would be not so much philosophy per se which radical immanence serves to delimit and circumscribe through its suspension of auto-decisional transcendence, but rather the various forms of transcendental synthesis invoked by correlationism (cf. Chapter 3), as well as every variety of dialectics, whether positive or negative.[20] It then becomes possible to re-interpret the term 'decision' in Laruelle's work as a synonym for transcendental synthesis, or more generally, as a cipher for correlationism. By the same token, Laruelle's account of decision can be seen to provide us with something like correlationism's genetic code. If this is conceded, the critical purchase of Laruelle's work becomes at once much narrower and far more perspicuous: his contribution can be seen to consist in the elaboration of a coherently articulated anti-correlationist stance – but one which abjures any resort to intellectual intuition – rather than a 'non-philosophy'. In this regard, Laruelle can be interpreted as a kind of renegade Kantian whose internal subversion of transcendental idealism not only rehabilitates the possibility of transcendental realism but also provides Kantianism's posthumous rejoinder to Hegelian idealism in all its guises – even that of such a heterodox dialectician as Badiou. We shall see below how the unbinding of transcendental synthesis effected by radical immanence amounts to a non-dialectical logic of negation, rather than to a neutralization of philosophy per se.

5.6   The evacuation of the real

Where Kant's delimitation of metaphysics rendered reason dependent upon sensibility, Laruelle's circumscription of decision renders the supposedly absolute autonomy of ontological transcendence or 'being' dependent upon the unobjectifiable immanence of what he calls 'the human'. This is Laruelle's attempt to radicalize finitude – one which, as we have already observed, in certain respects simply supplements Heidegger's existential radicalization of Kant with Michel Henry's phenomenological critique of Heidegger. Thus, in *The Philosophies of Difference*, Laruelle presents a Henry-influenced reading of Heidegger wherein *Dasein*'s finite transcendence functions as the unobjectifiable determinant of objectification (Laruelle 1986: 55–120). Clearly, Henry's phenomenological exacerbation of *Dasein*'s 'mineness' (*Jemeinigkeit*) as auto-affecting ipseity provides the obvious philosophical analogue for the unobjectifiable immanence of the human, which Laruelle cites as the ultimate determinant for ontological transcendence. But unlike Heidegger, Laruelle maintains that the essence of the real qua radical immanence remains non-ontological. And unlike Henry – whose influence he acknowledges even as he underscores the distance between their respective agendas – Laruelle insists on the necessity of evacuating immanence of every residue of phenomenological substance liable to render it susceptible to ontologization – precisely the egological substance which Henry continues to characterize in terms of the radical passivity of affect, pathos, and imprint. For Henry's dualism of pathos and concept leaves him incapable of explaining why the absolute passivity of auto-affecting Life should ever externalize itself in the intentional objectifications of consciousness or the ekstatic transcendence of being-in-the-world. Thus Laruelle charges Henry with indulging in a phenomenological idealization of radical immanence which renders the latter dependent upon the very conceptualization which it is supposed to abjure. This idealization engenders a dilemma for Henry. If pathic immanence repels conceptual transcendence as something entirely extraneous to it, its autonomy becomes co-constituted by the transcendence whose repulsion it requires in order to remain absolute. As a result, the existence of this constituting transcendence, and hence of conceptualization, is at once presupposed and rendered inexplicable. But if pathic immanence is 'always already' the determining precondition for conceptual thought, then the putatively irreversible disjunction between its unobjectifiable pathos and objectifying thought becomes

ultimately reversible, and the disjunction between real and ideal, immanence and transcendence, is re-encompassed in a decisional synthesis
(Laruelle 1996: 133–43). It is precisely in order to counter this synthetic
idealization of radical immanence that Laruelle insists on de-phenome-
nologizing and de-substantializing it the better to transform it into a
univocal vector of axiomatic abstraction:

> Once it has been rigorously defined rather than given over to the
> realm of unitary, metaphysical or anthropological generality; once it
> has been axiomatically determined rather than presupposed through
> vague theses or statements, what we are calling 'man' as identity is
> so in-consistent, so devoid of essence as to constitute a hole in noth-
> ingness itself, not just in being. [...] Real identity is impoverished,
> impoverished to an extent that is unimaginable for philosophy, but
> it is not impoverished because all alterity has been abstracted from it
> or because it has been stripped bare through a process of alienation.
> It is indeed articulated through a symbol, and its effects are in turn
> articulated through a play of symbols, but to confuse the real with its
> symbol is precisely the mistake of theoreticist idealism and the root
> of all philosophical illusion. [...] The expression 'One-in-One' or
> 'vision-in-One' indicates the absence of any operation that would
> define the latter; the fact that it is not inscribed within an opera-
> tional space or more powerful structure; its immanence *in* itself
> rather than *to* anything else; its naked simplicity as never either
> exceeding or lacking, because it is the only measure required, but one
> that is never a self-measurement, one that measures nothing so long
> as there is nothing to measure.
>
> (Laruelle 2003: 175–6)

Yet Laruelle's insistence on identifying the unobjectifiable immanence of the real with 'the human' surreptitiously re-ontologizes it. For
while it may be perfectly coherent to claim, as Laruelle does, that I am
identical-in-the-last-instance with radical immanence, or that I think in
accordance with the real and that my thinking is determined-in-the-
last-instance by it, it does not follow from this that I am the real qua
One, in the same way in which, for Heidegger, I am my *Dasein* as that
being which is in each case mine. To privilege, as Laruelle does, the
irrecusability of the 'name-of-man' over and above the contingency of
other occasional nominations of the last-instance, is effectively to confuse the real with its symbol by reintroducing a 'rigid designator' which
is supposed as sufficient for fixing the essence of the real in a manner

ultimately indistinguishable from its co-constitution via decision.[21] The slide from 'I think according to my ultimate identity with a real that is already given' to 'this real of the last-instance is the human that I am' is as precipitate as the more familiar leap from 'I think' to 'I am'. This slide envelops what by Laruelle's own lights amounts to a decision: 'I am human'. But what can 'being-human' mean given that the radically in-consistent real is not? What I think I am can have no privilege vis-à-vis the identity of a real already given independently of anything I may happen to think about it. To claim that I harbour some sort of pre-ontological understanding of my own being-human is to plunge straight back into Heidegger's hermeneutics of *Dasein*. Alternatively, to assert, as Laruelle is wont to, that one already 'knows' oneself to be human in and through radical immanence, is simply to misuse the verb 'to know', to reintroduce thought into the heart of radical immanence and hence to render thought co-constitutive of the real, exactly as Henry does. The privileging of the nomenclature 'man' to designate the real cannot but re-phenomenologize and re-substantialize its radical in-consistency and invest it with a minimal degree of ontological consistency. By insisting that 'the human' remains the invariable site of the last-instance, Laruelle risks regressing back into Henry's pathetic transcendental egology. Worse, this ultimately arbitrary identification of the real with the human individual threatens to reduce Laruelle's vaunted non-philosophical radicalism to a transcendental individualism wherein each human self becomes the ultimate determinant of philosophy; a position which is all too redolent of Fichtean solipsism to be convincingly described as non-philosophical. It is this punitively solipsistic identification which must be abolished in order to definitively separate the real from being. To think oneself in accordance with a real which is without essence does not mean to think oneself to be this rather than that; a human being rather than a thing. To think oneself according to an inconsistent real which punctures nothingness itself means to think oneself as identical with a last-instance which is devoid of even the minimal consistency of the void. The real is less than nothing – which is certainly not to equate it with the impossible (Lacan) or with Sartre's nihilating 'for-itself' puncturing the opacity of the 'in-itself'. Ultimately, to concur with Laruelle's claim that the real knows no contraries or opposites is to identify it with the 'being-nothing' which Badiou sought (problematically, as we saw in Chapter 4) to define subtractively, rather than with any variety of 'non-being'. The real is not the negation of being, since this would be to re-constitute it in opposition to something, but rather its degree-zero. What is given 'without-givenness', or 'non-auto-decisionally', suspending the entwinement of givenness and given, neither withdraws from presence nor subtracts itself from presentation; for it is precisely in doing so that it becomes transcendently co-constituted by the relation to its own contrary. Rather, it is immanently given as 'being-nothing'.

5.7   Determination in the last instance

The real qua being-nothing is not an object but that which manifests the inconsistent or unobjectifiable essence of the object = X. Thus 'objectivity' can be redefined to index the reality which subsists independently of conditions of objectification tethered to transcendental subjectivity, whether the latter be called 'Dasein' or 'Life'. What is truly original in Laruelle's work resides not in 'non-philosophy' understood as an aggravation of deconstruction compounded by an overdose of phenomenological solipsism – which is precisely what his obsession with fixing the essence of philosophy threatens to reduce it to – but rather in defining conditions under which thinking does not intend, reflect, or represent its object but rather mimes its unobjectifiable opacity insofar as the latter is identical-in-the-last-instance with a real which is 'foreclosed' to objectification. This is what Laruelle calls 'determination-in-the-last-instance' – thought's effectuation of the object's unobjectifiable essence in its non-synthetic identity with the real:

[D]etermination-in-the-last-instance is the causality which renders it universally possible for any object X to determine its own 'real' cognition, but only in the last instance [...] X [...] is not known in exteriority, in idealist fashion, but by itself without this identity between the real and its cognition assuming a dialectical form (real = rational, etc.) since it takes the form of determination-in-the-last-instance. There is no transcendent subject; cognition is the subject, its 'own' subject so to speak, as much as its own object, but only by virtue of the 'last-instance' of the real. It is as though we were to insist that the 'matter' of materialism should cognize itself and be capable of its own theorisation without having to pass through dialectical identity or some other philosophical apparatus designed to ensure the reversibility between the known object and the knowledge of the object. [...] Cognition is heterogeneous to the known object, but it is the latter which determines it in the last instance. The object X is at once – though without being divided philosophically – cause-of-the-last-instance of its own knowledge and known object. [...] The old problem of the possibility of knowledge is not resolved by invoking a transcendental subject or foundation but by the real's being-foreclosed to knowledge, or by every object's being-foreclosed to its own cognition; a being-foreclosed which does not render knowledge possible but rather determines it.

(Laruelle 2000: 48–9)

For Laruelle then, idealism is not circumvented by subtracting intellectual intuition from the reality to which it provides access, but by short-circuiting the transcendental difference between thinking and being so that what is foreclosed to thought in the object coincides (albeit non-synthetically) with what is foreclosed to the object in thought. Once shorn of the thetic or auto-positional mechanisms of reflection and representation, thinking becomes the vehicle for the causality of an un-intuitable real. Determination-in-the-last-instance involves an ascesis of thought whereby the latter abjures the trappings of intellectual intuition as well as of objectifying representation. By submitting to the logic of determination-in-the-last-instance, thought ceases to intend, apprehend, or reflect the object; it becomes non-thetic and is thereby turned into a vehicle for what is unobjectifiable in the object itself. The object becomes at once the patient and the agent of its own cognitive determination. Rather than looking to intellectual intuition to provide an exit from the correlational circle – a move which threatens to re-invoke some sort of pre-established harmony between thinking and being – determination-in-the-last-instance unbinds correlational synthesis in order to effectuate (rather than represent) an identity without unity and a duality without distinction between subject and object. It effectuates a non-correlational disjunction between unobjectifiable reality and ideal objectification by instantiating the identity-of-the-last-instance between the being-foreclosed of the object and that of the real qua being-nothing. Identity without unity and duality without distinction are the hallmarks of determination-in-the-last-instance insofar as its structure is that of what Laruelle calls a 'unilateral duality'. By effectuating a unilateral duality between thought and thing, determination-in-the-last-instance manifests a non-correlational adequation between the real and the ideal without re-incorporating the former within the latter, whether through the machinery of symbolic inscription or the faculty of intellectual intuition.

5.8 The thinking object

Determination-in-the-last-instance is the conjoining of two causes: immanence as real cause and objectification as occasional cause. But this conjunction assumes the disjunctive structure of a unilateral duality. The agency of the real as cause-of-the-last-instance manifests itself as a unilateralizing force. Unilateralization is not to be confused with unilaterality. Unilaterality is well known in philosophy: X distinguishes itself unilaterally from Y without Y distinguishing itself from X in return. Various neo-Platonists, Hegel, Heidegger, Derrida, and Deleuze have all evoked this logic in different contexts. But in these standard philosophical contexts, the unilaterality of X is always reinscribed in a bilateral relation with Y at the supplementary meta-level available to reflection, which enjoys a position of overview vis-à-vis X and Y and continues to see both terms in relation to one another at the same time. Thus, X's unilaterality relative to Y is only operative at the level of X and Y, not for reflection, which exempts itself from this immanent relation through transcendence. Reflexive thought is always a spectator which views everything (terms and relations), including itself, from above. It is this supplementary dimension of overview which is the characteristic of thetic reflexivity.

But unilateralization is foreclosed to reflection: it can only be effectuated non-thetically, that is to say, non-auto-positionally. Being-nothing does not distinguish itself from being; it is not transcendent. Rather, it is being qua auto-positional transcendence which distinguishes itself absolutely from being-nothing. Since being-nothing is foreclosed to thought, and since thinking presupposes a minimum degree of objectifying transcendence as its element, it is not the real which causes thought, but rather objectifying transcendence. Thinking needs to be *occasioned* by objectifying transcendence in order for it to be able to assume the real as its unobjectifiable cause-of-the-last-instance. For thinking to effectuate the foreclosure of its real cause, it must first be occasioned *by* its ideal cause. The real qua cause-of-the-last-instance can only become effective for thinking – or more exactly, *in* and *as* thinking – if thinking has already been caused by transcendence. Thus determination-in-the-last-instance requires objectifying transcendence even as it modifies it. And it modifies it by bequeathing the unilateralizing force of the last-instance to the object which has been transcendently given or objectified: instead of being objectively manifest as the correlate of an objectifying act, the object becomes the subject which determines its own objective manifestation; it is taken up *in* and *as* the agent of thinking which unilateralizes its own transcendent objectification. Determination-in-the-last-instance thus converts the object qua agent of the occasional cause into a subject qua patient of the real cause. The object becomes the place-holder or non-thetic representative of the last-instance which causes objectification to distinguish itself absolutely from it even as it remains indistinguishable from objectification. The object = X unilateralizes its own transcendent objectification by instantiating the identity (without synthesis) between its being-foreclosed and that of the real; as well as the duality (without distinction) between this unobjectifiable identity and the difference between its objective being and its being-nothing.

Accordingly, determination-in-the-last-instance effectuates the unilateralizing identity of the object X, while objectification instantiates the unilateralized difference of X's being insofar as it distinguishes itself absolutely from X's being-nothing. Consequently, it is not X's identity-of-the-last-instance with being-nothing that distinguishes itself unilaterally from X's objective being, but rather the latter which distinguishes itself unilaterally from the former. But in X qua unilateralizing identity, the supplementary dimension of reflexivity through which objectifying thought is able to oversee the relation between object and objectification, X and Y, is effectively reduced and rendered inoperative. Thus the unilateral relation between X and Y itself becomes unilateralized, shorn of its bilateral envelopment within objectifying thought, leaving only X's unilateralizing identity as known object which determines its own knowing subject, and the unilateralized difference between X and Y as synthesis of object and objectification. X is at once the determining subject and the determined object, and remains radically indifferent to the difference between X and Y, object and objectification (or determined object and subjective determination). Ultimately, where correlationism guarantees the ubiquity of the object by insisting that thinking remain unobjectifiable, determination-in-the-last-instance dismantles objectification by turning thought itself into a thing.

5.9   Transcendental unbinding

Unilateralization hamstrings dialectics. A unilateral duality is a structure comprising non-relation – the object X as unilateralizing identity – and the relation of relation and non-relation – objectifying thought as unilateralized difference between X and Y, identity and difference. Unlike more familiar instances of unilaterality in philosophy, which ultimately always retain two sides, the unilateral duality effectuated by determination-in-the-last-instance is a duality with only one side: the side of objectification as difference (relation) between X (non-relation) and Y (relation). Accordingly, where dialectics invariably orbits around the relation of relation and non-relation as apex of reflexivity – which is also the apex of idealist narcissism, since it converts every 'in-itself' into a 'for us' – the unilateral duality effectuated by determination-in-the-last-instance exemplifies an irreflexive and hence non-dialecticizable disjunction between objectifying transcendence and unobjectifiable immanence; one which embodies the non-relation of relation and non-relation. Unlike every variety of reflection, whether transcendental or dialectical, determination-in-the-last-instance effectuates a unilateral duality with only one side – the side of objectifying transcendence. Since the latter is always two sided, i.e. dialectical, determination-in-the-last-instance effectively unilateralizes dialectics. Thus unilateralization cannot be dialectically re-inscribed.

Moreover, the radical separation or unilateral duality between being-nothing as already-manifest and ontological transcendence as mixture of manifest and manifestation is itself already-manifest (but without-manifestation). In other words, at the deepest level of analysis, the unilateralizing force (or non-dialectical negativity) proper to Laruelle's 'non-' does not merely consist in separating X's unobjectifiable immanence from its transcendent objectification in the form of a unilateral duality, but more fundamentally, in separating the objectification of the dyad 'objectifiable/unobjectifiable' from the already-manifest unilateral duality separating dyadic objectification from unobjectifiable duality. In other words, not only is the difference between unobjectifiable immanence and objectifying transcendence only operative on the side of the latter; more importantly, the duality between this difference and the real's indifference to it becomes operative if, and only if, thinking *effectuates* the real's foreclosure to objectification by determining the latter in-the-last-instance. The difference/indifference distinction is an objectifiable difference; but it becomes unobjectifiable and hence transcendental when determination-the-last-instance effectuates the real's indifference to objectification. More exactly, it becomes transcendental through what Laruelle calls the 'axiomatic ultimation' whereby determination-in-the-last-instance assumes the ultimate identity between the object as transcendently given cause and the real as already-given cause without positing or presupposing this identity via an act of synthesis. Only by being effectuated as ultimate cause for thinking does the real qua last-instance become capable of determining the difference/indifference distinction as a unilateral duality. This is why Laruelle characterizes determination-in-the-last-instance as a 'transcendental' operation: it determines every difference posited and presupposed through objectifying synthesis as the object's indifference to determination – an indifference which is now effectuated in and as the subject of thought. In this regard, if objectifying synthesis is transcendental, then the unilateralization of such synthesis is meta-transcendental: it determines determination as such. More precisely, it determines transcendental determination qua synthesis of real object and ideal objectification as a disjunction which unbinds objective synthesis in the unilateral duality comprising the identity of X's unobjectifiable reality and the difference between X's ideal objectification and its unobjectifiable reality. Accordingly, unilateralization is tantamount to a transcendental unbinding.

5.10 Absolute and relative autonomy

(This section provides a necessary but somewhat technical clarification about the precise functioning of unilateralization. Readers who find it excessively turgid are encouraged to skip to the following section, which is slightly more digestible.) Unilateralization as 'determination of determination' must be understood in terms of the conjunction of two causes: the real qua necessary but non-sufficient cause and the ideal as supposedly sufficient cause. In other words, unilateralization is the non-dialectical conjunction of an absolute or necessary cause and a relative or occasional cause. Whereas the former is already-given as *determining*; the latter is already-given as *determinable*. Thus objectification is already-given as the occasional cause to be determined by the real as cause-of-the-last-instance. Nevertheless, the real qua cause-of-the-last-instance is effectuated as transcendentally determining for thought only if thought is occasioned by objectification. But objectification is an occasion because it is already-given by the real, with which it is identical-in-the-last-instance. Consequently, determination-in-the-last-instance exists as the unilateral duality of real cause and occasional cause; a duality which is effectuated in and as thinking. The agency of the real cause only becomes effective when it is occasioned by the ideal cause. The object X becomes the subject of its own determination because its objectification provides the occasional cause which converts its unobjectifiable identity into the real agent of its determination.

Accordingly, even the supposed autonomy of objectification is nevertheless relative-in-the-last-instance to being-nothing. Being qua ontological transcendence is only posited-as-given by petitioning an unobjectifiable immanence which is already-given. Thus being as supposedly sufficient condition for ontological synthesis remains relative-in-the-last-instance to being-nothing qua necessary but non-sufficient condition. The absolute, self-positing autonomy of ontological transcendence is only relatively autonomous vis-à-vis the radical autonomy of that which is already-given. It remains relative to that radically autonomous last-instance which it petitions as already-given in order to effect its transcendental synthesis of object and objectification. In Laruelle's words:

> Real immanence neither absorbs nor annihilates transcendence, it is not opposed to it, but is capable of 'receiving' it and of determining it as a relative autonomy. Real immanence is so radical – rather than absolute – that it does not reduce the transcendence of the world – whether philosophically or phenomenologically – it does not deny or limit it but on the contrary gives it – albeit in accordance with its own modality: as that being-given-without-givenness of transcendence which, whilst remaining 'absolute' or auto-positional in its own register, acquires a relative autonomy with regard to the real.
>
> (Laruelle 2000: 50–1)

Consequently, ontological transcendence is never just given as an absolutely autonomous 'in-itself' in terms of the metaphysical dyad 'objectifying transcendence/unobjectifiable immanence'. It is also already given-without-givenness as relatively autonomous – which is to say, given as an occasional cause for determination-in-the-last-instance. It is this heteronomous or non-auto-donational giving of transcendence as an occasional cause – the fact that its self-positing autonomy is given-without-givenness as a merely relative autonomy – which suspends its pretension to absolute sufficiency and turns it into a determinable material. The putative autonomy of transcendence – its supposed sufficiency for ontological synthesis – is suspended once it is understood that the necessity of objectification has already been heteronomously given as no more than a relatively sufficient condition; an occasional but non-determining cause to be determined-in-the-last-instance by the real qua necessary but in-sufficient cause.

It is this suspension of the absolute autonomy of reflexive transcendence which explains the possibility of determination-in-the-last-instance as non-dialectical synthesis of known object and object of knowledge. Yet it is also that aspect of it which remains the most difficult to understand from the viewpoint of reflexivity and correlationism more generally. For doesn't thought's putative 'effectuation' of a real which is supposed to remain radically foreclosed to it re-institute a reciprocity – and thereby a bi-lateral determination – between real and ideal, thinking and being? In order to appreciate why this is not the case, it is important to remember that the real's foreclosure to objectifying synthesis entails that it is already separate-without-separation from every dyadic opposition, such as for instance the opposition between thinkable and unthinkable. Thus the real's foreclosure to the dyadic alternative between thinkable and unthinkable does not render it 'unthinkable'. Being-nothing's foreclosure to thought means that it knows neither opposition nor negation because it is identical-in-the-last-instance with being qua objectification. It is this unilateralizing potency which allows it to determine the objective opposition between thinkable and unthinkable, objectifiable and unobjectifiable, being and non-being – oppositions which ultimately undermined Michel Henry's phenomenology of absolute immanence – as the occasional cause which converts the foreclosure of being-nothing into an identity-of-the-last-instance with the foreclosure of objectified-being.

Thus the distinction between the real's foreclosure to thought and determination-in-the-last-instance as a transcendental effectuation of that foreclosure is not a dyadic distinction between different reifiable 'things'. Neither the being-foreclosed of the real nor its effectuation as determination-in-the-last-instance can count as philosophically distinguishable 'things'. There is only one 'thing': objectifying transcendence as occasional cause. 'Between' the real's foreclosure to objectification and determination-in-the-last-instance's foreclosure to objectification there is neither identity nor difference but only an identity-of-the-last-instance occasioned by objectification itself. The real's foreclosure is effectuated as determination's foreclosure to objectification on the basis of the latter as occasional cause. Objectification remains the single hypostatized instance here. The real qua cause-of-the-last-instance is already-given as determinate but it has also already-given the synthesis of object and objectification as the occasion which causes its own determination. This determination is simply the unilateralization of transcendental synthesis. And it is the prefix 'non-' which ultimately condenses the unilateralizing force of determination-in-the-last-instance as a non-dialectical negativity.

5.11   Non dialectical negativity

Nevertheless, the prefix 'non-' is fundamentally equivocal. On the one hand it is supposed to express the positivity of the real as sufficient, autonomous, and necessary in and of itself, and it is this positivity which allows it to suspend and determine, rather than cancel and destroy, the supposed sufficiency of ontological transcendence. The latter's pretension to absolute autonomy turns out to be an illusion which already presupposes the agency of real immanence, its binding power, in order to achieve the transcendental synthesis of given and givenness which secures its autonomy. Thus the transcendence of being at once petitions and disavows being-nothing; it presupposes and denies it simultaneously. By way of contrast, being-nothing allows ontological transcendence to be given, albeit without-givenness. Yet these positive characteristics of the real, its radical sufficiency, autonomy, and necessity, remain essentially negative until they are effectuated through determination-in-the-last-instance. Thus the last-instance remains a universally necessary but non-sufficient condition. It does not assume a determining role unless objectifying transcendence occasions its own determination, and this necessitates the intervention of thought – albeit a thought which undoes objectification by turning itself into a thing. The real's negative sufficiency, autonomy, and necessity do not become positively operative until they are effectuated in and as determination-in-the-last-instance. Only via the latter does the real transmit its negative sufficiency to the absolute sufficiency of objectification, suspending the circle of synthesis rather in the way in which a speed restriction is lifted. This is the merely negative positivity of 'non-' as allowing the synthesis of given and givenness to be given 'without-givenness'.

Yet at the same time, this negative positivity continues to retain a more emphatically negative sense as annulment: for the 'non-' not only suspends the autonomy of synthesis but also dismembers it through unilateralization, eliminating the reciprocity, correlation, and correspondence associated with reflexivity. Thus the real continues to harbour a positive negativity; a power of incision or dismemberment, which finds expression when its negative positivity becomes effectuated in and as determination-in-the-last-instance. This positive negativity underwrites the real's unilateralizing force.

But it is precisely this positive negativity harboured by determination-in-the-last-instance – its potential for intra-philosophical incisiveness, so to speak – which Laruelle disavows on the grounds that it threatens to compromise the putative incommensurability between philosophical and non-philosophical thinking. Yet as we have seen, it is only Laruelle's own insistence on equating philosophy with decision which shores up this alleged incommensurability. Once the dichotomy between philosophy and non-philosophy has been recast as a contrast between correlationalist and non-correlationalist thinking, the rationale for disowning any potentially intra-philosophical consequences of the real's positive negativity simply evaporates. In fact, Laruelle's disavowal of the latter amounts to an attempt to neuter his work's latent philosophical potency on the grounds that this would compromise non-philosophy's supposed indifference towards philosophical decision.[22] But it is necessary to insist, against Laruelle himself, that it is precisely the positive negativity of the 'non-' which expresses the real's non-dialectical negativity. It is the non-contradictory coincidence of the real's positivity and negativity which sustains unilateralization's capacity for non-dialectical negation, insofar as it simultaneously suspends and incises, rather than cancels and preserves, every form of synthetic unity.

Thus it is precisely because it is rooted in the real qua being-nothing that the 'non-' can function as an index of positive negativity, and of a power of negation that knows neither opposition nor contradiction. But this is only possible so long as unilateralization involves the coincidence of suspension and incision. For the fact that the real qua being-nothing has always already suspended the sufficiency of objectification leaves everything as it is; it does not suffice to determine the illusory sufficiency of ontological transcendence – a sufficiency which is only operative within that objectifying transcendence – unless the real's indifference is converted through determination-in-the-last-instance into a power of unbinding. The fact that the latter operates by prefixing familiar transcendental locutions with modifiers, such as 'non-', 'without-', and 'already-', underscores the extent to which any positivity claimed for 'non-philosophy' derives not just from the suspension of auto-position, but rather from its dismemberment. This is precisely what unilateralization means: not just the suspension of thetic reflexivity and the generation of new concepts which somehow 'float' above philosophical discourse, supposedly irreducible to the element from which they are generated (as Laruelle seems to assume), but rather a surgical intervention upon the body of transcendental synthesis, severing terms from relations, amputating reciprocity, and sharpening one-sidedness. Every synthesis is double-edged and hence reversible, but to unilateralize synthesis means to endow it with a capacity for achieving an irreversible, one-sided cut.

In this regard, the account of unilateralization which we have extracted from the work of Laruelle consolidates and deepens the logic of subtraction we examined in Badiou (cf. Chapter 4). But where the latter remains ontological, the former is transcendental. The transcendental ratification of subtractive ontology occurs via a decision which allows one to assume being-nothing as the real presupposition which determines ontological discourse. Thus the decision that being is nothing can obviate the recourse to the primacy of the subtractive signifier Ø when it is determined by a real instance which is identified as being-nothing independently of discourse. It is the real as zero degree of immanence which determines its ideal nomination as void. The decision that ontology is mathematics, for instance, can only be ratified via theory's non-mathematical – i.e. non-discursive – suture to the real qua being-nothing. Philosophy thereby abjures its metaontological role as transcendent mediator between science and reality, discourse and world. The full-force of Badiou's ontological thesis – viz., that being is nothing – is only realized when it is supplemented by the transcendental hypothesis which we have extracted from Laruelle – viz., that there is an identity-of-the-last-instance between the foreclosure of being-nothing and the being-foreclosed of thought. The thesis we have drawn from Badiou pertains to 'what is': being is nothing. The hypothesis we have deployed using Laruelle pertains to the relation between thought and what is (which Badiou subordinated to the logic of inscription): through determination-in-the-last-instance, philosophy sutures itself to nothing in order to effectuate a void. This 'voiding' is another way of describing the unilateralizing potency of determination-in-the-last-instance. We will distinguish the void as unilateral duality from the being-nothing in which it is rooted as indivisible zero. Where dialectics proceeds by the One dividing into two, unilateralization consists in the two of the void effectuating the zero of being-nothing. Non-dialectical negation is this 'voiding' and the logic of its effectuation is that of the unilateral duality, the irreversible cut.

5.12   The identity of space-time

The originality of a philosopher is usually gauged in terms of *what* he thinks. By way of contrast, Laruelle's singular contribution only becomes appreciable when it is understood that he proposes to transform *how* philosophers think. His innovation is fundamentally formal: it consists in the invention of a new kind of transcendental logic whose conceptual depth (if not extensive breadth) at once equals and challenges that of Hegel's dialectical logic. In this regard, the non-dialectical negativity uncovered by Laruelle provides the key to understanding the diachronicity inherent in what Meillassoux called 'absolute time' in Chapter 3. As we saw there, Meillassoux's invocation of intellectual intuition in his account of thought's grasp of the absolute threatened to compromise the autonomy of the latter by re-inscribing it within a correlational synthesis. What we have tried to suggest in the foregoing is that absolute or non-correlational objectivity is better understood in terms of an asymmetrical structure which the discontinuity of the object imposes upon thinking. Metaphysics conceived of the autonomy of the object in terms of the model of substance. But successive critiques of the hypostatization of substance from Kant to Heidegger have undermined the plausibility of metaphysical (substance based) realism, thereby securing the triumph of correlationism. Laruelle's work challenges this correlationist consensus by proposing a version of transcendental realism wherein the object is no longer conceived of as a substance but rather as a discontinuous cut in the fabric of ontological synthesis. It is no longer thought that determines the object, whether through representation or intuition, but rather the object that seizes thought and forces it to think it, or better, *according* to it. As we have seen, this objective determination takes the form of a unilateral duality whereby the object thinks through the subject.

This unilateralization lies at the heart of the diachronicity which, as we saw in Chapter 3, indexes the asymmetry of thought and being. Where correlationism ontologizes temporal synthesis at the expense of space – whether as *ekstasis* or *durée* – diachronicity expresses the identity of space-time; but a discontinuous or unilateralizing identity proper to the autonomous object. The discontinuity of space-time unilateralizes thought and expresses the nihilating force of being-nothing as that which unravels the correlationist synthesis of space and time. In the next chapter, we will examine how the transcendental syntheses of time elaborated by Heidegger and Deleuze subordinate objective space-time to a form of ontological temporality commensurate with the subjectivity of *Dasein* or 'Life'. Against the correlationist privileging of transcendental temporality, speculative (post-metaphysical) realism must uphold the autonomy of a space-time that is independent of the correlation of thinking and being; a space-time whose incommensurability with the spans of human or even biological duration is no longer a function of chronological discrepancy (as it seems to be for Meillassoux) but of a diachronicity rooted in the voiding of being-nothing. But first we must examine the different ways in which Heidegger and Deleuze have radicalized Kant's transcendentalization of time. Ironically enough, this radicalization has been carried out through an *ontologization* of time which institutes the latter as the veritable transcendental subject, in the form of *Dasein* and 'Life' respectively.

Part III   The End of Time

6
The Pure and Empty Form of Death

6.1   Who is time?: Heidegger

In his 1924 lecture 'The Concept of Time'[1], which has been called the 'Urform' of *Being and Time*[2], Heidegger begins with the question 'What is time?' and shows how it gradually transforms itself into the question '*Who* is time?' Time cannot be grasped by means of the question of essence, which enquires into 'the what' (*das Was*) of things. The traditional understanding of 'whatness' or 'essence' operates on the basis of a prior hypostatization of time as presence. *Ousia* is understood as *Vorhandenheit*, presence-at-hand (though Heidegger is not yet using this vocabulary in 1924). Thus the question 'What is time?' prejudges the very nature of the phenomenon about which it enquires by reducing it to the status of a specific way of being in time: being-present. But time is precisely that which is never merely present: its way of being cannot be grasped on the basis of being-present. So we cannot simply assume that time's way of being is that of intra-temporal entities. To understand how time is and how its way of being differs from that of intra-temporal entities, we must first understand how we originally come to grasp the various senses of temporal being, how temporal things are. But this entails grasping the intimate relation between those varieties of temporal being and our own being as that within which temporal phenomena are encountered. Thus for Heidegger the enquiry into how time is necessitates an enquiry into the way of being of that entity on whose basis we originally come to access the varieties of temporal being. That being is of course our own: *Dasein*. Its defining characteristics are temporal specificity (*Jeweiligkeit*) and mineness (*Jemeinigkeit*). *Dasein* is always mine: 'The specificity of the "I am" is constitutive for *Dasein*. Just as primarily as it is being-in-the-world, *Dasein* is therefore also my *Dasein*. It is in each case its own and is specific as its own' (Heidegger 1992: 8E). But if the temporal specificity of *Dasein* is in each case mine, this is to say that each of us *is* time and that time as such is in each case mine. And this is indeed precisely the conclusion Heidegger draws towards the close of his lecture: '[The question] "What is time?" became the question "Who is time?" More closely: "Are we ourselves time?" Or closer still: am I my time?'(Heidegger 1992: 22E). For Heidegger at this juncture, to ask 'Am I my time?' is to ask 'Am I my *Dasein*?' And as we know, this is to enquire into the 'propriety' of *Dasein*'s being as defined in terms of its 'ultimate' and 'most extreme' possibility: death. *Dasein* becomes properly individuated insofar as it appropriates death as its own. Already in this 1924 lecture, it is *Dasein*'s appropriation of death as its own most extreme possibility, its 'running ahead of itself toward its own past', which authentically individuates it and thereby singularizes its time. The appropriation of death allows the past to be seized out of the future. In *Being and Time* of course, this 'running-ahead' will be characterized in terms of the 'resolute anticipation' exhibited in *Dasein*'s being-towards-death. Despite all the significant nuances which Heidegger will subsequently add to this account in *Being and Time*, the intimate link between individuating death and temporal singularization remains the defining feature of *Dasein*'s 'finite transcendence'. For the early Heidegger at least, death provides *Dasein*'s, and therefore time's, ultimate principle of individuation. The key question in this regard would seem to be whether death and time can be said to be 'mine' authentically or inauthentically.

Yet though 'The Concept of Time' prefigures the core of Heidegger's celebrated magnum opus in charting this movement from time's 'what' to its 'who', it is clearly distinguished from *Being and Time* by its explicit disavowal of any attempt to conduct an enquiry 'back beyond time into its connection with the other categories' (Heidegger 1992: 2E). Insofar as it abjures any explicit thematization of the relation between *Dasein*'s time and the temporal character of being in general, Heidegger will even go so far as to claim that the enquiry conducted in 'The Concept of Time' is not strictly philosophical in tenor (Heidegger 1992: 2E). It is the attempt to articulate the relation between *Sein* and *Dasein* and more specifically, the connection between *Dasein*'s temporal self-understanding and the temporal understanding of being in general that distinguishes the project undertaken in *Being and Time* from its germinal prefiguration in the 1924 lecture. In *Being and Time* the three structural 'moments' of *Dasein*'s being-in-the-world constitute the originary 'ekstases' of temporalization: time is nothing but the process of *Dasein*'s self-temporalizing in the threefold unity of being-already, being-alongside, and being-towards. In Heidegger's words: 'The phenomena of the "toward...", the "to...", the "alongside...", make temporality visible as the "ekstatikon" pure and simple. Temporality is the primordial "outside-of-itself" in and for itself' (Heidegger 1962: 377).[3] This last formulation is particularly significant because it neatly encapsulates what will turn out to be the key difficulty for fundamental ontology. Recall that the existential analytic of *Dasein*, outlining the ekstatico-horizonal structure of finite transcendence, was to be developed into an account of the relation between the individuated temporality (*Zeitlichkeit*) of *Dasein* – the time which is in each case mine – and the Temporality (*Temporalität*) of being in general. Being in general, we tentatively assume, cannot simply be coextensive with *Dasein*, which is in each case mine. It must harbour some pre-individual dimension. And indeed Theodore Kisiel has pointed out[4] that this pre-individual dimension of being had been an abiding concern of Heidegger's throughout the decade preceding *Being and Time* (hence long before his so-called turn of the 1930s), citing as evidence Heidegger's recurrent use of the impersonal pronoun 'It' in sentences such as 'It worlds' in his attempt to evoke the pre-theoretical and pre-worldly event of being qua 'primal something' (*Ur-etwas*).

But if *Dasein's* temporality is the primordial ekstatikon 'in and for itself', a formulation that makes it sound remarkably like the Idealist absolute, does this not imply that the only time is *Dasein's* time, my time? In this regard, a particularly cryptic passage from 'The Concept of Time' already seems to prefigure this tendency to render ontological time entirely subservient to existential temporality. Heidegger writes:

> *Dasein* is time, time is temporal. *Dasein* is not time, but temporality. The fundamental assertion that time is temporal is therefore the most authentic determination – and it is not a tautology because the Being of temporality signifies non-identical actuality [...] Insofar as time is in each case mine, there are many times. 'Time itself' is meaningless; time is temporal.
>
> (Heidegger 1992: 21E)

From Heidegger's point of view here, the notion of 'time itself' is presumably meaningless precisely insofar as it is tantamount to no-one's time. Confronted with the difficulty of articulating the distinction between temporality as we experience it and time in general, the temptation – to which Heidegger himself seems to have succumbed while elaborating the project of fundamental ontology, however audaciously he may have struggled with it before and after – is simply to deny the ontological autonomy of 'time itself' and to reduce it to our temporality.

6.2   Ekstasis and ekstema

To see how this may have come about, let us quickly recapitulate Heidegger's account of *Dasein's* threefold ekstasis in *Being and Time*. (1) As ahead of itself, *Dasein* is becoming its ownmost possibility. Existentiality is grounded in futurity. *Dasein* is always already coming towards itself. (2) But in becoming that possibility – going forward – *Dasein* is a returning to and a reappropriation of what it already was – its facticity. By going out towards its ownmost possibility in resolute anticipatoriness, *Dasein* returns to its always-already-having-been, thereby authentically taking over its intrinsic finitude. (3) And it is by becoming what it already was that *Dasein* gains access to entities in the '*Augenblick*': the moment of authentic 'empresenting' or making-present.[5] Thus the temporalization of temporality, understood as the synthesis of the 'ahead of', the 'already', and the 'alongside' – or future, past, and present – occurs through *Dasein's* resolute anticipation of death as its ownmost possibility – one which, in Heidegger's words, is 'non-relational' and 'not be outstripped'. Being-towards-death integrates and individuates *Dasein* as that structure which is otherwise continually fleeing from its ownmost potentiality for being via dispersion in 'the they'. Since *Dasein's* being is that of time understood as ecstatic temporality, the individuation of *Dasein* is also the individuation of time as 'the *ekstatikon* in and for itself'. Indeed, being-towards-death is the distillation of time as pure un-actualizable possibility, for 'higher than actuality stands possibility' (Heidegger 1962: 63). Thus being-towards-death as possibility of impossibility is the uttermost modality of *Dasein's* thrown-projection and hence the 'ur-project' which potentiates *Dasein's* ownmost potentiality for being. It is in the pure possibility of death that *Dasein's* 'Self' is revealed as the answer to time's 'Who?'[6]

But as we know, Heidegger distinguishes the temporality of existence – *Zeitlichkeit des Dasein* – from the temporality of being – *Temporalität des Seins*. And the project of *Being and Time* famously falters precisely at the point where it becomes necessary to explain the precise character of their connection. This was reserved for the projected but never written third division. Nevertheless, Heidegger provides a glimpse of how he envisaged the nature of this connection in his 1927 lecture course *The Basic Problems of Phenomenology*.[7] There Heidegger maintains that *Dasein* as finite transcendence is not 'beyond' but rather a 'stepping beyond'. In Heidegger's own words: '*Transcendere* means to step over; the *transcendens,* the transcendent, is that which oversteps as such and not that toward which I step over [...] *Dasein* itself oversteps in its being and thus is exactly not immanent' (Heidegger 1982: 299). *Dasein's* temporal ekstasis is a transcending, a stepping-beyond; but every such removal or displacement possesses a determinate orientation, a 'whither' as that towards which *Dasein* steps over. That 'towards which' *Dasein* steps over is presumably being, which Heidegger refers to in *Being and Time* as 'the *transcendens* pure and simple' (Heidegger 1962: 62) – though as we shall see, it is precisely this distinction which become problematic. The temporality of being is the 'ekstematic' correlate implied by *Dasein's* ekstatic transcendence.[8] Heidegger is careful to distinguish this relation between ekstasis and ekstema, which he takes to be constitutive of ontological transcendence, from what he considers as the merely ontic reciprocity between *noesis* and *noema* as correlated through the transcendence of intentionality. Intentional transcendence, whose trajectory goes from immanent consciousness to transcendent object, is according to Heidegger merely a derivative mode of this more originary temporal transcendence. The ekstematic-horizonal 'whither' is precisely not an objective correlate for *Dasein's* transcendence because it cannot be described as something which 'is'. Yet Heidegger insists that ekstasis does not thereby become a transport towards nothing:

> Rather as removal to [...] and thus because of the ekstatic nature of each of them, [the three ekstases] each have a horizon which is prescribed by the mode of the removal, the carrying-away [...] and which belongs to the ekstasis itself. Each ekstasis as removal to [...] has at the same time within itself and belonging to it a pre-delineation of the formal structure of the whereto of the removal.
>
> (Heidegger 1982: 302)

Thus the ekstematic horizon for temporal ekstasis is not to be understood as a circular visual limit but as that with which transcendence encompasses and delimits the bounds of its own stepping-beyond. Consequently, the ontological horizon cannot be located in subjectivity, nor in time, nor in space; it is no-thing. Moreover, if, as Heidegger clearly seems to suggest, the ontological horizon belongs to the ekstasis as a stepping-beyond, then this surely implies that it has been somehow 'generated' or 'produced' in and through ekstatic transcendence. And indeed the whole thrust of Heidegger's project in *Being and Time* seems to be devoted to showing how the structure of transcendence, bringing together the unity of the temporal ekstases in the ekstematic unity of their horizons, reveals a 'productivity' specific to ekstatic temporality and from which being-in-the-world 'results'. To interpret this ontological productivity as something which is simply 'beyond', independent of *Dasein*'s 'stepping-beyond', would be to turn the 'temporality of being' into a transcendental objective correlate for *Dasein*'s ekstatic transcendence, and thus to hypostatize the temporality proper to being as *something* which is transcendental, over and above *Dasein*'s movement of transcendence. But this would be to compromise the latter's specifically ontological and therefore unobjectifiable character.

6.3   Finite possibility and actual infinity

However, this refusal to hypostatize the distinction between ekstasis and ekstema confronts Heidegger with a dilemma: how can we conceive the difference between ekstasis and ekstema without objectifying the latter, but without collapsing it into the former? To hypostatize the ekstematic correlates proper to the temporal understanding of being in general would be to compromise their strictly ontological status; but to characterize them as entirely constituted through ekstasis would effectively be to subordinate *Sein* to *Dasein*. Fundamental ontology claimed to have outstripped metaphysical subjectivism, yet now finds itself confronted by the choice between objective or subjective idealism. The structure of temporal transcendence seems to harbour some sort of intrinsic originary differentiation between a subjective and an objective pole; yet this differentiation proves inordinately difficult to configure on the basis of Heidegger's own phenomenological premises without relapsing into the very distinctions between transcendence and the transcendent, noesis and noema, which Heidegger claimed to have 'overcome'. What is ironic about Heidegger's critique of metaphysical subjectivism is that it is precisely his refusal to hypostatize the world as present-at-hand object of representation that precipitates him towards the arch-idealist conclusion according to which 'If no *Dasein* exists, no world is "there" either' (Heidegger 1962: 417).[9] Or as he puts it even more explicitly in his *Introduction to Metaphysics*:

> [S]trictly speaking we cannot say: there was a time when there were no human beings. At every time, there were and are and will be human beings, because time temporalizes itself only as long as there are human beings. There is no time in which there were no human

beings, not because there are human beings from all eternity, but because time is not eternity, and time always temporalizes itself only at one time, as human, historical *Dasein*.

(Heidegger 2000: 88–9)

But as we saw in Chapter 4, this is a prototypical correlationist conceit, which is refuted both by the fossil record and the possibility of human extinction. Just as the space-time wherein *Dasein* arises and perishes cannot be turned into an ekstematic correlate generated through *Dasein*'s ekstatic temporalization, so the annihilation of thought indexed by cosmological disintegration cannot be turned into a possibility coextensive with *Dasein*'s being-towards-death. Yet in *Being and Time*, it is death as the impossibility of possibility which provides the ultimate condition of possibility for presencing: death is the impossibility of presencing which renders presencing possible. Thus it is precisely the fact that *Dasein* is always already dying that disqualifies the possibility of death from being interpreted as an empirical or 'ontic' occurrence – when properly or 'authentically' understood, death is a pure ontological possibility, not an ontic 'fact': 'Death *is* as *Dasein*'s end, *in* the being of this entity toward its end' (Heidegger 1962: 303, my emphasis). Death is *in* and *as Dasein*'s structure of ontological possibility, rather than any merely ontic actuality: 'The closest closeness which one may have in Being toward death as a possibility, is as far as possible from anything actual' (Heidegger 1962: 306–7). To be actual is to be represented as present-at-hand, which is merely a derivative and 'inauthentic' mode of presencing supervening upon the structure of pure possibility coextensive with *Dasein*'s transcendence. But to say that death 'is' precisely insofar as it is never actual is to say that though *Dasein* is always already dying, it can never actually die, since death is its transcendental and hence unactualizable condition of (im-)possibility. The actuality of bio-physical death is incommensurable with *Dasein*'s specific mode of being, which is pure possibility. Thus, it becomes apparent that the ontological difference between presencing and presence is intimately tied to the transcendental disjunction between death as pure ontological possibility and death as biological actuality,[10] a disjunction which is a function of temporalization. Moreover, the disjunction ensuring that the actualization of pure possibility remains perpetually deferred also guarantees the *de jure* reciprocity (or 'co-propriation') between the transcendence of *Sein* and the ekstasis of *Dasein*. The temporalization of existence brought about through the resolute anticipation of death involves a 'static synthesis' of the three temporal ekstases

of past, present, and future, and it is as the potentiation of pure possibility that this synthesis perpetuates the deferral of the actualization
which would reduce presencing to presence. But as a result, the very
synthesis which produces finite transcendence as the transcendental
disjunction between ecstatic possibility and static actuality does so by
generating an incommensurability between death as ontological possibility and death as biological actuality which bears all the hallmarks of
an actual infinity. For just as there can be no intra-temporal point in the
history of the human organism when its mode of being shifted from
not-*Dasein* to *Dasein* – i.e. from intra-temporal to temporalizing – so
there can be no intra-temporal point in the future when *Dasein* will
cease to be temporalizing. Temporality as pure potentiality 'to be' neither arises nor perishes in time – there can be no intra-temporal transition from inexistence to existence for the temporalization which
conditions intra-temporal succession. Moreover, just as there can be no
transition at the level of the human individual, there can be no transition at the level of the history of the human species. Hence Heidegger's
insistence on the unbridgeable abyss that separates those beings that
have a world from those that do not.[11] But consequently the transcendence of *Dasein*'s 'always already being ahead of itself' becomes difficult
to distinguish from the transcendence of eternity. To say that this transcendence, and hence the existential disjunction between temporality
and time, is 'timeless' rather than 'eternal' or 'infinite' changes little, for
either this 'timelessness' neither begins nor ends, which is tantamount
to saying it has always and will always obtain, in which case it is difficult to see in what its 'finitude' consists; or temporalization itself
emerged within time, in which case we are owed an explanation as to
how and when – precisely the questions which Heidegger's account of
Dasein's transcendence rules out of court (there can be no genesis of 'the
originary' and 'the primordial', Heidegger's favoured adjectives whenever characterizing *Dasein*). Ironically enough, Heidegger's ontologization of *Dasein*'s 'primordial' historicality erases the very history within
which *Dasein*'s emergence and perishing is rendered intelligible.[12]
Consequently, at the level of temporalization itself, all that is left to
ensure the transcendental efficacy of the disjunction between pure
ontological possibility (absolute potentiality) and mere present-at-hand
actuality is an actually infinite abyss between the time of death and the
temporality of dying. This unavowed yet infinite separation between
ontological and bio-physical time is required in order to perpetuate
the transcendent disjunction between potentiality and actuality; it is
what precludes the cancellation of the difference between presence

and presencing, time and temporality – a cancellation implied by the reality of physical death. But as we argued in Chapter 3, every attempt to stipulate a transcendental disjunction between ontological temporality and bio-physical time surreptitiously occludes the empirical conditions of instantiation through which the former supervenes upon the latter. And as we have seen throughout the preceding chapters, the categories to which Heidegger ascribes an ontological valence – 'meaning', 'mineness', 'unity', 'presencing', 'transcendence' – are in the process of being dismantled by a discourse of objectification whose empirical and speculative resources exceed those of the objectivating discourse which Heidegger believes himself to be at once subverting and founding.

It is this occlusion of temporality's bio-physical instantiation which inflates phenomenological death into an impossible possibility – but an impossibility which is recoded as the condition for the possibility of everything else. Yet to say that impossibility is the ultimate condition of possibility is still to say that it never happens. Just as the transcendental conditions of representation cannot be represented, so death as (quasi-)transcendental condition for all happening cannot itself happen. This sophism points not so much to the un-actualizability of death as to the irreality of the phenomenological attempt to absolutize the disjunction between its possibility and its actuality. I can certainly anticipate the actuality of my own death; but the reality of the latter cannot be reduced to my anticipation of its actuality because the reality of the time of death remains incommensurable with the temporality of its anticipation. More precisely, the reality of the time of death implies the inexistence of the temporality in which it is anticipated. And because the time of death precedes and succeeds the temporality of existence, the reality of the former cannot be reduced to the anticipation of its actualization within the latter. It is precisely the conflation of the reality of the time of death with the anticipation of its impossible actualization which encourages phenomenologists to subordinate death's bio-physical reality to its existential anticipation. But the real disjunction is not between death as pure possibility and death as biological actuality but rather between the temporality of thought and the time of death.

Ultimately, Heidegger's account of *Dasein*'s finite transcendence unfolds entirely in the domain of hermeneutic sense; thus its fealty is to the requirements of appropriate or 'authentic' (*Eigentlich*) interpretation, rather than to those of impartial stringency. In matters of interpretation, talent outweighs rigour and finesse overrules stringency. Where Kant felt obliged to justify his appeal to a transcendental difference in his attempt to account for the possibility of objective knowledge, Heidegger simply stipulates ontological difference as the appropriate inter-pretative horizon required for the excavation of *Dasein*'s pre-theoretical self-understanding and dismisses requests for its justification as symptoms of the forgetting of this difference. Similarly, there can be no question of demonstrating the necessity of the absolute disjunction between biological and existential death which lies at the root of Heidegger's account of finite transcendence; this disjunction is a precondition of Heidegger's interpretative strategy, not its result. Heidegger does not argue for ontological transcendence; he insists upon it, then castigates those who would deny it for remaining in thrall to metaphysics and/or representation. Contra Heidegger, the preceding chapters have lain out a rudimentary case against this stipulation of transcendence. Thus, Chapter 1 outlined reasons to be chary of any attempt to transcenden-talize our supposedly pre-theoretical access to the 'meaning' of phe-nomena; Chapter 4 called into question the presuppositions underlying the characterization of being as 'presencing'; lastly, Chapter 5 under-mined some of the principal assumptions propping up Heidegger's construal of being as 'transcendence'. Moreover, by absolutizing tran-scendence under the aegis of the disjunction between the two faces of death, biological and ontological, Heidegger effectively deprives himself of any means for explaining how transcendence comes about. It is in this regard that Deleuze's treatment of the relation between death and time in *Difference and Repetition*[13] becomes particularly salient. Like Heidegger, Deleuze distinguishes between death's merely material aspect and its properly ontological dimension, but unlike Heidegger, Deleuze's account is geared towards showing how this disjunction, and hence transcendence, is not originally given as the precondition for ontology, but rather something that emerges within it.

6.4   Deleuze: time in and for itself

Like *Being and Time*, *Difference and Repetition* overhauls Kantian tran-scendentalism on behalf of an ontology of temporal difference, more precisely, an ontology wherein being is understood as temporal differ-entiation. Deleuze rehabilitates the thesis of ontological univocity such that it is being qua time that is 'said in one and the same sense of all its individuating differences or intrinsic modalities' (Deleuze 1968: 53, 1994: 36) – though those differences or modalities remain divergent.[14] Yet although it is often cited as evidence of Deleuze's allegiance to a variety of materialist monism, Deleuze's re-interpretation of univocity in terms of time actually necessitates a privileged role for a special kind of being, an exceptional modality of individuation, that of the psyche. Thus, it is in the human psyche that individuation becomes fully *potentiated* as the differentiator of difference. This potentiation of difference is played out in the third synthesis of time, which Deleuze explicitly associates with Freud's 'death-instinct'. However, contrary to any interpretation of the latter which would see in it the expression of a compulsion to return to the inorganic, Deleuze flatly denies that death can be understood as a material phenomenon: 'Death has nothing to do with a material model' (Deleuze 1968: 28, 1994: 17). Moreover, in a surprising endorsement of the Heideggerean distinction between death and dying,[15] Deleuze goes on to distinguish between death as a bare objective repetition and death as an 'intensive' form of subjective individuation: 'Death does not appear in the objective model of an indifferent, inanimate matter to which what is living would "return"; it is present in the living as a differentiated subjective experience endowed with a prototype. It does not pertain to a state of matter; on the contrary, it corresponds to a pure form that has abjured all matter – the empty form of time' (Deleuze 1968: 148, 1994: 112 tm). Thus though he suspends consciousness's transcendental privileges, Deleuze turns thinking into the privileged locus for an apocalyptic individuation whereby, in a striking re-inscription of Heidegger, the future 'ungrounds' the past and death becomes the subject of a time that splits the self. Ultimately, for Deleuze, death, like time, is no-one's.

Difference and Repetition can be usefully (albeit only partially) summarized as a particularly audacious rewriting of Kant's 1st Critique in the light of Bergson's *Matter and Memory*.[16] But Deleuze uses the scalpel of a refined Bergsonism to re-arrange the body of Kantianism. Representation is subjected to a critique which annuls the mediating function of conceptual understanding vis-à-vis reason and sensibility. Thus in *Difference and Repetition* the tripartite structure of the 1st Critique ostensibly undergoes an involution which folds the Transcendental Dialectic directly into the Transcendental Aesthetic. The mediating role of the Transcendental Analytic is supplanted by an account of spatio-temporal individuation which provides the sufficient reason for a non-conceptual synthesis of reason and sensibility. With the unifying function of the understanding suspended, the aesthetic manifold need no longer be subjected to conceptual subsumption; it now incarnates the dialectical structures of ideal multiplicity. Rather than being specified via the representational logic of subsumption, wherein the concept is always too 'baggy' to fit the particular object, the individuated entity is the actualization of a virtual multiplicity, and it is individuation as ultimate determinant of actualization which ensures the exact coincidence of the ideal and the real, and hence a precise fit between ideal genesis and empirical actuality. In seeking out the ideal conditions capable of generating the individual entity of actual experience, rather than the particular object of possible experience, Deleuze's 'transcendental empiricism' treats the concept (i.e. the Idea as virtual multiplicity) as the object of an encounter which is no longer governed by the logic of recognition: thus Deleuze declares, 'concepts are the things themselves, but things in their free and untamed state, beyond "anthropological predicates"' (Deleuze 1968: 3, 1994: xxi–ii tm).

6.5   The intensive nature of difference

The key component in this renegotiation of the Platonic–Kantian dyad, aesthetic-dialectic or sensibility-ideality, is provided by Deleuze's theory of intensive difference, through which he finesses Bergson's bald dichotomy between matter and memory, space and time. It is this dichotomy which is recoded in the conjunction of 'difference' and 'repetition' in the book's title. Initially at least, it seems as though the discussion of difference is rooted primarily in conceptual issues, while the account of repetition has more of a bearing on questions of perception and sensibility. Thus the critique of the representational concept of 'difference' and the account of non-conceptual difference seem to pertain principally to thought, and to be consummated in Chapter 4's theory of Ideas ('The Ideal Synthesis of Difference'[17]). Similarly, the critique of bare repetition and the account of 'clothed' repetition (*répétition vétue*)[18] seem to pertain primarily to the realm of the sensible and to find their fulfilment in Chapter 5's theory of individuation ('Asymmetrical Synthesis of the Sensible'). Though this superficial impression is not entirely inaccurate, it quickly becomes apparent how profoundly difference and repetition, ideality and materiality, are reciprocally enveloped, both within and across chapters. Each is shown to inhabit the other: material repetition turns out to be inhabited by passive syntheses which extract ideal differentiations from it, and ideal differentiation is implicated in material repetition. More profoundly, the initial divergence between the trajectories of temporal difference and material repetition is merely the preliminary to their intersection in the book's account of individuation. Thus the apparent absence of any discernible architectonic structure in what is effectively an astonishingly ambitious philosophical treatise belies the intricate coherence of the book's serial organization. Though successive chapters focus alternately on the themes of difference or repetition, each implicates and envelops the other: the theme of repetition recurs throughout the discussions of difference and the topic of difference crops up throughout the discussion of repetition. The extended critique of the representational image of philosophical thought in the book's central chapter ('The Image of Thought') is at once its point of equilibrium and its methodological fulcrum, stapling its two halves together and ensuring their communication by mirroring each into the other.

Accordingly, both 'difference' and 'repetition' harbour a double aspect, depending on whether they are viewed from the side of representation or grasped in and for themselves. The representational characteristics of difference are identity in the concept, opposition in the predicate, resemblance in perception, and analogy in judgement. But difference in itself, as exhibited in the Idea, is simulacral, dialectical, intensive, and univocal. Similarly, from the viewpoint of representation, repetition is bare, material, extrinsic, and reproductive. But viewed for itself, it is clothed, spiritual, intrinsic, and productive. Difference in the concept marks the limit of conceptual identity; repetition outside the concept marks the blockage of conceptual difference – only when the concept of difference in itself is repeated for itself is representation undone. Thus and crucially, for Deleuze '*Repetition is a condition for action before being a concept of reflection*' (Deleuze 1968: 121, 1994: 90 – italics in original). This imperative to repeat, through which thought shifts from the contemplative reflection of identity to the active production of difference, finds expression in the third synthesis of time as affirmation of eternal recurrence.[19]

As we shall see, it is psychic individuation that ultimately catalyses this repetition of difference in itself. However, the interaction between each of the four aspects outlined above – difference in the concept, concept of difference, repetition without a concept, repetition of difference – is intricate; it cannot be reduced to some Manichean opposition between temporal heterogeneity and spatial homogeneity, virtuality and actuality. Ideas as virtual multiplicities are at once expressed by intensive repetitions and enveloped by them, but at the same time they are actualized as species and parts through the same process whereby intensive quantity is explicated as extensive quality. Deleuze alleviates Bergson's blunt dualism of quantity and quality, difference in degree and difference in kind, arguing that it is pointless to try to object to mechanism by insisting on the irreducibility of life to extensity, quality to quantity. The difference between difference in degree and difference in kind is not reducible to either: 'between the two are all the degrees of difference, under both lies the whole nature of difference: the intensive' (Deleuze 1968: 299, 1994: 232). The degrees and/or nature of difference are intensive quantities. Where the value of extensive quantities, such as energy, mass, volume, or entropy, is proportional to the size of the system which they measure and governed by the logic of part/whole, the value of intensive quantities, such as speed, density, pressure, or temperature, is measured by the ratio of two quantities and is governed by the logic of co-variation. Deleuze characterizes intensity in terms of three fundamental characteristics: it is unequalizable, affirmative, enveloped and enveloping. We shall briefly recapitulate each of these in turn.

First, intensity is the 'uncancellable' in quantitative difference and hence the 'unequalizable' in quantity; or the quality proper to quantity (Deleuze 1968: 299, 1994: 232). It is not a species of the genus 'quantity' but rather the moment of essential inequality which is constitutive of every variety of quantity. Thus every type of number is constructed on the basis of an essential inequality which it retains within itself relative to the type upon whose inequality it has been constructed. For example, fractions express an inequality in the relation between two magnitudes which cannot be reduced to a whole number; likewise, irrational numbers express the impossibility of determining a common quotient between integers. But though the fraction ostensibly cancels the inequality upon which it is based in the equality of its quotient, and though the irrational number seems to cancel the inequality which founds it in the equality of a purely geometrical relationship, the intensive inequality remains implicated in the quantitative extension – that of the fraction or the irrational number – in which it is explicated. Consequently, there is an essential asymmetry between the intensive and the extension to which it gives rise, because although extensity explicates and cancels intensity, the inequality proper to the latter remains implicated within it.

The second characteristic of intensity is to be essentially affirmative. Since equivalence can be defined by affirming inequality ($\neq$) rather than by stipulating identity ($A = A$), two numbers A and B can be defined as equivalent by affirming the distance ($\neq \neq$) separating them from a third number C: if A is distant from every number C which is distant from B, then $A = B$. This distance affirmed in asserting inequality is intrinsic to intensity. Since the latter is always constructed out of at least two series of differences, which are implicated within it, and these series in turn are constructed out of further series of differences, which are likewise implicated within them, the intensive synthesis whereby intensity is explicated in the discrete qualities and parts of extensive magnitude involves the affirmation of a continuous distance or 'depth' implicated in extensity but proper to the unequal. To affirm the inequality of intensity is also to affirm the distance or depth which is implicated within it.

The distance implicated in intensity expresses its third fundamental characteristic: as enveloping and enveloped. Intensive difference is never negated by its qualitative equalization because it remains implicated and implicating, or enveloped and enveloping, within itself: intensity is primarily and intrinsically implicated in itself as enveloping difference and enveloped distance; and only secondarily or extrinsically implicated in the qualities and parts of extensity: 'Difference in depth is composed of distances, but "distance" is not an extensive quantity but an indivisible asymmetrical relation, ordinal and intensive in nature, which is established between series of heterogeneous terms and which expresses each time the nature of what does not divide without changing nature' (Deleuze 1968: 306, 1994: 238). It is this distance enveloped in intensive difference which renders the latter indivisible into discrete extensive parts. Thus intensive magnitude constitutes a continuum which cannot divide without changing in state. Intensive distance explicates itself as the three dimensions of spatial extensity: left and right, up and down, figure and ground; yet it remains implicated within extensive space as the pure depth of the intensive *spatium*.

Moreover, it is the intensive nature of difference itself and its explication in extensity which generates the illusion whereby physical systems can be represented as moving from a differentiated to an undifferentiated state, or from disequilibrium to equilibrium. Entropy is a transcendental physical illusion which arises when representation conflates intensity's extrinsic implication in extensity with its intrinsic implication in itself:

The paradox of entropy is the following: entropy is an extensive factor, but unlike all other extensive factors, it is an extension or 'explication' which is implicated as such in intensity; one which only exists as implicated and which does not exist independently of implication; and this because its function consists in rendering possible the general movement through which the implicated is explicated or extended. There is thus a transcendental illusion essentially tied to the *qualitas* Heat and to the extension, Entropy.

(Deleuze 1968: 295, 1994: 229 tm)

For Deleuze, the postulation of an entropic principle is paradoxical because it involves positing an extensive factor in order to account for the explication of intensity, but one which is ascribed a purely intensive existence as implicated in intensity. Instead of paradoxically implicating an extensive factor within intensity in order to account for its explication, Deleuze insists that it is necessary to grasp how it is of the nature of intensity to explicate itself, but to remain implicated within itself even as it does so: 'For difference has not ceased to be in itself, to be implicated in itself, even when it is explicated outside itself' (Deleuze 1968: 294, 1994: 228 tm). This is to say that 'difference is essentially implicated, that the being of difference is implication' (Deleuze 1968: 293, 1994: 228 tm).

As we shall see, it is because intensity is essentially individuating that difference explicates itself. Moreover, we shall re-examine this denunciation of entropy as a transcendental physical illusion when we come to scrutinize *Difference and Repetition*'s endorsement of vitalism below (by 'vitalism' we simply mean the claim that physical and chemical principles cannot explain biological functions and processes). But first we must consider the link between the aforementioned claim that 'the being of difference is implication' and the claim that intensity constitutes 'the being of the sensible' (Deleuze 1968: 305, 1994: 236). Deleuze recodes the notion of ontological difference in the distinction between the virtual differen*t*iation of Ideas as problematic multiplicities and their actual differen*c*iation into the parts and qualities of extensity. Being is not given in the representation of the actual; it corresponds to the problematic dimension of virtual differen*t*iation whose differen*c*iation generates the actual as its (always partial) solution. Thus being is problematic because it is at once fully differen*t*iated yet un-differen*c*iated. Intensity is the paradoxical instance in sensibility which corresponds to this problematic ideality of being – it is at once what cannot be sensed and what can only be sensed. It cannot be sensed because it is not the given but rather that through which the given is produced (Deleuze 1968: 305, 1994: 236). As we have seen, the explication of intensity generates the three dimensions of spatial extensity within which perception operates: left and right in the first dimension, up and down in the second dimension, figure and ground in the third dimension. But intensive depth is implicated in the three dimensions of spatial extensity as that which is at once the imperceptible in perception, yet also what can only be sensed. Moreover, intensity as the imperceptible (*sentiendum*) which can only be sensed awakens memory to the immemorial (*memorandum*) which can only be remembered, and this in turn forces thought to confront the un-thought (*cogitandum*) which can only be thought (Deleuze 1968: 183, 1994: 140–1). As the imperceptible which generates sensation, intensity is the catalyst for that discordant exercise of the faculties whereby each is forced to transcend its own limit in the confrontation with the paradoxical instance which defines the being of its proper object: 'From the *sentiendum* to the *cogitandum* there develops the violence of that which forces us to think [...] Instead of all the faculties converging and contributing to the common effort to recognize an object, we witness a divergent effort, each faculty being confronted with what is "proper" to it in what essentially concerns it' (Deleuze 1968: 298, 1994: 231 tm). Yet 'transcendent' here does not mean that the faculty is referred to an object beyond the world but rather that it is forced 'to seize that in the world which concerns it exclusively, and which makes it be born to the world' (Deleuze 1968: 186, 1994: 143). It is through this transcendent-discordant as opposed to empirical-concordant exercise that each faculty accesses its own problematic-ontological dimension: thus the *sentendium* indexes the ontological dimension of sensibility; the *memorandum* points to the onto-logical dimension of memory; while the *cogitandum* indicates the onto-logical dimension of thinking. The transcendent exercise of the faculties thereby marks the juncture at which thinking is forced into being and being is encountered in thinking (Deleuze 1968: 252, 1994: 195). Yet as the faculty through which we originally access the intensive, sensibility retains a privilege as source of the encounter with what forces us to think: 'From the intensive to thought, it is always by means of an inten-sity that thought comes to us. If sensibility enjoys a privilege as origin it is because that which forces feeling and that which can only be felt are one and the same in the encounter, whereas the two instances are distinct in the other cases' (Deleuze 1968: 188, 1994: 144–5 tm). Consequently, while the illusion of entropy is generated in accordance with the requirements of good sense and common sense, which govern the empirical exercise of the faculties and allow intensity to be grasped only insofar as it is already explicated in extensive quality, this illusion is exposed when the facultative concord is interrupted by the 'discordant accord' wherein the *sentendium* gives rise to the *cogitandum* and the con-comitant discovery that 'intensity remains implicated in itself and con-tinues to envelop difference at the very moment when it is reflected in the extensity and the quality which it creates, which implicate it only sec-ondarily, just enough to "explain it".' (Deleuze 1968: 309, 1994: 240 tm).

Accordingly, if entropy can be called a transcendental physical illu-sion it is because the explication of intensity which is the precondition for the representation of entropy points to an objective reality, rather than a merely subjective deception. Yet as we have seen, intensity only explicates itself outside itself, while remaining implicated in itself as enveloping difference and enveloped distance. The question then is: Why is intensity driven to externalize itself in the first place? Why does it not simply remain self-enveloped and enveloping without ever externalizing itself in extensity? The answer lies in Deleuze's theory of individuation.[20] It is individuation which accounts for the process whereby intensity is explicated in qualitative extensity and which explains why intensity does not simply remain in itself. For not only is intensity 'the determinant in the process of actualization' (Deleuze 1968: 316, 1994: 245), it is the intensive nature of individuating difference which binds virtual and actual, the ideal and the sensible, and provides the sufficient reason for actualization: 'It is individuation which ensures the embedding of the two great dissimilar halves [i.e. virtual and actual]' (Deleuze 1968: 358, 1994: 280). Actualization occurs along three series: spatial, temporal, and psychic (Deleuze 1968: 284, 1994: 220). Accordingly, individuation has a spatial, a temporal, and a psychic aspect. Moreover, it is the intensive nature of individuation which determines the actualization of the Idea in the form of its spatio-temporal 'dramatization'. Where Heidegger called into question the metaphysical determination of being as presence-at-hand which prejudges the enquiry into the 'whatness' or essence of things, Deleuze displaces the question 'What is X?', along with the analogical distribution of being which underlies it, with a 'method of dramatization' in which the *eidos* (Idea) is no longer grasped as a unit of representation but as a problematic multiplicity whose salient features correspond to questions such as 'Who?', 'How?', 'When?', 'Where?', 'How many?' (Deleuze 1968: 236, 1994: 188).[21] But since individuation is the determinant for the actual differenciation of virtual differentiation, 'it is individuation that answers the question "Who?" just as the Idea answered the questions "How?" and "How many?" "Who?" is always an intensity' (Deleuze 1968: 317, 1994: 246 tm). Thus, 'all individuality is intensive' (Deleuze 1968: 317, 1994: 246). Accordingly, it is intensity as individuating difference which provides the key to the rehabilitation of ontological univocity proposed by Deleuze in *Difference and Repetition*. If being can be 'said in one and the same sense of all its individuating differences or intrinsic modalities' (Deleuze 1968: 53, 1994: 36), it is because intensity relates univocal being directly to its individuating differences. Deleuze's critique of representation allows him to circumvent the Kantian problematic of cognitive access, but his rehabilitation of univocity effectively short-circuits the Heideggerean problematic of ontological access precisely insofar as psychic individuation, announced by the transcendent exercise of the faculties and consummated in the third synthesis of time, marks the point of intersection at which the dialectic of ideas and the aesthetic of intensities, or ideality and sensibility, ultimately converge in a double genesis of thinking and being. Yet since individuating difference is precisely what slips through the meshes of representation, the thinking of individuation necessitates an individuation in and of thinking.[22] This is the function of the third synthesis which Deleuze associates with the affirmation of eternal return. Thinking is individuated through its intensive repetition of ontological difference; more precisely, thinking is individuated by repeating being's individuating differences, a repetition which effects thought's shift from contemplative representation to ontological production: 'In the eternal return, univocal being is not only thought and even affirmed but effectively realized' (Deleuze 1968: 60, 1994: 41–2). By realizing univocal being, thinking transcends representation and accesses the intensive noumenon underlying the extensive phenomenon. Thus the reciprocal presupposition between the thinking of individuation and the individuation of thinking marks the point at which univocal immanence is articulated with ontological transcendence.

6.6   Individuation and the individual

Deleuze characterizes the inherently dynamic nature of individuation in terms of spatio-temporal dynamisms: 'They are the actualizing, the differenciating agencies' (Deleuze 1968: 276, 1994: 214). Intensities are spatio-temporal dynamisms: 'It is intensity which is immediately expressed in the fundamental spatio-temporal dynamisms and which determines an 'indistinct' differential relation in the Idea to incarnate itself in a distinct quality and a distinguished extensity' (Deleuze 1968: 316, 1994: 245 tm). Intensities are individuals, but individuals are not to be confused with individuation. Individuation is dynamic process characterized by a positive feedback loop between an intensive individual and the pre-individual singularities borne by Ideas. Thus a field of individuation marks the juncture between the static perplication of differential relations in the realm of the Idea and the dynamic implication of intensities in the realm of the sensible. Consequently, 'intensities presuppose and express only differential relations; individuals presuppose only Ideas' (Deleuze 1968: 324, 1994: 252). Ideas are characterized as both distinct and obscure. They are distinct insofar as they are perfectly differentiated – via the reciprocal determination of relations and the complete determination of points – but obscure because they are not yet differenciated – since all Ideas coexist with one another in a state of virtual perplication. By the same token, intensities are at once clear and confused. They are clear insofar as they are enveloping and confused insofar as they are enveloped. Thus the clarity of enveloping depth is inseparable from the confusion of enveloped distance. Accordingly, in individuation, the perplication of ideas is expressed by the implication of intensities. Enveloping depth clearly expresses distinct relations and points in the Idea, while enveloped distance confusedly expresses their obscure indifferenciation. Moreover, enveloping depth constitutes the field of individuating differences, while enveloped distances constitute the individual differences. Intensity is individuating precisely insofar as it expresses the Idea, but this expression[23] is a function of thinking: 'To the distinct-obscure as ideal unity corresponds the clear-confused as individuating intensive unity. The clear-confused is not a characteristic of the Idea but of the thinker who thinks it or expresses it. For the thinker is the individual as such' (Deleuze 1968: 325, 1994: 253 tm). Intensity as spatio-temporal dynamism implies an individual thinker precisely insofar as it is the expression of an Idea. Thus Deleuze insists, the Idea finds expression in the realm of the sensible because intensity *thinks* and is inseparable from thought; albeit a thought that is no longer a function of representational consciousness:

> Every spatio-temporal dynamism marks the emergence of an elementary consciousness which traces directions, doubles movements and migrations, and is born at the threshold of those singularities condensed relative to the body or the object of which it is the consciousness. It is not enough to say that consciousness is consciousness of something; it is the double of this something and each thing is consciousness because it possesses a double, albeit very distant and very foreign to it.
>
> (Deleuze 1968: 316, 1994: 220 tm)

Yet what precisely is the relation between the elementary consciousness that emerges in every spatio-temporal dynamism and the body or object which it 'doubles'? What is the nature of this enigmatic 'doubling'? The answer lies in the correlation between intensity as 'expressing' and the Idea as 'expressed'. The movement of actualization corresponds to a fork in being between the intensive individual's clear-confused thought as 'expressing' and the distinct-obscure difference in the Idea as 'expressed'

(Deleuze 1968: 326, 1994: 253). In actualization, univocal being splits between the expressing thought of the intensive thinker – the 'larval subject' of the spatio-temporal dynamism – and the expressed Idea. Thus the difference between thought and thing, thinking and being, is not a transcendent condition of access to things, as it is for the philosophy of representation, but is rather internal to things themselves. In actualization, each thing is at once the expression of an Idea and the thought through which that Idea is expressed: 'Every body, every thing thinks and is a thought insofar as, reduced to its intensive reasons, it expresses an Idea whose actualization it determines' (Deleuze 1968: 327, 1994: 254 tm). Thus things themselves determine their own actualization insofar as they are the loci of spatio-temporal dynamisms inhabited by larval subjects whose thought is the clear-confused expression of a distinct-obscure difference in the Idea. The larval subject of spatio-temporal dynamism is the thinker of individuating difference insofar as it clearly expresses a distinction in the Idea. Accordingly, individuating difference is the thought that 'makes the difference' (Deleuze 1968: 43, 1994: 28). It is the 'differenciator of difference', the 'dark precursor', through which difference in the Idea communicates with difference in intensity (Deleuze 1968: 154, 1994: 117). The intensive individual or larval subject is the thinker whose clear expression of distinct relations and points in the Idea generates the individuating difference through which the virtual is actualized.

Thus individuation does not proceed from abstract universal to concrete particular through the gradual specification of genera and the continuous division of parts, but rather via discontinuous ruptures and abrupt transitions in a metastable system comprising differences in potential between two heterogeneous series: that of the reciprocal determination of differential relations and the complete determination of singular and remarkable points in the Idea; and that of the explication of intensity into the differenciated parts and qualities of extensity. The individuating difference expressed by the larval subject of the spatio-temporal dynamism is the agent of differenciation through which the disparity in potential between these heterogeneous series crosses a critical threshold of disequilibrium, resulting in a sudden exchange of information whereby ideal differentiation enters into a relation of internal resonance with extensive differenciation. Individuating difference determines actualization as the resolution of a disparity in potential between virtual and actual, through which a differential relation becomes differenciated as a physical qualification or biological organization and the corresponding distribution of singular and remarkable points become incarnated in a physical partition or a biological specification. Individuating difference is 'the disparate' or the dark precursor as differenciator of difference; the disparate generated by 'the disparity' of intensive difference.[24]

Ultimately then, individuation determines actualization, which unfolds according to the fork in being between expressing thought and expressed Idea. This fork is a function of the nature of intensity as enveloping and enveloped. Consequently, the distinction between individuating and individual difference depends upon Deleuze's account of intensity as essentially implicating. Moreover, not only is the larval subject of spatio-temporal dynamism the catalyst for individuation, and hence for actualization, since it is his clear expression of a distinction in the idea that 'makes the difference'; it is the larval subject that provides the conduit for this fork in actualization insofar as it is at once the patient of individuation, or the expression of the Idea, and the individuating agent, or the expressing thought. But how do spatio-temporal dynamisms and the larval subjects associated with them come about? What underlies this correlation between expressing thought and expressed Idea? As we shall see, both the former and the latter are to be explained in terms of a series of passive syntheses of space and time.

6.7   The syntheses of space and time

Intensity synthesizes time and space: it is the yoking of the three syntheses of time – present, past, and future – and the three syntheses of space – explication, implication, and ungrounding. The first synthesis of time is the contraction of the living present in the passive synthesis of habit. The living present of habit consists in the contraction of a difference between two bare or spatial repetitions (repetition *partes extra partes*) contemplated by what Deleuze refers to as a 'passive self':

> The passive Self is not just defined by receptivity, i.e. by the capacity to undergo sensations, but by the contracting contemplation which constitutes the organism itself before constituting its sensations [...] These selves are larval subjects; the world of passive syntheses constitute the system of the self in conditions to be determined, but the system of the dissolved self.
>
> (Deleuze 1968: 107, 1994: 78 tm)

The larval subject of habit is not only the fundamental component of all organic life but also provides the foundation from which all other psychic phenomena, including representational consciousness, derive (Deleuze 1968: 107, 1994: 78) This fundamental contraction of the living present in habit constitutes the originary presentation of repetition, embodied in an elementary consciousness which is neither representative nor represented but which is presupposed by all representation. Consequently, the contracted present is retention of a past and expectancy towards a future both of which remain internal to this living present. It expresses a direction wherein the arrow of time moves from past to future, from particularity to generality, from disequilibrium to equilibrium, and as such is the synthesis which constitutes good sense, measuring the time it takes for intensity to cancel itself out in extensity[25] (Deleuze 1968: 289, 1994: 224). Accordingly, the contraction of the present corresponds to the spatial synthesis whereby intensity is explicated in extensity.

Yet the paradox of the living present, Deleuze maintains, is that it constitutes the present in a time which is itself un-constituted. The living present is the empirical foundation of time, but that foundation requires a transcendental ground in the form of a synthesis of the past constituting the time wherein the present can pass (Deleuze 1968: 108, 1994: 79). For if the past had to wait for a new present in order to become past then it would prove just as impossible for the old past to recede as for the new one to arrive. Thus, following Bergson, Deleuze insists that the past must be constituted as past 'at the same time' as it is constituted as present – the present can only pass if it is already contemporaneous with the past which it 'will be'. This contemporaneity with the present constitutes the first paradoxical aspect of the pure past. But if every past is already contemporaneous with the present which it 'has been' then it is the past as a whole which co-exists with each present since it can no more be said to be contained in the actual present relative to which it is now past than to follow 'after' the past present which it 'has been' (Deleuze 1968: 111, 1994: 81–2). Thus every actual present is merely the most contracted point of the past as a whole. Co-existence with the present is the second paradoxical aspect of the pure past. Moreover, though it allows the old present to pass and the new one to come forth, the pure past is precisely that which neither comes into nor out of being: 'One cannot say: "It was". It no longer exists, it does not exist, yet it insists, it consists, it *is*' (Deleuze 1968: 111, 1994: 82 tm). Consequently, the pure past pre-exists the passing present as the a priori element of all time. This is its third paradoxical aspect. Accordingly, transcendental memory is the passive synthesis of these three paradoxical aspects of the pure past: contemporaneousness with the present which it has been, co-existence with the present relative to which it is past, and pre-existence vis-à-vis the passing present.

Yet this passive synthesis of memory harbours a double aspect for not only does it ground the passive (sub-representational) synthesis of habit, it also provides the precondition for the representation of the past in the active synthesis of memory. Following Husserl, Deleuze distinguishes the retention of the past in the living present from its reproduction in memory. The past that is retained in the living present is a particular past belonging to an actual present which constitutes the element of generality oriented towards the future of which it is the anticipation. But the past that is reproduced in memory constitutes the element of generality within which particular presents, both the past present and the actual present, are mediated. Thus particularity resides in the past present as what 'has been', whereas the pure past constitutes the element of generality, the 'was' within which this particularity is intended. Accordingly, the pure past is the element of generality within which the old present can be represented in the actual present. But every representation of a past present in the actual present also involves the representation of the present in which this past is. Thus representation always represents itself (Deleuze 1968: 109, 1994: 80). Consequently, the relationship between the past present and the actual present in representation is not that of two successive instants on a line; rather, the actual present always enjoys a supplementary dimension through which it not only represents the past present but also represents itself as actual: the actual present reflects itself in the same act through which it recollects the past present. Thus the active synthesis of memory entails two dimensions, the reproduction of the past present and the reflection of the actual present, both of which are deployed in every representation.[26] Yet the pure past cannot be reduced to the past which is reproduced in representation; it is at once the condition of representation and the ground of the sub-representational synthesis upon which representation is founded. Where the passive synthesis of habit constitutes time through the contraction of instants under the condition of the present, the active synthesis of memory constitutes time as the embedding of presents within one another under the condition of the pure past; consequently, the latter not only provides the ground for the passive constitution of the living present but also the precondition for the active reproduction of the past within the present (Deleuze 1968: 110, 1994: 81). Moreover, whereas past and future remained internal dimensions of the living present, both the actual present in which the past is reproduced and the future present which is reflected in the actual present are now dimensions internal to the pure past. This is why the latter is not a dimension of time, but rather the synthesis of time as a whole. As ground for the reproduction of the past present and for the representation of the actual present, it is the condition for the temporal structure of representation; but it cannot itself be represented. The active synthesis of memory represents the present according to the dual aspect of the reproduction of the past present and the reflection of the actual present. But the element of the pure past within which both past and future presents are intended remains in itself even as it grounds the representation of these past and future presents.

Following Bergson once more, Deleuze characterizes the manner in which the past as a whole is conserved in itself in terms of the vertical co-existence of different degrees of contraction and dilation of duration. Duration is internally differentiated in accordance with a multiplicity of temporal rhythms indexing distinct rates of actualization. Thus the pure past constitutes a virtual totality of coexistence within which the degrees of contraction and dilation of duration repeat one another at different but superimposed levels (each degree expressing a set of differential relations and singular points in the Idea). Accordingly, every present has two faces: it is at once the most contracted point of duration insofar as it is grounded in a memory wherein the past as virtual whole is intensively repeated; but also its maximal dilation insofar as it is founded upon the repetition of habit which contracts difference from a bare or spatial repetition: 'The present is always a contracted difference; but in one case it contracts indifferent instants, while in the other, by going to the limit, it contracts a differential level of the whole which is itself one of dilation or contraction' (Deleuze 1968: 114, 1994: 84 tm). The articulation between the contraction of the present in habit and the contraction of the past in memory provides the key to understanding the way in which intensive difference is implicated in extensive repetition. Every articulation between the contraction of bare repetition in habit and the contraction of clothed repetition in memory is determined by a larval subject whose thought of individuating difference determines an actualization of the virtual past. Variable rhythms of actualization are a function of the reciprocal variation between enveloping intensity's clear expression of distinct relations and points in the Idea and enveloped intensity's confused expression of their obscure perplication. Variations in rhythms of actualization determine the different degrees to which intensity is implicated in itself and explicated in extensity. The former is the latter's external envelope: the bare repetition of extensity explicates clothed repetition, while clothed or intensive repetition remains implicated in bare repetition (Deleuze 1968: 370, 1994: 289). Intensity is implicated and implicating in itself according to its clear-confused expression of Ideas as virtually co-existing degrees of duration, while its explication in extensity corresponds to the bare repetition of habit. Yet bare or spatial repetition is grounded in the passive synthesis of memory which implicates intensive difference in extensity. Accordingly, the synthesis of space whereby intensive depth is implicated in extensity rests upon the synthesis of memory (Deleuze 1968: 296, 1994: 230). The intensive *spatium* is space's memory of time. The contraction of memory constitutes the originary sub-representational depth of intensive difference without which the contraction of habit in extensity would be impossible. Moreover, since the latter is merely the envelope of the former, extensive space is merely the de-differentiation – more precisely, the individualizing actualization or 'indi-different/ciation' – of intensive time. Accordingly, the relation between space as maximal contraction of temporal intensity and time as minimal dilation of spatial extensity is entirely internal to time. If time qua duration pertains essentially to mind (*'esprit'*), it is precisely the mind of the larval subject, whose thinking of individuating difference determines the actualization of the virtual as a contraction of memory. Thus for Deleuze, as for Bergson, matter is to be understood 'as the dream of mind or as mind's most dilated past' (Deleuze 1968: 114, 1994: 84 tm). The larval subject of spatio-temporal synthesis dreams matter into being through the individuating difference of his thought insofar as it clearly expresses a distinction in the Idea.

6.8   The fracture of thinking

Yet how does this correlation between expressing thought and expressed Idea come about? What generates the correspondence between intensity and Idea through which actualization occurs? Deleuze characterizes the relation between the first and second passive synthesis as one between an empirical foundation of time and a ground of time that is at once transcendental and metaphysical. The synthesis of memory harbours a transcendental aspect insofar as it constitutes the being of the past which makes the present pass, but it also harbours a metaphysical aspect because it invokes the 'in-itself' of this pure past as the ground of the consciousness of the present (Deleuze 1968: 374, 1994: 293). Thus the contraction of habit founds the physical presentation of time in the organism, but the contraction of memory grounds its metaphysical representation in consciousness. This grounding is metaphysical precisely to the extent that it allows the past relative to which every present passes to be represented as the originary model for the latter. Representation institutes a series of concentric presents expanding outward in ever-widening arcs from an originary but always already past present. As a result, the relation between the a priori past and the presents which it grounds becomes one of resemblance and the difference between past and present is subordinated to an identity in the concept (Deleuze 1968: 351, 1994: 274). But actualization occurs through an individuating difference which is the determination of a differentiation in the Idea, not the specification of a difference in the concept. Thus actualization is the determination of the difference between two differences: the extrinsic difference between instants contracted in the present and the intrinsic difference between the degrees of contraction of memory. The difference between the past and the present resides in the difference between these two contractions of difference – between the repetition in extensity of extrinsically related successive instants (*partes extra partes*) and the repetition in intensity of internally related co-existing levels of the past (Deleuze 1968: 114, 1994: 84).

Actualization as determination of the difference between the contraction of habit and the contraction of memory implies a third synthesis, and it is the latter that institutes a correspondence between expressing and expressed, thought and Idea. Between the determination of thought in the passive self of the larval subject and the indetermination (i.e. indifferenciation) of problematic being in the Idea lies the pure and empty form of time as the transcendental condition under which the indeterminate becomes determinable (Deleuze 1968: 220, 1994: 169). It is 'pure' because it is the exclusively logical time internal to thinking, rather than the chronological time in which thought unfolds. It is 'empty' because it is devoid of empirical content (the living present of habit), as well as of metaphysical substance (the contractions and dilations of ontological memory). And it is 'transcendental' because it ensures the a priori correspondence between thinking and being as expressing and expressed. Accordingly, it establishes the correlation between the determination of thought as individuating difference borne by the intensive thinker, and the determinability of being as differentiated but undifferenciated pre-individual realm. Thus it is the third synthesis of time which accounts for the genesis of ontological sense as that which is expressed in thought,[27] and which relates univocal being directly to its individuating difference as the expressed to its expression. In this regard, it is indissociable from the transcendent exercise of the faculties through which the Idea is generated (Deleuze 1968: 251, 1994: 194).

The third synthesis is the properly ontological synthesis which determines actualization as the different/*c*iation that generates the future
through the division between past and present. Moreover, as actualization of the future, it conditions the actualizations comprised in the past
and the present because it generates the correspondence between
thought and Idea which is already presupposed in them. Thus the third
synthesis not only generates the specifically ontological difference
between two sorts of difference – the extrinsic difference that separates
instants contracted in the present and the intrinsic difference that
separates the contractions of memory – it also brings together what
it separates since it establishes a correspondence between the larval
thought contracted in the present and the Idea embodied in the degrees
of contraction of ontological memory. The 'fracture' of pure and empty
time conjoins thinking and being even as it separates the past and the
present which are retained as degrees of contraction in the Idea: 'For
just as difference is the immediate gathering and articulation of what
it distinguishes, so the fracture retains what it splits, and Ideas also
retain their sundered moments' (Deleuze 1968: 220, 1994: 170 tm).
Accordingly, thinking is never the activity of a constituting consciousness.
Likewise, transcendental synthesis is not anchored in the subject of
representation. Rather, both thinking and the subject of thought are
engendered through the empty form of time that fractures the 'I' which is
supposed to lie at the origin of thinking and correlates it with the larval
consciousness which crystallizes through the contractive contemplation
of pre-individual singularities (the un-differenciated 'groundlessness' of
the Idea):

> It is the empty form of time that introduces and constitutes Difference
> in thought; the difference on the basis of which thought thinks, as
> the difference between the indeterminate and determination. It is the
> empty form of time that distributes along both its sides an I that is frac-
> tured by the abstract line [of time], and a passive self that has emerged
> from the groundlessness which it contemplates. It is the empty form of
> time that engenders thinking in thought, for thinking only thinks with
> difference, orbiting around this point of ungrounding.
> (Deleuze 1968: 354, 1994: 276 tm)

Between the determination of the passive self and the indetermination of the I fractured by the Idea lies the difference generated by
thinking, and it is through the latter that the pure form of time establishes the correlation between expressing intensity and expressed Idea

(Deleuze 1968: 332, 1994: 259). Thus the key distinction (though it remains unstated in Deleuze's text) is that between the specifically onto-logical different/*c*iation carried out by *thinking* and the clear-confused *thought* of the larval subject which expresses that difference. Yet think-ing is an act, precisely 'the most intense or most individual act' (Deleuze 1968: 285, 1994: 221) insofar as it overthrows the identity of the I and the resemblance of the self (Deleuze 1968: 283, 1994: 219).

6.9   The caesura of the act

The act that engenders thinking within thought occurs in the wake of the encounter with intensity (the *cogitandum*) and the transcendent exercise of the faculties. Accordingly, thinking is not the act of a pre-constituted, already individuated psychic agent but rather something that is provoked by intensive difference; it is the effect of a transcendent exercise of the faculties wherein the psyche is folded back into its own field of individuation in such a way as to usurp its specification in the I and its organization in the self (Deleuze 1968: 330, 1994: 257). If think-ing is the most intense and most individual act it is because it precludes the habitual differenciation of psychic singularities into the form of the I and the explication of psychic intensities in the matter of the self, through an act that implicates the psyche back into its own process of individuation. In the act of thinking, claims Deleuze, 'what the self has become equal to is the unequal in itself' – in other words, intensity or intensive individuation as such (Deleuze 1968: 121, 1994: 90). Thinking is the most individual act because it flashes forth as the determination which correlates larval consciousness with pre-individual singularities (or determinate thought and indeterminate Idea) in an individuation that raises up the latter's unconscious, pre-individual depths to shatter the surface of actual consciousness (Deleuze 1968: 197, 1994: 151–2). Thus psychic individuation involves an act in which the intensive realm of pre-individual singularities surfaces within individuated psy-chic actuality, usurping the specification of consciousness in the I and its organization in the self. Thinking is that act wherein the individual becomes adequate to its own individuation by accessing the individu-ating realm of pre-individual singularities and implicated intensities through the fracture of time that splits the I from the self: 'The individ-ual in intensity finds its image neither in the organization of the self nor in the specification of the I but, on the contrary, in the fractured I and the dissolved self [i.e. the larval subject], and in the correlation between the fractured I and the dissolved self' (Deleuze 1968: 332, 1994: 259). In becoming equal to the domain of intensive individuation as the unequal in itself, the thinker becomes 'the universal individual' who affirms eternal recurrence: 'The thinker, doubtless the thinker of eternal recurrence, is the individual, the universal individual' (Deleuze 1968: 327, 1994: 254).

This affirmation of eternal recurrence involves an act of ontological repetition. Bearing in mind Deleuze's dictum that 'repetition is a condition for action before it is a concept of reflection', it is clear that thinking's break with the requirement of reflection and the strictures of representation is inseparable from an act of ontological repetition which 'makes the difference' between the psychic repetition of the past and the physical repetition of the present (Deleuze 1968: 374, 1994: 293). While the actualization established by the synthesis of habit restricts the psychic individual to the repetition of the present, and the actualization brought about by the synthesis of memory confines him to the repetition of the past, the third synthesis involves an actualization through which the psychic individual produces the future according to a repetition of the past which eliminates the latter as repeated condition, and a repetition of the present which eliminates the latter as repeating agent. Between the physical repetition of the past in habit and the psychic repetition of the present in memory comes the ontological repetition which produces the future in the form of a 'repetition of repetition' that determines the difference between these repetitions while eliminating both the past, as the repeated condition of repetition, and the present, as the repeating agent of repetition:

> Repetition now pertains imperatively to repetitions; to modes or types of repetition. Thus the frontier or 'difference' has been singularly displaced; it is no longer between the first time and the others, between the repeated and the repetition, but between these types of repetition. It is repetition itself which is repeated.
>
> (Deleuze 1968: 377, 1994: 295 tm)

It is this act of ontological repetition that produces thinking as a 'caesura' in the order of time, which in turn introduces the fracture of time into thinking: 'It is the caesura, and the before and after which it ordains once and for all which constitute the fracture of the I (the caesura is precisely what gives birth to the fracture)' (Deleuze 1968: 120, 1994: 89 tm). The caesura establishes an order, a totality, and a series of time. It effects an ordination of time that distributes a 'before', a 'during', and an 'after' relative to the act in the simultaneity of a static synthesis which separates time's pure form from its chronologically sequenced empirical content. It determines the totality of time by fixing an image or symbol for the act that configures time as a whole in the static synthesis of the 'before', the 'during', and the 'after' (eternal recurrence is precisely such an image or symbol). Lastly, it establishes the series of time by determining the difference between the repetition founded in the present and the repetition grounded in the past through the act that repeats these repetitions while eliminating the repeated past and the repeating present (Deleuze 1968: 379, 1994: 297).

Thus the caesura effects an ordination which, as Deleuze puts it, throws time out of joint (Deleuze 1968: 119, 1994: 88). Time's joints are those cardinal points which subordinate it to periodic movement according to a measure of succession: 1st, 2nd, 3rd; past, present, future. Moreover, the relation of succession obtains not only between terms in a single series – the 1st, 2nd, 3rd in the 1st series – but also across series – 1st series, 2nd series, 3rd series – as well as between terms in successive series – 1_1, 1_2, 1_3. Thus while time is jointed and subordinated to the number of movement it continues to be articulated according to successive cycles of repetition and coordinated according to relations of intra-cyclic repetition (2 repeats 1, 3 repeats 2, etc.) or inter-cyclic repetition (1_2 repeats 1_1, 2_2 repeats 2_1, etc.). Relations between repeated terms within a series, or between repeating series themselves, are determined in conformity with the strictures of analogy and resemblance. Thus, whether intra-cyclic or inter-cyclic, repetition performed under the aegis of jointed time remains subordinated to identity and hence external to the repeated (Deleuze 1968: 376–7, 1994: 294–5). But in springing time free from its joints, the caesura orders series according to a fixed and static synthesis that is no longer bound by the requirements of representation and the dynamic determinations of time's empirical content. It distributes both terms and series independently of any measure of movement or order of succession, and hence in such a way as to preclude the subsumption of their differences under judgements of analogy or perceptual resemblances. By introducing the fracture of pure time into consciousness, the caesura of thinking establishes time as a structure wherein what is repeated is no longer identity but a repetition that already harbours difference within itself. The past that is repeated is no longer the model for its repetition in the present, and the repeating present is no longer a copy dependent upon what it repeats. Thus the difference established by the caesura is not a difference between past, present, and future understood as the difference between an originary 'first instance' and its successive repetitions (1st, 2nd, 3rd ...) in accordance with a relation of succession in representation, but rather a difference between the repetition that only repeats 'once and for all' and the repetition that repeats an infinity of times for every time. The repetition that only repeats once is eliminated by the repetition which can only repeat what has already been repeated an infinity of times.

The time 'before' the caesura is the condition for the act but a condition whose existence is retroactively determined by the act which it conditions; similarly, the time 'during' which the act occurs serves as its agent, but an agent whose existence is retroactively cancelled by the time which it produces as coming 'after' it:

> The Before and the During are and remain repetitions, but repetitions which only repeat once and for all. It is the third repetition which distributes them in accordance with the straight line of time, but which also eliminates them, determining them to operate only once and for all and keeping the 'all times' for the third time alone [...] The frontier is no longer between a first time and the repetition that it renders hypothetically possible, but between the conditional repetitions and the third repetition or *repetition in the eternal return*, which renders the return of the other two impossible [...] As we have seen, the condition of the action by default does not return; the condition of the agent by metamorphosis does not return; what alone returns is the *unconditioned* in the product as eternal return.
>
> (Deleuze 1968: 379–80, 1994: 297 tm)

Thus what the affirmation of eternal recurrence eliminates is the repetition of the identical, while what it produces is the future as the 'unconditioned'; the instance of absolute novelty which Deleuze explicitly associates with works of art (Deleuze 1968: 374–5, 1994: 293) as simulacra or 'systems wherein the different relates to the different through difference itself' (Deleuze 1968: 383, 1994: 299 tm). The caesura of time effects a selection wherein repetition in intensity and differentiation in the Idea are separated from the repetition of habit and the difference in the concept. It marks the point at which difference in itself is repeated for itself. The future as unconditioned or absolute novelty emerges through the fracture of time that allows individuation to rise up to the surface of consciousness in the gap between its specific form and its organized matter. But it is the caesura that generates this fracture in consciousness and hence the act of the thinker that produces the new. Thus it seems that the act through which consciousness is fractured by the form of time in such a way as to introduce novelty into being is a peculiar privilege of complex psychic systems. Only consciousness can be folded back into its own pre-individual dimension; only the psychic individual can become equal to its own intensive individuation. Ultimately, it is the thinker – the philosopher-artist – who is the 'universal individual'.

6.10   The two faces of death

In this regard, the psychic individuation which occurs in the caesura of thinking is intimately connected to an experience of dying which remains irreducible to bio-physical death. For there are two deaths: one, external and extensive; the other, internal and intensive. The former is defined as 'the disappearance of the person and the cancellation of the difference represented by the I and the self' (Deleuze 1968: 149, 1994: 113 tm), or more fundamentally, as 'the living's quantitative and qualitative return to inanimate matter', whose definition is merely 'extrinsic, scientific, and objective' (Deleuze 1968: 147, 1994: 111 tm). But the latter is defined as 'the state of individual differences when they are no longer subjected to the form imposed upon them by the I or self and when they develop in a figure which excludes my own coherence along with that of any identity whatsoever' (Deleuze 1968: 149, 1994: 113 tm). This death is never 'my' death but the anonymous experience of dying in which 'one dies'; it is the death which is no-one's since it coincides with the surfacing of pre-individual singularities in the Idea and impersonal individuations in intensity through the fracture of time within the psyche. Here Deleuze refers approvingly to Blanchot's inversion of Heidegger: where death remains a personal possibility, dying is the impossibility of personal possibility wherein the self is disintegrated into an anonymous pre-individual realm (Deleuze 1968: 148–9, 1994: 112–13).[28] Yet for Deleuze, unlike Blanchot, it is precisely insofar as this pre-individual realm remains the true locus of individuation that its emergence within the psyche coincides with the latter's maximal individuation. In this regard, dying is 'individuation, a protest by the individual who has never recognized himself within the limits of the Self and the I, even when these are universal' (Deleuze 1968: 333, 1994: 259 tm). The 'one' who dies in the scission between the fractured I and the passive self is the thinker as universal individual.

Thus Deleuze contrasts the death which emerges from within the psyche as the maximization of difference through the fracture of time to the death which arrives from the physical realm as the minimization of difference through its explication in extensity. Where the former represents the apex of intensive individuation, the latter represents the nadir of extensive in-differentiation. Thus 'every death is double through the cancellation of the big difference it represents in extension; and through the swarming and the liberation of the little differences that it implicates in extensity' (Deleuze 1968: 333, 1994: 259 tm). But it is intensive death that harbours the veritable face of the 'death-instinct', which *pace* Freud, is not to be understood in terms of a compulsion to return to the inorganic, but rather as the maximal potentiation of the difference between intensive differentiation and extensive de-differentiation, or mind and matter. For Deleuze, far from being an expression of the compulsion to return to the inorganic, the death-instinct testifies to everything that renders psychic 'life' irreducible to its physical envelope. The death-instinct is not a function of inorganic compulsion but of the act of thinking which 'makes the difference' between repetition in intensity and repetition in extensity, thereby rendering clothed psychic repetition definitively irreducible to bare material repetition. It is inextricably linked with the affirmation of recurrence precisely insofar as it 'promises and implies "once and for all" the death of that which is one' (Deleuze 1968: 152, 1994: 115 tm). Accordingly, the death-instinct which finds expression in the affirmation of eternal recurrence is precisely a function of negentropic time; the pure time in which only difference is repeated: 'The time which is empty and out of joint, with its rigorous formal and static order, its crushing totality, and its irreversible series, is precisely the death-instinct' (Deleuze 1968: 147, 1994: 111 tm).

Ultimately, the caesura of thinking, the fracture of time, the affirmation of recurrence, and the experience of death through which the psychic individual becomes re-implicated in individuation, all point towards a fundamental ontological conversion wherein consciousness frees itself from the strictures of representation to become the catalyst for the eternal repetition of difference-in-itself. For it is through the caesura of thinking that the implication of intensity is finally prised free from its explication in extensity and intensive difference finally becomes liberated from extensive repetition. Moreover, the ontological selection effected in and through the act of thinking cannot be confined to the life of the psyche, for given Deleuze's claim that 'every thing thinks and is a thought', together with his account of the fundamental role of the third synthesis in determining the correlation between expressing thought and expressed Idea, it is clear that the caesura cannot but affect all three dimensions of actualization – physical, temporal, psychical – thereby implying not only a transformation in the life of the psychic individual but also a metamorphosis in nature itself.

6.11   The fusion of mind and nature

We have seen how Deleuze carefully distinguishes between physical, temporal, and psychic layers of actualization. But he also distinguishes between physical, biological, and psychical systems in terms of the distinct orders of differentiation in the Ideas which they incarnate; their distinct rates of individuation – 'all at once and only at their boundaries for physical systems, while the biological system receives successive influxes of singularities and involve its entire internal milieu in the operations which occur at its outer limits' (Deleuze 1968: 328, 1994: 255 tm) – and by the different figures through which differenciation occurs in them: qualification and partitioning in physical systems, specification and organization in biological and psychic systems (Deleuze 1968: 328, 1994: 255). All actualization entails a double cancellation of difference: first in the explication of intensity, then in the disintegration or death of an actual physical or biological system. The first corresponds to the annulment of differentiation as productive difference, the second to the effacement of differenciation as produced difference. Thus actuality testifies to the governing role of explication as an entropic principle directing this cancellation of producing and produced difference. Nevertheless, Deleuze insists, explication as entropic principle cannot account either for the conditions of production of the actual or for the differenciation it exhibits. Although it explains everything, it accounts for nothing. Certainly, it enjoys an empirical validity insofar as it governs the functioning of a qualified extensive domain; but it is intensive difference which creates that domain and which accounts for the fact that explication holds sway in it. Explication is the empirical principle upon which actual extensity is founded; but intensive difference is the transcendental principle which provides the ground for that foundation insofar as it creates the extensive domain and generates the conditions in accordance with which the empirical principle governs it (Deleuze 1968: 310, 1994: 241). Intensive difference as transcendental principle does not govern any domain, it remains implicated in itself beyond the purview of any empirical principle as that which grounds the latter and generates their domains of application. Thus beneath the laws of nature catalogued by the natural sciences lies the depth of intensive difference as transcendental *spatium*. Accordingly, 'at the same time as the laws of nature govern the surface of the world, the eternal return ceaselessly rumbles in this other dimension, that of the transcendental or of the volcanic *spatium*' (Deleuze 1968: 311, 1994: 241 tm). Consequently, far from being a law of nature, 'the eternal return unfolds in a depth or depthlessness wherein originary nature resides in its chaos, beyond the jurisdictions and laws which are only constitutive of second nature' (Deleuze 1968: 312, 1994: 242–3 tm). Thus the 'universal ungrounding' unleashed by the eternal return cannot be confined to the psychic domain as the transfiguration of consciousness wherein mind throws off the shackles of representation; it points to a fundamental metamorphosis in nature whereby the intensive depths rise up to engulf the surface of extensity and dissolve all empirical laws and jurisdictions. However, this claim seems to harbour the fantastic implication that physical qualification and partitioning, as well as biological specification and organization, can simply be eliminated through an act of thinking. In an attempt to stave off this unwanted implication, Deleuze distinguishes between two states of quality and extensity:

> One in which quality flashes forth as a sign in the distance or interval of a difference in intensity; the other in which quality is an effect which already reacts against its cause and tends to cancel difference. One in which extensity remains implicated in the enveloping order of differences; the other in which extensity explains the difference and cancels it in the qualified system. This distinction, which cannot be effectuated in experience, becomes possible from the viewpoint of the thinking of the eternal return.
>
> (Deleuze 1968: 314, 1994: 243–4 tm)

Moreover, by transfiguring qualities into 'pure signs' and retaining of extensity only what remains implicated in the originary depth of the *spatium*, the eternal return promises to bring forth

> Qualities which are more beautiful, colours more brilliant, stones more precious, extensions more vibrant; because, being reduced to their seminal reasons and having broken with every relation to the negative, they shall remain forever affixed onto the intensive space of positive differences – then Plato's final prediction in the *Phaedo* shall be realized; the one in which he promised to the sensibility which has been freed from its empirical exercise temples, stars, and gods which have never been seen; unheard of affirmations.
>
> (Deleuze 1968: 314, 1994: 244 tm)

Beauty, brilliance, preciousness, and vibrancy are aesthetic rather than cognitive qualifications. The transfiguration envisaged here betrays the perspective of a transcendental aestheticism. The selection operated by the caesura of thinking in the eternal return overthrows the sovereignty of identity in representation and the jurisdiction of explication in actuality the better to affirm the point of convergence between the dialectic of ideas and the aesthetic of intensities, thereby reuniting a purified thought and a refined sensibility. What Deleuze refers to above as a 'sign' is obviously neither an object of recognition nor a particular property of an object, but rather the intensive noumenon as *sentendium* which gives rise to the *cogitandum* in the transcendent exercise of the faculties.[29] Similarly, to grasp extensity insofar as it remains implicated in the intensity which envelops it is to reach beyond the given to the intensive difference through which the given is produced. Again, this is only possible through the transcendent exercise of the faculties. Thus, by Deleuze's own admission, the distinction between the two states of quality and extensity – quality as differenciated property and quality as intensive sign; extensity as explicated difference and intensity as implicated in difference – are a function of the transcendent exercise of the faculties generated by the act of thinking. But these distinctions, which seemed designed to stave off the implication that the subversion of identity in representation entails the collapse of differenciation in actuality, suggest that it is only from the perspective of a purified thought and a refined sensibility that intensive nature is liberated from the double cancellation of difference entailed by the empirical principle of explication. This renders the precise ontological status of differenciation in actuality, whether of physical parts and qualities, or of biological species and organs, profoundly ambiguous. On the one hand, Deleuze's text strongly suggests that these are objectively 'real' physical phenomena, empirically founded by the principle of explication and transcendentally grounded by difference in intensity. Yet at the same time, Deleuze's distinction between the two 'states' of quality and extensity implies that the empirical law of explication which governs these phenomena ceases to be binding for the thought that has been purified and the sensibility that has been refined through the transcendent exercise of the faculties. Thus it is the transcendent exercise of the faculties which guarantees the coincidence between the overthrowing of representation in the psyche and the ungrounding through which intensive nature casts off the yoke of explication. But if it is the transcendent exercise of the faculties which guarantees the juncture between psychic individuation and intensive nature, then contrary to the aforementioned 'realist' account of differenciation, the implication seems to be that the empirical reality of explication is merely a function of representation, and hence that its founding role for empirical experience collapses along with the subversion of identity in representation. And indeed, it is because of Deleuze's empiricist emphasis on the primacy of experience that the transcendent exercise of the faculties must play this mediating role between ideality and sensibility as that which links a transformation in the psyche with a metamorphosis in nature. Thus the underlying premise for this convergence between the subversion of identity in representation and the usurping of explication in nature is provided by Deleuze's empiricist substitution of 'concrete' (sub-representational) conditions of experience for 'abstract' (epistemological) conditions of reality. Deleuze commends empiricism for starting 'in the middle' and remaining within the concrete, rather than invoking conceptual oppositions between abstract principles in order to explain the concrete.[30] Moreover, it is precisely insofar as the bounds of actual experience are porous and metamorphic, extending all the way from organic habit to psychic act, that experience refuses to conform to the categorial structures of representation or the intentional schemas of phenomenology. Accordingly, the primary datum in *Difference and Repetition* is a field of experience that is neither subsumed under the form of the object of recognition nor co-ordinated by a knowing subject. Deleuze plunges into the sub-representational dimension of experience that subsists beneath the abstractions of knower and known, subject and object, to excavate the passive syntheses which generate the receptivity of sensibility, the activity of consciousness, and the empirical congruence between the differenciation of actuality and the categories of representation. At the same time, he ascends beyond the merely given differences in actual experience to explore their genesis in the dimension of transcendental synthesis that implicates the ideal within the sensible. Thus, it is because 'experience' is the mediating term between the dialectic of ideas and the aesthetic of intensities – between the psychic and the physical – that the principle of explication which is eliminated by the transformation in thought and sensibility is not an 'objective' aspect of bio-physical reality but rather an empirical dimension of experience. Since the latter is generated by transcendental synthesis, it can be reconfigured by it.

Consequently, Deleuze's empiricism rules out any 'realist' interpretation of his account of physico-biological extensity. But it also leaves his account of the scope of the ontological selection performed in the eternal return equivocating between transcendental and absolute idealism. The selection can be construed in transcendental terms as applying to our experience of things, rather to things in themselves. According to this interpretation, the selection merely eliminates the representation of physical parts and qualities, and of biological species and organs, within experience, rather than the actual parts and qualities of physical systems or the actual species and organs of biological systems. But this implies that physico-biological extensity as described by the natural sciences, along with the principle of explication, is a transcendental illusion generated by representation to occlude the chaos of the intensive *spatium*. Moreover, it seems to invite the correlationist conclusion that phenomena such as the physical qualification and partitioning that occurred during the accretion of the earth, or the biological specification and organization that occurs in embryogenesis, have no reality independently of representation. Yet though Deleuze's text does not preclude such an interpretation, the decisive role ascribed to the transcendent exercise of the faculties in effecting thought's conversion from representation to production seems to point towards an absolutist construal of the scope of selection. Accordingly, if the latter is construed in absolute rather than merely relative terms, then it must be understood as effecting an elimination of differenciation in actuality, rather than in representation, precisely insofar as the caesura of thinking fuses intensive thought with noumenal nature. It is by virtue of this fusion that intensive signs can be definitively separated from extensive qualities, and implicated extensity finally divorced from explicated intensity. But if this is the veritable ontological scope of the third synthesis, it is only possible insofar as the correlation between intensity and Idea, and hence the conditions under which being relates to its individuating differences, is ultimately determined by the caesura of thinking in the third synthesis. In this regard, the determining role allotted to thinking in absolutizing the correlation between ideality and sensibility is characteristic of absolute idealism.

Thus, underlying the empirical correspondence between identity in representation and differenciation in actual experience is the absolute correlation between intensive thinking and noumenal nature in the transcendent exercise of the faculties.[31] The first synthesis establishes the conditions for the sub-representational experience of actuality, the second establishes the conditions for the representation of actuality in consciousness, but the third synthesis releases experience from the yoke of representation in the conjunction between the caesura of thinking and the ungrounding of extensity. Accordingly, the third synthesis brings about a fusion of the psychic and the physical beyond the adjudications of representation and the legislatures of explication. It releases intensive generation from the fetters of physical degeneration by re-implicating its individuating differences back into the pre-individual realm through the fracture of time in the psyche. Psychic life escapes from the entropic domain of physical death through an experience of dying whereby it becomes a medium for pre-individual singularities in the Idea and impersonal individuations in intensity:

> Such is the world of the 'ONE' or the 'they'; a world which cannot be assimilated to that of everyday banality, but on the contrary, one wherein encounters and resonances unfold; the ultimate face of Dionysus and the true nature of the depth and groundlessness which overflows representation and brings forth simulacra.
>
> (Deleuze 1968: 355, 1994: 277 tm)

6.12   The expression of complexity

Physical, biological, and psychic systems are not only distinguished by the order of Ideas incarnated in them, their rates of individuation, and their figures of actualization. They are also distinguished by the fact that they express increasing degrees of complexity. Deleuze defines the latter in terms of what he calls the 'values of implication' or 'centres of envelopment' present within a system as it undergoes individuation and actualization (Deleuze 1968: 329, 1994: 255). These centres of envelopment 'are not the intensive individuating factors themselves, but their representatives within a complex system in the process of its explication' (Deleuze 1968: 329, 1994: 256 tm). They have three characteristics. First, they are signs, flashing between two series of difference in intensity, the latter constituting the 'signal system' which generates the sign (Deleuze 1968: 286–7, 1994: 222). Second, they express the sense of the Idea incarnated in the system. And third, insofar as they envelop intensity without explicating it, these centres testify to local increases in negentropy, defying the empirical law of entropic explication. Thus what distinguishes complex systems is their incorporation of individuating differences: though the latter are never directly expressed in the extensity whose actualization they determine and in which they are partially explicated, they are enveloped within it insofar as they subsist in a state of implication in signal-sign systems. These constitute the centres of envelopment for intensive difference within an extensive system, or as Deleuze puts it, the phenomenon closest to the intensive noumenon (Deleuze 1968: 329, 1994: 256).

Accordingly, the complexity of a system in extensity can be measured by the extent to which its individuating factors become discretely segregated from the pre-individual continuum and incorporated within it as signal-sign systems. Where the intensive factors that individuate physical extensity remain extrinsic to the latter, so that the physical qualification and partitioning of a system occurs 'all at once' and only at its edges, those that individuate biological systems are enveloped within the organism (as genetic factors for instance) so that the specification and organization of the latter occurs in successive stages, through influxes of singularities involving dynamic interaction between the organism's internal milieu and its external environment.[32] Thus, Deleuze concludes, 'the living pays witness to another order; one that is heterogeneous and of another dimension – as though its individuating factors or atoms considered individually according to their power of mutual communication and fluent instability, benefited from a superior degree of expression in it' (Deleuze 1968: 329, 1994: 255 tm). For Deleuze, the intensive factors enveloped in living organisms enjoy a 'superior degree of expression' because their biological incorporation implicates them in extensity without exhaustively explicating them. Centres of envelopment harbour an un-explicated residue of implicated intensity. Consequently, Deleuze considers the complexity exhibited by the living to be fundamentally 'heterogeneous' to the inorganic precisely insofar as the former 'expresses' intensity to a higher degree than does the latter. Here as throughout *Difference and Repetition*, Deleuze's use of the term 'expression' is quite specific. 'Expression' is explicitly defined as 'that relation which essentially comprises a torsion between an expressor and an expressed, such that the expressed does not exist apart from the expressor, even though the latter relates to the former as to something entirely other than it' (Deleuze 1968: 334, 1994: 260 tm). As we have seen, the expressive torsion between expressor and expressed is articulated in the correlation between individuating intensity and pre-individual Idea generated through the fracture of time. More precisely, the ontologically 'expressive' relation between univocal being and its individuating differences is a function of the correlation between intensity in sensation and sense in ideation which is effectuated through the caesura of thinking. Thus the 'expression' of intensive difference provides the obverse to its 'explication': where the latter corresponds to its degree of dilation in physical space, the former corresponds to its degree of contraction in psychic time. Accordingly, only in the psychic dimension does the expressive relation between sensible repetition and ideal difference attain its consummate realization. It is in the psyche, and in psychic individuation more particularly, that intensive difference achieves its fullest expression. The psychic realm not only represents an exponential increase in complexity vis-à-vis the domain of the living but rather the definitive potentiation of intensive difference precisely insofar as it is in psychic individuation – as exemplified by the third synthesis and the caesura of thinking – that the expressing becomes commensurate with the expressed. As we know, Deleuze explicitly identifies the act of thinking with the experience of intensive death or dying. In dying, the factors of psychic individuation are enveloped in the structure of 'the other' (*autrui*). It is the a priori other, the psychic individual who is no longer representable as another I in analogy with me or as another self in resemblance with mine, who emerges as the centre of envelopment for psychic intensities in the split between the fractured I and the passive self (Deleuze 1968: 335, 1994: 261). This a priori other is defined solely by its expressive value as enveloping intensity: 'This is why, in order to grasp the other as such, we were entitled to demand very specific conditions of experience, no matter how artificial; namely, the moment wherein the expressed does not yet have any existence independently of that which expresses it – the Other as *expression of a possible world*' (Deleuze 1968: 335, italics in original, 1994: 260–1 tm). The other envelops pre-individual singularities and the psyche's expression of the other in the experience of dying marks the point at which the expressor becomes fully adequate to the expressed; the point at which the expressed is enveloped in an expression that has been purified of its explicative aspect. Far from being abstracted from actuality in representation, the 'possible world' expressed by the other is a sheer virtuality; an intensive sign existing purely in a state of implication or envelopment within the other.[33] Dying expresses this virtuality enveloped by the other without explicating it. The death indexed by the other in me is no longer represented as the dissolution of my I or self but experienced as the emergence within the psyche of the intensive individual who is 'no-one'. Yet it is through the anonymity of dying that expression finally becomes commensurate with the expressed. In dying through the other, the expressed Idea is enveloped in expressive thought while at the same time thought is re-implicated back into the pre-individual dimension of the Idea. Thus the correlation between thought and Idea is no longer subject to physical or biological explication but is folded back into the psychic dimension that originally generated it. Where the sensible and the ideal had been extrinsically correlated via the act of thinking that determines physico-biological actualization, they are now reciprocally enveloped in the expression of thinking as adequation between expressing intensity and expressed Idea. Far from signalling the disintegration of the psyche or testifying to the sovereignty of physical entropy, the experience of dying defies the law of entropic explication governing physico-biological extensity and marks the apex of psychic life as vector of negentropic complexification.[34]

6.13   The life of the mind

For Deleuze then, the manifestation of the 'death-instinct' in the psyche testifies to an act of thinking generated through the transcendent exercise of the faculties. The death-instinct gives rise to an act of onto-logical repetition (the dice-throw as affirmation of recurrence) whereby the psychic expression of difference is definitively emancipated from its bio-physical explication. Like Heidegger, Deleuze sees in a certain experience of death the fundamental locus for the relation between time and ontological difference. Heidegger stipulates *Dasein*'s ontological transcendence as condition of access to entities in the world, but the pure potentiality 'to be' (*Seinkönnen*) exhibited in *Dasein*'s transcendence only becomes fully potentiated through the resolute anticipation of being-towards-death: time is temporalized through *Dasein*'s appropriation of death. Similarly, for Deleuze, time as ontological differentiation is likewise potentiated through the act of thinking that engenders the affirmation of intensive death. Yet unlike Heidegger, it seems that for Deleuze the act of thinking resulting from the transcendent exercise of the faculties emerges from a more rudimentary level of physico-biological repetition. However, though the expression of intensive difference concomitant with ontological repetition emerges from bio-physical repetition as a result of the transcendent exercise of cognitive faculties possessing a well specified empirical function, there is a sense in which this maximal psychic repetition of difference is already latent in the habitual repetitions carried out by the larval subjects of passive synthesis. Thus although ontological repetition arises out of bio-physical repetition, it ultimately eliminates its bio-physical basis by bringing about a definitive separation between bio-physical explication and the psychic expression of difference. Once again, it is Deleuze's empiricist appeal to the primacy of 'experience' that provides the rationale for this separation between entropic explication and negentropic expression in the third synthesis.

We have seen how, instead of presupposing consciousness as a unitary locus of experience, Deleuze atomizes it into a multiplicity of larval subjects. In so doing, not only does he render an elementary form of consciousness ontologically ubiquitous, thereby endorsing a variety of panpsychism, he also injects intensive duration into physical extensity by making the psychic contraction of difference into the precondition for spatial repetition. Though intensity is implicated in space, its nature is essentially temporal as the multiplicity which cannot divide without changing in nature.[35] Thus Deleuze finesses the Bergsonian dualism of temporal heterogeneity and spatial homogeneity by implicating the former at the heart of the latter in the shape of elementary psychic syntheses which precede constituted individual organisms as well as the individuated subject of consciousness. The claim that intensive difference originates in an elementary form of psychic contraction is the crucial empiricist premise (derived from Deleuze's reading of Hume) which will allow Deleuze to attribute a transcendental function to time understood as intensive difference and to construe the latter as the precondition for space construed as extensive repetition:

> In each instance, material repetition is the result of a more profound repetition which unfolds in depth and produces it as a result, like an external envelope or a detachable shell, but one which loses all its sense and all its capacity to reproduce itself once it is no longer animated by its *cause* or by the other repetition. Thus it is the clothed that lies beneath the naked, and that produces or excretes it as the effect of its secretion.
>
> (Deleuze 1968: 370, 1994: 289 tm)

The repetition which unfolds in depth is the intensive repetition between the virtually coexisting degrees of difference in ontological memory. Thus the clothed or intensive repetition of duration inhabits bare or physical repetition as its enabling condition. Accordingly, it is the empiricist premise that time implies the psychic registration of difference, and hence that temporal difference is a function of psychic contraction, that provides the precondition for the transcendental claim according to which the intensive noumenon furnishes the sufficient reason for the extensive phenomenon. Consequently, it seems at least initially that the vitalism which Deleuze will quietly but unequivocally endorse towards the close of *Difference and Repetition* – 'the living bears witness to another order, to a heterogeneous order, and to another dimension' – follows from a panpsychism which is rooted in a form of radical empiricism.

Yet there is a fundamental ambiguity concerning the relation between the organic and the psychic in *Difference and Repetition*. On one hand, Deleuze seems to attribute a fundamental status to the larval thinker as 'universal' intensive individual and to thought itself as ultimate individuating factor: 'every body, every thing thinks and is a thought insofar as, reduced to its intensive reasons, it expresses an Idea whose actualization it determines' (Deleuze 1968: 327, 1994: 254 tm). To reduce something to its 'intensive reasons' is to reduce it to its constituting spatio-temporal dynamisms, of which the larval subject is at once the patient and the agent whose individuating thought catalyzes the actualization of Ideas (Deleuze 1968: 156, 1994: 118–19). Assuming that not every body or every thing is organic, this would then imply the absolute ubiquity of larval subjectivity and hence the existence of passive syntheses proper to the inorganic realm. Yet this does not seem to be the case, for all the textual evidence indicates that the passive syntheses executed by larval subjectivity are peculiar to the organic domain. Consider the following three passages:

[I]in the order of constituting passivity, perceptual syntheses refer back to organic syntheses as to the sensibility of the senses, to a primary sensibility which we are. We are made of contracted water, earth, and light, not only prior to recognizing or representing them, but prior to perceiving them. Every organism is, in its receptive and perceptual elements, but also in its viscera, is a sum of contractions, retentions, expectations.

(Deleuze 1968: 99, 1994: 73 tm)

What organism is not made up of elements and cases of repetition, of contemplated and contracted water, nitrogen, carbon, chlorides and sulphates, thereby intertwining all the habits of which it is composed? Organisms awake to the sublime words of the third *Ennead*: all is contemplation!

(Deleuze 1968: 102, 1994: 75)

A soul must be attributed to the heart, to the muscles, nerves and cells, but a contemplative soul whose entire function is to contract a habit. This is no mystical or barbarous hypothesis. On the contrary, habit here manifests its full generality: it concerns not only the sensory-motor habits that we have (psychologically), but also, before these, the primary habits that we are; the thousands of passive syntheses of which we are organically composed [...]
Underneath the self which acts are little selves which contemplate and which render possible both the action and the active subject. We speak of our 'self' only in virtue of these thousands of little witnesses

which contemplate within us: it is always a third-party who says 'me'. These contemplative souls must be assigned even to the rat in the labyrinth and to each muscle of the rat.

(Deleuze 1968: 101–3, 1994: 74–5 tm)

These and other similar passages which constantly reiterate the intimate connection between larval subjectivity and the organic domain strongly suggest that Deleuze's claims concerning the necessary role of passive synthesis in the constitution of the present, and of larval subjectivity in individuation, point not towards their ubiquity across the organic and inorganic realms, but rather towards the much stronger vitalist thesis that it is insofar as everything is ultimately organic and/or 'living' in some suitably enlarged sense that everything 'thinks' in some equally expanded sense. Despite initial appearances, Deleuze does not anchor his endorsement of vitalism in panpsychism; his assertion of panpsychism is rooted in his commitment to vitalism. Deleuze's claim is not, contrary to what one might expect, that some minimal form of consciousness is implicated even in the inorganic realm, and that this provides the precondition for the emergence of organic sentience, the latter being understood as a complexification of this more primitive inorganic 'prehension' (of the sort envisaged by panpsychists like Whitehead and, more recently, David Chalmers).[36] Rather, Deleuze seems to assert (1) that a primitive form of organic time-sentience, understood as the psychic expression of temporal difference – as effectuated in the correlation between thought and Idea – provides the precondition for the actual *experience* of individuated extensity, where 'actual experience' is understood as simultaneously comprising an unconscious or sub-representational level and a conscious or representational level, and 'individuated extensity' is construed in terms of the physico-biological explication of intensity; and (2) that the psychic expression of temporal difference concomitant with this time-sentience only attains its ultimate ontological dignity in a specifically psychic dimension of individuation. Within this continuum of experience that runs from the sub- representational to the representational level, organic contraction provides the originary juncture between the virtual dimension of the pre-individual and the actual realm of constituted individuals. Thus the contraction of habit yields the originary organic synthesis from which the two divergent continua of empiria – i.e. ideality and sensibility – derive. More precisely, given the two diagonal axes around which *Difference and Repetition* is structured, ideal-sensible and virtual-actual, organic contraction marks the point of inception of difference in experience from which these two diagonals originally diverge before ultimately converging again in the ontological repetition which generates the transcendental difference that splits experience by separating psychic expression from physical explication.

Nevertheless, Deleuze's insistence on casting psychic expression as the sufficient reason for physical explication puts him in a position where he is constantly equivocating between the claim that he is providing an account of the genesis of actual experience and the claim that he is giving an account of the genesis of actuality *tout court*. The two are not coextensive. In response to Deleuze's claims that the synthesis of the present (organic contraction) constitutes extensity in actual experience, and that the psychic expression of difference determines the physical as well as the biological actualization of Ideas, it is necessary to point out that, for all its much vaunted audacity, Deleuze's excavation of the sub-representational and unconscious dimensions of experience still leaves vast tracts of actual reality completely unaccounted for. For even if organisms are composed of contracted water, nitrogen, carbon, chloride, and sulphates, these elements are not themselves composed of organic contractions – thus the neutrinos, photons, gluons, bosons, and muons which compose physical space-time cannot plausibly be construed as contractions of organic habit. Nor can galaxies, gravitational fields, or dark matter. Whatever their ultimate ontological status – whether they are patronized as useful idealizations or admitted as indispensable constituents of actuality – these are precisely the sorts of physical entity that cannot but be ignored by the empiricist bias of Deleuze's account of the constitution of space and time. It might be objected that these and other supposedly 'theoretical' entities do enjoy a real generative status for Deleuze as the ideal components of virtual multiplicities.[37] But the only reason for confining them to the domain of ideality – unlike the heart, muscles, nerves, and cells to which Deleuze ascribes a privileged role as loci of passive syntheses – is the empiricist prejudice that insists on contrasting the putative 'concretion' of experience to the abstraction of cognitive representation. Deleuze radicalizes empiricism, widening the ambit of actual experience to include sub-representational and unconscious depths; nevertheless, it is precisely the assumption that experience invariably comprises 'more' than whatever can be cognitively represented and the ensuing contrast between conceptual abstraction and perceptual concretion that encourages him to include muscles and water within the ambit of actual experience, but not galaxies and electrons. It is because the actual extensity whose genesis Deleuze attributes to the operations of passive synthesis has been circumscribed as a domain of experience, and hence necessarily tethered to the organic, that the muscles of rats are deemed more appropriate sites for the larval subjects of spatio-temporal dynamisms than are electrons. And it is Deleuze's empiricist bias towards the genesis of actuality as constituted in experience that explains his restriction of the ambit of passive synthesis to differences that can be organically registered. In this regard, it is important to note how the autonomy Deleuze attributes to the realm of ideality as virtual reservoir of pre-individual singularities is nevertheless anchored in the empiricist claim that temporal difference presupposes psychic contraction and that contraction requires an organic substrate. For it is the organic contraction effected by the larval subject that is responsible for the expression of the Idea: 'Larvae bear Ideas in their flesh, while we are still at the stage of the representations of the concept' (Deleuze 1968: 283, 1994: 219 tm). The speculative audacity with which Deleuze upholds the rights of virtual ideality should not blind us to the curiously conservative nature of this empiricist premise.

Ultimately, the vitalism which is endorsed at the close of *Difference and Repetition* is indissociable from the empiricism which is embraced at its opening, and the epistemological shortcomings of the latter are aggravated rather than ameliorated by the considerable conceptual ingenuity displayed in pursuing the ontological ramifications of the former. Vitalism may or may not be compatible with physics, but it behoves the vitalist to make at least some sort of attempt to reconcile them. Yet although discussions of biology abound in *Difference and Repetition* – notably developmental biology – physics is conspicuously underrepresented, and where it is invoked, albeit metonymically in the form of thermodynamics, this is only in order to be lambasted for consecrating entropy. Moreover, Deleuze's characterization of entropy as a transcendental illusion presupposes his account of the implication of intensive difference through the synthesis of memory – it is the latter which implicates time as uncancellable difference in actual extensity. But this is based on an account of time as duration which remains vitiated by the empiricist premise that insists on locating the constituting syntheses of time and space at the juncture between the organic and psychic realms.

In the absence of any physicalist corrective to vitalist hubris, biocentrism leads infallibly to noocentrism. Physical qualification and partitioning is determined by the correlation between intensity and Idea, larval thought and ontological memory. Thus Deleuze's account of spatio-temporal synthesis begins by ascribing a privileged role to organic contraction in the 1st synthesis of the present, proceeds to transcendentalize memory as cosmic unconscious in the 2nd synthesis of the past, and ends by turning a form of psychic individuation which is as yet the exclusive prerogative of homo sapiens into the fundamental generator of ontological novelty in the 3rd synthesis of the future. Matter is relegated to 'a dream of the mind' whose representation in extensity presupposes its animation by a temporal difference that generates inanimate extensity as its blockage. The empiricist premise that the life of thought must already be implicated in insensate matter insofar as the latter is *experienced* underlies Deleuze's vitalist claim that physical space-time harbours an impetus towards complexification belying the reign of entropy in actuality. The contrast with which Deleuze presents us, between actuality as an entropic junkyard yoked beneath the iron collar of representation, and an actuality transformed into an inexhaustible reservoir of ontological novelty as the result of what effectively amounts to an idealization of matter, continues to assume that the experience of time is irreducible to the objectifying representation of space. As we saw in Chapter 1, this assumption seems to be grounded in the conviction that first-person experience, in both its conscious and unconscious aspects, cannot as a matter of principle be integrated into the third-person perspective of scientific objectification. This is one of the abiding intuitions that fuels correlationism, whose ontologization of temporal difference remains complicit with the denial of the autonomy of absolute time. Nevertheless, the latter cannot be subsumed within duration by positing a synthesis of space and time that continues to ascribe an unalloyed privilege to the experience of time.

Deleuze palliates the Bergsonian dichotomy of space and time, quantity and quality, at the cost of reabsorbing the former into the latter in what ultimately amounts to an idealist monism. Psychic individuation in the act of thinking defines the point at which experience is transected by pre-individual singularities in the Idea and impersonal individuations in sensibility. Hence, in a peculiar echo of Heidegger, the psychic experience of dying marks the moment wherein time, i.e. being, is folded back into itself. Transcendental access to the sense of being is internalized within experience through the transcendent exercise of the faculties that generates Ideas as the *intensional* correlates of larval thought (albeit a 'sense' which is indissociable from non-sense).[38] As we have seen, it is the transcendent operation of the faculties, provoked by the encounter with individuating intensity as the unthinkable proper to thought, which gives birth to the act of thinking through which the Idea is generated:

> It is nevertheless true that Ideas have a very special relationship to pure thought [...] The para-sense or violence which is transmitted from one faculty to another according to an order assigns a particular place to thought: thought is determined such that it grasps its own *cogitandum* only at the extremity of the fuse of violence which, from one Idea to another, first sets in motion sensibility and its *sentendium*, and so on. This extremity might just as well be regarded as the ultimate origin of Ideas. In what sense, however, should we understand 'ultimate origin'? In the same sense in which Ideas must be called 'differentials' of thought, or the 'Unconscious' of pure thought, at the very moment when thought's opposition to all forms of common-sense remains stronger than ever. Ideas, therefore, are related not to a Cogito which functions as ground or as a proposition of consciousness, but to the fractured I of a dissolved Cogito; in other words, to the universal *ungrounding* which characterizes thought as a faculty in its transcendent exercise.
>
> (Deleuze 1968: 251, 1994: 195 tm)

Thus the Idea in which the sense of being is expressed is the unconscious of pure thought understood as ontological memory. The double genesis of thought and being in the encounter with intensity which gives rise to the act of thinking produces the divergent lines of actualization in the real according to the distinct senses in which thinking expresses being: 'The attributes effectively operate as qualitatively different senses, which relate back to substance as to a single designated; and this substance in turn operates as an ontologically unified sense relative to the modes which express it, and which subsist within it as individuating factors or inherent intense degrees' (Deleuze 1968: 59, 1994: 40 tm). Thus Ideas have an attributive status as expressed in actualization, yet ideal sense is generated by the act of thinking. Deleuze uses Bergson to reconcile Kant's discovery of the transcendental status of time with Spinoza's monism. While Spinoza cannot deduce the number and nature of fundamental differences in substance, which he calls 'attributes', Kant deduces these differences, which he calls 'categories', by de-substantializing them and yoking them to representation. Yet the Bergsonian method of intuition offers Deleuze a way of identifying the wellspring of ontological differentiation by characterizing differences in nature in terms of divergent series of actualization. Moreover, these divergences in actualization are not merely empirically given since they are engendered in and through thinking as expressed senses of being. Being is said in a single sense of everything that is, yet everything that is differs, and this modal difference in everything that is is a function of divergences in actualization corresponding to the distinct senses in which being is expressed in thought: the Ideas. Thus for Deleuze, the key to grasping ontological differentiation, or the real differences in being, lies in seizing the differences in actualization, but this in turn hinges on grasping the way in which the larval subject of spatio-temporal dynamism is the bearer of individuating differences, clearly enveloping distinct differences in the Idea, as well as individual differences, which confusedly envelop the Ideas' obscure perplication. Yet the individuating expressions of being occur in and as thought: from the germinal thought of the larval subject to the fully potentiated thinking of the fractured I. For Deleuze then, being is nothing apart from its expression in thought; indeed, it simply *is* this expression.

Deleuze's vitalism boils down to a single fundamental conviction: time makes a difference that cannot be erased. Yet in Deleuze's account, the only difference which time makes is a difference in and as thought, a difference which is indissociable from thinking. The alternative is not that time makes no difference but rather that it should not be privileged over space and that neither time nor space should be reduced to any variety of difference which depends for its expression on thinking. As suggested in the previous chapter, the task is to uncover the identity of space-time in the form of an objectivity which is at once determining for thought and irreducible to thinking; an objectivity that is no more reducible to the trajectory of entropic dissolution than to that of creative differentiation. Space-time should not be posited as an ontological principle, whether as entropic dissolvent or negentropic differentiatior; it should only be presupposed as an identity, but an identity devoid of ontological substance and hence commensurate with the real as being-nothing. To refuse vitalism is not to favour the stasis of indifference over the movement of difference but to affirm the irreducible reality of physical death along with the autonomy of absolute space-time as identity of difference and indifference, life and death (though as we saw in Chapter 5, this identity should be understood non-dialectically). The reality of the object can be made to yield the ultimate determinant for philosophical thought, but in the form of an identity that unbinds the correlational synthesis of thinking and being, just as it separates the irrecusable reality of physical death from its vitalist idealization. In the next chapter, we will suggest that this identity instantiates the diachronicity of absolute space-time in the form of a subject which carries out a 'voiding' of being. This voiding can be understood in terms of a cosmological re-inscription of Freud's account of the death-drive. Ultimately, the abrogation of time's transcendental privileges necessitates an unbinding of temporal synthesis whereby thought becomes the locus for the identity of absolute objectivity and impersonal death.

7
The Truth of Extinction

Once upon a time, in some out of the way corner of
that universe which is dispersed into numberless twin-
kling solar systems, there was a star upon which clever
beasts invented knowing. That was the most arrogant
and mendacious minute of 'world history', but nevertheless, it was only a minute. After nature had drawn
a few breaths, the star cooled and congealed, and the
clever beasts had to die. – One might invent such a
fable, and yet he still would not have adequately illus-
trated how miserable, how shadowy and transient,
how aimless and arbitrary the human intellect looks
within nature. There were eternities during which it
did not exist. And when it is all over with the human
intellect, nothing will have happened.

(Nietzsche 1873)[1]

Let us guard against saying death is the opposite of
life; the living creature is simply a kind of dead creature, and a very rare kind.

(Nietzsche 1882)[2]

7.1   Nietzsche's fable

Nothing will have happened: Nietzsche's 'fable' perfectly distils nihilism's
most disquieting suggestion: that from the original emergence of
organic sentience to the ultimate extinction of human sapience 'nothing
will have happened'. Neither knowing nor feeling, neither living nor
dying, amounts to a difference that makes a difference – 'becoming aims

at *nothing* and achieves *nothing*'.[3] Yet Nietzsche's entire philosophy is dedicated to overcoming this nihilistic conjecture. It is nihilism understood as the triumph of indeterminate negation, as assertion of the ultimate indifference or convertibility of being and becoming, truth and lie, reality and appearance, that Nietzsche seeks to vanquish by affirming the coincidence of being (identity) and becoming (difference) in a gesture that would simultaneously overthrow both their metaphysical distinction and their nihilistic indistinction. The instrument of this overturning and the focus of this affirmation are provided by the hypothesis of eternal recurrence, Nietzsche's 'thought of thoughts',[4] which is poised at that 'mid-point'[5] of (Western) history marking not only the culmination of European nihilism, but also the possibility of its overcoming.

According to Nietzsche, nihilism reaches its apogee in the pivotal moment when truth, hitherto the supreme value, turns against itself – for it is 'truthfulness' itself that calls the value of 'truth' into question, thereby subverting all known and knowable values, specifically the valuing of reality over appearance and knowledge over life.[6] But truth, the venerable guarantor of value, is also the patron of belief, since for Nietzsche every form of belief is a 'holding-something-true'.[7] Consequently, the self-undermining of truth calls the very possibility of belief into question: 'The most extreme form of nihilism would be the view that *every* belief, every holding-something-true is necessarily false because there is no *true world*' (1968: §15). Yet as Nietzsche recognized, the collapse of belief in the true world also entails the dissolution of belief in the apparent world, since the latter was defined in contradistinction to the former.[8] Disbelief in any reality beyond appearance cannot be converted into belief in the reality of appearance. Since the collapse of the reality–appearance distinction undermines the intrinsic connection between belief and truth, it is not something that can be straightforwardly endorsed or 'believed in'. Thus nihilism appears to undermine itself because it is incompatible with any belief – it seems that it cannot be believed in, for if nothing is true, then neither is the claim that 'nothing is true'. As a self-proclaimed 'perfect nihilist',[9] Nietzsche refuses to retreat from this aporia and insists that it must be traversed, for nihilism can only be overcome from within. How then are we to think the apparently unthinkable thought that nothing is true, which, for Nietzsche, looms at the nadir of nihilism, yet also harbours the key to its overcoming?

For Nietzsche, this aporia of nihilism is simultaneously crystallized and dissolved in the thought of eternal recurrence.[10] The thought of recurrence is at once the ultimate nihilistic conjecture – 'existence as it is, without meaning or aim, yet recurring inevitably without any finale of nothingness'[11] – and what vanquishes nihilism by turning momentary transience into an object of unconditional affirmation and thereby into a locus of absolute worth:

> Becoming must be explained without recourse to final intentions; becoming must appear justified at every moment (or incapable of being evaluated, which comes to the same thing); the present must not be justified by reference to the future, nor the past by reference to the present. [...] Becoming is of equivalent value at every moment; the sum of its values always remains the same; in other words, it has no value at all, for anything against which to measure it, and in relation to which the word 'value' would have meaning, is lacking. *The total value of the world cannot be evaluated* [...]
>
> (1968: §708)

Accordingly, the affirmation of recurrence coincides with the *transvaluation* of all existing values. Transvaluation should not be understood as an operation of inversion, the substitution of the lowest and least valued for the highest and most valued and vice versa. Rather, as Deleuze points out in his ingenious (although controversial) *Nietzsche and Philosophy*,[12] transvaluation points to a fundamental *qualitative* transformation in the will to power – the 'differential genetic element' which produces values. Since all known (and knowable) values consecrated by Judeo-Christian culture are a function of those reactive forces animated by the negative will to nothingness, whose evaluations are governed by the norm of truth, the affirmation of eternal recurrence is at once the annihilation of all known values and the creation of unknown values. It exterminates all known values because it is the assertion of absolute eternal indifference, without even a 'finale of nothingness' to punctuate the sequence or to distinguish between beginning and end. In this regard, eternal recurrence is a 'demonic' hypothesis precisely insofar as it entails the evacuation of all meaning and purpose from existence, and hence the recognition of its ultimate valuelessness.[13] Yet at the same time it also marks the discovery of a previously inconceivable kind of value because it asserts the absolute, invaluable worth of every moment of existence as such – it is no longer possible to separate one moment from another or to subordinate the value of the vanishing present to that of a cherished past or longed-for future. The transitoriness of the instant which was considered worthless in the old mode of valuation, where becoming was deemed deficient with regard to the transcendent value of eternal being, becomes the focus of ultimate worth in the new one – transcendence is revoked and with it the possibility of appraising the worth or worthlessness of existence from some external vantage point.

Accordingly, nihilism is overcome through a transvaluation whereby the pointlessness of becoming is embraced beyond its opposition to the supposed purposefulness of true being – aimlessness is affirmed in and for itself, without appeal to extrinsic justification. Thus the affirmation of eternal recurrence marks the coincidence of 'midday and midnight'[14]: it is at once the apex of affirmativeness – the eternalization of transience – and the nadir of negativity – the negation of all purposefulness. Yet as Deleuze and Heidegger both underline, despite their otherwise incompatible interpretations of Nietzsche, this is a conjunction of opposites which refuses the conciliatory mediation of dialectical negativity: rather, it affirms the immediate, irreconcilable coincidence of absolute value and valuelessness, affirmation and negation, immanence and transcendence. Moreover, this discordant conjunction of opposites finds expression in the antinomy inherent in the attempt to believe in recurrence, or 'hold-it-as-true'. For the assertion of recurrence claims that the world is nothing but ceaseless becoming, without rest or fixity, and hence that there is no cognizable being underlying becoming, no final truth upon which belief could find a secure footing. Since Nietzsche identifies truth with permanence, and permanence with being, it follows for him that to believe that the world is nothing but becoming, without ever becoming something, is to believe that there is no truth and therefore to 'hold-it-as-true' that nothing is true. It is in fact a contradictory belief, one that cancels itself out, and as such is equivalent to the *unbelief* which refuses to hold anything as true. This is why the thought of eternal recurrence is an expression of what Nietzsche himself calls 'the most extreme form of nihilism'. Belief in eternal recurrence provides the definitive expression of the nihilistic belief that nothing is true; more precisely, it is the only way of holding-it-as-true that nothing is true. The paradoxical structure of this belief in the impossibility of belief betrays a fault-line in the folk-psychological construal of rationality; one which already prefigures the paradox of eliminativism we encountered in Chapter 1. We saw there how the apparent contradiction inherent in the 'belief' that there are no beliefs vanishes once it is understood that belief is neither the substrate nor the vehicle of this assertion. Moreover, it is precisely insofar as the critique of FP introduces a reality–appearance distinction into the phenomenal realm that it becomes possible to distinguish the phenomenological experience of belief from its psychological reality. In this regard, although Nietzsche anticipated, as no one else did, the depth of the crisis of the manifest image, the scanty resources provided by nineteenth-century psychology prompted him to transpose what he correctly identified as the impasse in the folk-psychological conception of rationality into a metaphysical register which merely recapitulated the specious categories of the psychology it was supposed to supplant. Thus while Nietzsche's penetrating critiques of pseudo-psychological categories such as that of 'intention'[15] prefigure the critique of FP, his antipathy towards 'positivism' (combined with his debt to Schopenhauer) encourages him to replace it with a metaphysical surrogate – the 'will to power' – which exacerbates rather than palliates the poverty of the psychological register which it was called upon to supersede. As a result, the cognitive dilemma engendered by the collapse of the folk-psychological conception of truth is transcoded by Nietzsche into an axiological predicament necessitating a metaphysical transfiguration in the quality of the will whose symptom belief is supposed to be. In willing eternal recurrence, the will casts off the yoke of truth, which bridled it to those transcendent values that depreciated becoming, and is transformed into a will capable of embracing illusion: 'the lie – and *not* the truth – is divine!'[16]

Deleuze provides a particularly subtle account of this transformation in *Nietzsche and Philosophy*. In Deleuze's reading, the thought of recurrence is the focal point for the transmutation of the will to power. Deleuze distinguishes that aspect of the will according to which it is knowable – its *ratio cognoscendi* – from that aspect through which the will exists as 'the innermost essence of being' (Nietzsche 1968: §693) – its *ratio essendi*. The negative will to power, which underlies the will to nothingness, whose symptom is the ascetic ideal, is simply the will's *ratio cognoscendi*, the knowable aspect of the will from which all hitherto *known* values derive. Nihilism – including Nietzsche's own active nihilism, insofar as it proceeds by unmasking existing values the better to expose the will to power which produced them – renders the will to power knowable to us, but only in its negative aspect as will to nothingness. This is why for Deleuze's Nietzsche, the history of human consciousness (and a fortiori, of philosophy) is the history of nihilism understood as the triumph of *ressentiment*, bad conscience, and the ascetic ideal. But the decisive juncture in this history occurs when the negative will to nothingness, which is also the philosophical will to truth, turns against truth itself and forces thought to break its alliance with knowing, and a fortiori with those reactive forces which enforced the rule of knowledge and the norm of truth. In the thought of recurrence, the will which animates knowing is obliged to confront itself no longer according to its knowable aspect, but rather according to that aspect through which it *is*. But since, for Nietzsche, 'will to power' is a synonym for the world interpreted as a chaotic multiplicity of conflicting forces – 'This world is will to power – and nothing besides!'[17] – which is to say, a synonym for 'becoming', then to think the will in its being is to think the being of becoming in its essentially dissimulatory, inherently self-differentiating 'essence' as a flux of perpetual transformation. Thus, the affirmation of recurrence marks the moment when the will comes to know that it cannot know itself in itself because its knowable aspect necessarily corresponds to nothing – since there is nothing, no aspect of the will 'in-itself', for it to correspond *to* or adequately represent.[18] This is Deleuze's dexterous resolution of a latent dichotomy that threatened to undermine the minimal conceptual coherence which even Nietzsche's denunciation of rationality cannot do without – the dichotomy between the will's phenomenal aspect, understood as the evaluable and interpretable dimension of becoming, and its noumenal aspect, understood as the chaos of becoming 'in-itself', beyond evaluation and interpretation, to which Nietzsche often, but incoherently, alludes.[19] This dichotomy can be avoided, Deleuze suggests, once it is understood that the will which affirms recurrence does not affirm becoming as something 'in itself', subsisting independently of that affirmation; rather, in affirming becoming without goal or aim, the will affirms itself.

For who else is capable of willing this annihilation of transcendent meaning and purposefulness and of endowing every vanishing instant with absolute worth as an end in itself if not the will to power as such? The 'overman' whom Nietzsche proclaims as alone capable of affirming eternal recurrence would no longer be a species of the genus 'man' but rather a placeholder for that perpetual self-overcoming which characterizes the will to power. Thus – and contrary to what Nietzsche himself often seems to suggest – the selection effected by the test of eternal recurrence would not be between types of human individual – noble versus base, strong versus weak, etc. – but rather between the will subordinated to extrinsic ends, and the will whose only end is itself. Only the will itself is devoid of all those interests and purposes whose satisfaction requires the utilitarian subordination of present means to future ends. Unconditional affirmation of the present is not only incommensurable with human consciousness, it is incompatible with organic functioning, which is indissociable from the utilitarian trade-off between pleasure and pain, gratification and survival. Only the will to power, which wants nothing other than itself – which is to say, its own expansion, intensification, and self-overcoming – only this will which wants itself eternally is capable of willing the eternal recurrence of everything that is, without regard for the proportion of pleasure to pain:

> Did you ever say Yes to one joy? O my friends, then you said Yes to *all* woe as well. All things are chained and entwined together, all things are in love; if ever you wanted one moment twice, if ever you said 'You please me happiness, instant, moment!' then you wanted *everything* to return! [...] *For all joy wants – eternity!*
>
> (Nietzsche 1969: 332)

Thus the scope of the transvaluation required by the affirmation of recurrence is as profound as it is uncompromising: it entails a will for which a moment of unadulterated joy, no matter how brief, is worth aeons of torment, no matter how excruciating. But two difficulties arise here. First, it is far from clear whether it is possible to commensurate joy and woe in such a way that the former, no matter how fleeting, will always outweigh the latter, no matter how prolonged. Second, there seems to be a latent indeterminacy in the normative claim that the will capable of affirming 'all woe' is nobler than the will that is not.

With regard to the first difficulty, Nietzsche seems to disregard a basic asymmetry in the relationship between joy and woe. For however multi-faceted our experience of joy may seem to us, hampered as we are by the rather meagre descriptive resources available within the manifest image, our possibilities for physical pleasure, as well as for psychological enjoyment, can be demarcated within boundaries determined by a set of physiological and psychological constraints which, however complex the interplay between neurophysiological and psychosocial dynamisms, cannot be assumed to be limitless. Yet when compared with our relatively restricted capacity for experiencing physical and/or psychological 'joy', the sheer depth and breadth of our capacity for 'woe', both in terms of our vulnerability to physical pain and our susceptibility to psychological suffering, appears nigh-on unlimited. This discrepancy has been given a particularly striking formulation by the writer Jesús Ignacio Aldapuerta:

> Consider the capacity of the human body for pleasure. Sometimes it is pleasant to eat, to drink, to see, to touch, to smell, to hear, to make love. The mouth. The eyes. The fingertips. The nose. The ears. The

genitals. Our voluptific capacities (if you will forgive me the coinage) are not exclusively concentrated in these places, but it is undeniable that they are concentrated here. The whole body is susceptible to pleasure, but in places there are wells from which it may be drawn up in greater quantity. But not inexhaustibly. How long is it possible to know pleasure? Rich Romans ate to satiety and then purged their overburdened bellies and ate again. But they could not eat for ever. A rose is sweet, but the nose becomes habituated to its scent. And what of the most intense pleasures, the personality-annihilating ecstasies of sex? [...] Even if I were a woman and could string orgasm upon orgasm like beads upon a necklace, in time I should sicken of it. [...] Yet consider. Consider pain. Give me a cubic centimeter of your flesh and I could give you pain that would swallow you as the ocean swallows a grain of salt. And you would always be ripe for it, from before the time of your birth to the moment of your death. We are always in season for the embrace of pain. To experience pain requires no intelligence, no maturity, no wisdom, no slow workings of the hormones in the moist midnight of our innards. We are always ripe for it. All life is ripe for it. Always. [...] Consider the ways in which we may gain pleasure. [...] Consider the ways in which we may be given pain. The one is to the other as the moon is to the sun.

(Aldapuerta 1995: 52–3)

This fundamental deficit between our susceptibility to pleasure and our vulnerability to pain vitiates the attempt to commensurate them. Indeed, the assumption that humans possess a limitless sensitivity to physical pleasure, or an inexhaustible capacity for psychological enjoyment, is an unfounded spiritualist conceit. In this regard, Nietzsche's insistence that 'joy is deeper than heart's agony' (1969: 331) implies that in affirming the recurrence of any moment of joy, the finite human organism transcends its own determinate psychophysical constitution. Thus, the affirmation of recurrence is the moment when finite lunar joy eclipses boundless solar pain. Yet Nietzsche provides no explanation of what makes this transcendence possible, other than saying that it is a function of some sort of 'strength' and/or 'power', while leaving the source of this 'strength' or 'power' completely indeterminate, apart from attributing it to an inherent 'superiority' in the character of the will. But given that the capacity for withstanding and surmounting pain is part of Nietzsche's definition of 'superiority of will' – a 'will' whose psychophysical basis remains wholly indeterminate – it is difficult to see how this superiority, which is cashed out in terms of wholly traditional virtues such as fortitude, resilience, and resourcefulness, differs from the venerable definition of *spiritual* superiority: 'The discipline of suffering, of *great* suffering – you do not know that it is *this* discipline alone which has created every elevation of mankind hitherto?' (1990b: §225). This is simply to endorse, rather than undermine, the spiritualization of suffering; indeed it is difficult to see how it differs from familiar Judaeo-Christian paeans to the spiritually edifying virtues of suffering. Either one ascribes a redemptive function to suffering itself, as does Christian dolorism, or one reintroduces a spiritual economy of means and ends, where the experience of woe is compensated for by some past remembrance or future expectation of bliss. Neither option can be reconciled with the stated aim of Nietzsche's transvaluation, which was to overthrow the Judaeo-Christian register of evaluation altogether.

Moreover, to insist that the human organism is always capable of transcending suffering in principle, even if it does not do so in fact, is to stipulate an ethical norm which implicitly assumes the 'soul-superstition' according to which humans have been endowed with an infinite reservoir of spiritual energy which furnishes them with an inexhaustible capacity for physical resilience. Ultimately, it is difficult to divorce the positive evaluation of suffering from the claim that suffering *means* something, in accordance with the strictures which the manifest image imposes upon our understanding of meaning. But to invest suffering with the varieties of 'meaning' concomitant with the manifest image is to automatically reinscribe woe into a spiritual calculus which subordinates present suffering to some recollected or longed-for happiness. By way of contrast, to acknowledge the meaninglessness of suffering is already to challenge the authority of the manifest image, since it is precisely its senselessness that renders woe resistant to redemptive valuation.[20] Once the senselessness of suffering has been acknowledged, it becomes more apposite to insist that 'woe is deeper than heart's ecstasy'. This of course would be contrary to the explicitly stated goal of Nietzsche's transvaluation, viz., that suffering no longer be counted as an objection to life. Nevertheless, unlike its affirmative antithesis, to which, as we shall see below, Nietzsche attributes a redemptive function vis-à-vis suffering, it is precisely the refusal to affirm or redeem woe that challenges the authority of the manifest image.

The second difficulty in Nietzsche's attempted transvaluation of joy and woe follows on from the first. For whether woe is eclipsed by joy, or joy outweighed by woe, the question remains: whose joy; whose woe – mine or others? Construed as a test designed to effect the selection between noble and ignoble varieties of individual will, the hypothesis of eternal recurrence is fatally underdetermined. If the selection is confined to the individual level, then it has to be acknowledged that any able-bodied, materially privileged epicure who has successfully maximized pleasure over displeasure in his or her existence will be eager to embrace eternal recurrence. Even the 'last man',[21] whose 'miserable ease' ensures the preponderance of pleasure over displeasure in existence, might prove as likely to opt for eternal recurrence as the overman, whose affirmation of the entwinement of joy and woe is ostensibly an act of self-overcoming. Nietzsche seems not to have envisaged the possibility that the noble individual might not be the only one capable of welcoming the 'demonic' hypothesis of recurrence; he did not anticipate its potential appeal to the bovine hedonist, whose coarseness effectively inures him or her to the demonic aspect of the thought. Accordingly, the ethical-psychological interpretation of recurrence as selective hypothesis is only viable if it is the individual's acceptance of his or her own allotment of suffering that the affirmation of recurrence invites, rather than the suffering of others – otherwise sadists and sociopaths would be as eager to embrace it as the noble types supposedly envisaged by Nietzsche. Yet even if we specify that only the individual is qualified to affirm his or her own suffering, ambiguity persists. For who is to say what proportion of joy and woe affirmed in an individual life constitutes the appropriate measure of magnanimity and courage required in order to distinguish the noble from the ignoble? How much suffering, and of what kind, should an individual be capable of enduring, without rancour or resentment, in order to qualify as courageous, rather than merely hardened? How much joy should an individual be capable of experiencing, and under what circumstances, for his or her delight in existence to be deemed a sign of spiritual munificence, rather than a symptom of indulgent libertinism? So long as the selection effected by the thought of recurrence is construed ethically and/or psychologically, and confined to the individual level, then its selectiveness remains vitiated by indeterminacy. Ultimately, the scope of the affirmation required by the thought of recurrence cannot be commensurated with any apportioning of joy and woe concomitant with the realm of individual human existence. For even when construed as a reformulated categorical imperative, as it is by Deleuze – *whatever you will, will it in such a way that you also will its eternal return*[22] – the doctrine of recurrence furnishes no criterion that would allow us to discriminate between the ignoble will of the privileged libertine, whose affirmation of 'all woe' is a symptom of insouciance, and the noble will of the spiritual aristocrat, whose affirmation of 'all woe' is a sign of munificence.

This is why Deleuze and Heidegger are right to insist that the differentiation operated by the affirmation of recurrence is epistemological and ontological, rather than psychological and anthropological. It does not select between noble and ignoble varieties of human will, but between the willing that is subordinated as a means for the fulfilment of ends, and the willing which abjures the economy of means and ends and has no other object than itself. The will that wills the recurrence of the instant is the will that wills the recurrence of everything, but in willing the recurrence of everything, the will simply wills itself: '[W]hat does joy not want! It is thirstier, warmer, hungrier, more fearful, more secret than all woe, it wants itself; it bites into itself, the will of the ring nestles within it' (Nietzsche 1969: 332).[23]

Accordingly if, as Nietzsche claims, 'knowledge in-itself in a world of becoming is impossible' (1968: §617), then the will that evaluates and interprets becoming in the thought of eternal recurrence is no longer evaluating and interpreting under the aegis of truth and knowledge, but rather affirming the intrinsically dissimulatory character of its own *ratio essendi* – the fact that it has no cognizable essence – and thereby creating itself by overcoming its own will to know. In so doing, the quality of the will undergoes a transformation from negative to affirmative – by willing becoming as creativity,[24] the will wills itself and thereby becomes positive. It usurps truth and becomes autonomous or *causa sui*. Thus the only aspect according to which the will (becoming) *is* is that of affirmation. Consequently, for Deleuze's Nietzsche, it is no longer a matter of affirming what is (in the manner of Zarathustra's braying ass),[25] but rather of creating what is affirmed. Or as Deleuze puts it, it is not being that is affirmed via eternal recurrence, but the affirmation of eternal recurrence that constitutes being.[26]

7.2 The turning point

Ultimately, nihilism's consummation in the affirmation of eternal recurrence rescinds the privilege traditionally ascribed to knowing in favour of a premium on creative affirmation. For only the will that affirms indifference (recurrence as meaningless iteration of the 'in vain') is capable of making a difference by producing being, not as an object of representation, but as a creative power worthy of affirmation.[27] But as we have seen, the will that affirms being as a creative principle rather than as an object of knowing is the will that wills itself. Thus, in a curiously

Hegelian denouement, the point of transmutation through which nihilism overcomes itself corresponds to that moment wherein, by asserting the being of becoming, the will to power shifts from being 'in-itself' to being 'in-and-for-itself'. By affirming itself and undergoing the metamorphosis from negation to affirmation, becoming expels the negative will to nothingness whose symptomatic manifestation was the 'knowing' which fuelled the logic of nihilism that eventually undermined the authority of knowing as such. Accordingly, for Nietzsche, it is the self-affirmation of the will that produces the difference between difference and indifference, affirmation and negation, intensification and disintensification; and it is this difference in turn that validates the creative power of affirmation by engendering the active life that distinguishes itself from reactive death. For as Nietzsche famously insists, it is precisely because life remains the precondition for all evaluation, that the value of life cannot be evaluated.[28] Once we recognize that there are no transcendent cognitive criteria in terms of which we could find life wanting, we must concede that it is always life itself that appraises life; or more precisely, that every evaluation of life is symptomatic of the type of life that evaluates: either healthy or sick, strong or weak. Accordingly, for Nietzsche, nihilism, along with every variety of negative judgement of life, is overcome when the affirmation of life becomes *causa sui*: the negative will to knowledge, which led to the depreciation of life, eventually turns against itself and is converted into an affirmative will which produces itself by affirming the invaluableness of meaningless life as an end in itself. Thus the life that affirms being is itself the locus of being, and the affirmation of self-differentiating life (will to power) expels everything that constrained life (reactivity, *ressentiment*, bad conscience) in what effectively amounts to an autocatalysis of vital difference.[29]

But as Nietzsche recognized, nihilism is perceived as debilitating precisely insofar as it threatens to collapse those distinctions and categories through which we make sense of existence; not only the difference between meaning and meaninglessness, but also (and perhaps more menacingly) the difference between life and death. Unlike those conservatives who presume to excoriate nihilism from without in the name of supposedly indubitable values, Nietzsche's audacious philosophical gambit is the suggestion that the poison is also the cure, that untrammelled negativity harbours the seed of its own metamorphosis into an unprecedented power of affirmation and creativity: when pushed to its ultimate extremity, the destruction of difference unleashed by the will to nothingness turns against itself and yields a hitherto inconceivable variety of difference. Accordingly, Nietzsche's alleged 'overcoming' of nihilism hinges on his claim to have exhausted this logic of indifferentiation from within, and to have converted it into a productive logic of differentiation which does not rehabilitate some traditionally sanctified (or 'metaphysical') difference. The question then is whether the power of creative affirmation celebrated by Nietzsche (as well as by Deleuze, arguably his most influential philosophical disciple) is in fact a new variety of difference or merely an old kind in a new guise. In what sense precisely does Nietzsche's affirmative embrace of the meaninglessness of becoming amount to a difference that really makes a difference?

Central to Nietzsche's narrative about the overcoming of nihilism is the claim that this moment of affirmation marks a pivotal point which 'breaks the history of mankind in two'.[30] Thus, Nietzsche ascribes to it the power of *redeeming* past time, for by willing the recurrence of what is and shall be, the wills also wills the recurrence of everything that has been, and therefore of the entire temporal series that conditioned this moment of affirmation. In so doing, it effectively wills backward, transforming resentment towards the past's '*it was*' into a positive '*thus I willed it*'. Accordingly, redemption is no longer projected into the future but rather retrojected into the past: it is the dissolution of the will's vengefulness towards the ineradicable persistence of what *has been*.[31] We cannot hope to undo the past; we can only embrace it. But in redeeming the past through this embrace, the present has already redeemed itself as well as its future. Thus, redemption is a function of the power of unconditional affirmation. So long as affirmation remains conditional – 'I will recurrence *if...*' – then it is the spirit of revenge that continues to motivate the will. When faced with the prospect of eternal recurrence, it is the negative will that seeks to affirm joy over woe, good over evil – it affirms selectively, separating joy from woe, good from evil. It presumes to be able to split becoming into good and evil. However, in so doing, it fails the test, because it reveals itself to be incapable of affirming becoming *unconditionally*, or as an indivisible whole. The negative will's conditional affirmation seeks to operate a selection between good and evil on the basis of interests wherein becoming is reinscribed in an economy of means and ends: 'I will recurrence *if ...*' It is not selected by the affirmation of recurrence precisely because it wills a conditional selection. By way of contrast, the affirmative will successfully separates active from reactive forces by unconditionally affirming *all* of becoming. It operates the selection between active and reactive, difference and indifference, by refusing to select joy at the expense of woe.

Yet there is an underlying difficulty in ascribing this pivotal *redemptive* function to the affirmation of recurrence. For if the latter marks the focal point of becoming, the moment in which activity is prized free from reactivity, and affirmation released from negativity, then how are we to reconcile this axial role allotted to a particular moment of becoming, with the claim that this is also the moment that evacuates history of sense, *telos*, direction? How can the affirmation which is supposed to render every moment of becoming absolutely equivalent to every other, also be invested with the redemptive power capable of cleaving history in two and transforming the relation between all past and future moments? The affirmation of recurrence is supposed to be the lightning rod for the affirmative will through which all other moments are redeemed, and as we saw above, only the will itself is capable of affirming becoming unconditionally. But since Nietzsche has eliminated the hypothesis of the *an sich*, the notion of the 'will itself' remains empty, just as the idea of 'becoming-in-itself' is vacuous, until the will's *ratio essendi* is realized in the act that affirms it. For the 'will itself' is nothing independently of its realization in this affirmative act. But since the will to power is a synonym for becoming, this implies that becoming only *is* (in its *ratio essendi*) insofar as it is *reflected* into itself through this act – a claim which, as we have already noted, is uncannily reminiscent of the Hegelian thesis according to which *essential* being is coextensive with the act of its own reflexive self-positing.[32] However, if becoming *is* only insofar as it is posited in this act, then the whole of becoming is condensed in this affirmative instant – indeed, this is precisely why it is this act that *eternalizes* becoming. Accordingly, it is time as a whole or eternity as such that is *reflected* into itself through this affirmative instant. But if eternity is compressed and its being is *expressed* in and through this affirmation (in conformity with the Deleuzean logic of expression discussed in Chapter 6), this is to say that the whole of becoming is redeemed by thought. Thus, and despite having acknowledged 'how aimless and arbitrary the human intellect looks within nature', Nietzsche effectively renders the being of becoming dependent upon the existence of creatures capable of evaluating it. But to construe being as a function of affirmation, rather than an object of representation, is merely another way of making the world dependent upon thought. Since Nietzsche cannot acknowledge the reality of becoming-in-itself, he makes becoming orbit around affirmation, which is to say, evaluation. (The reverse, which would consist in making affirmation orbit around becoming, is not an option for Nietzsche since it would require the sort of metaphysical realism which he has abjured.)[33]

It is this insistence that becoming is not an object of knowledge, but rather a libidinal motor of evaluation, that encourages Nietzsche to translate the epistemological conundrum generated by the inadequacy of the manifest image of truth – a conundrum which Nietzsche himself correctly identifies as a consequence of the Enlightenment will to truth – into an axiological crisis inviting a transvaluation of values. Through this transvaluation, which deposes truth, the enlightened premium on disinterested knowing is diagnosed as a symptom of the will to nothingness, and supplanted by a symptomatology of forces which abrogates the privileging of knowledge – insofar as the latter invoked a world-in-itself indifferent to evaluation – in the name of a genealogy of values. Genealogy proceeds by positing the will to power as guarantor of the correlation between evaluation and a world that *is* only insofar as it is evaluated: the will is at once *evaluating* and *evaluated*, the *agent* of evaluation as well as its *patient*. Accordingly, for Nietzsche, the pivotal moment in the history of nihilism occurs at that juncture when the will's drive to eradicate value from the world in the name of truth exposes truth itself as just another value. This is the point at which the negative will to truth converts itself into the affirmative and evaluative *will to lie*; into a will which is willing to fabricate the value it bestows upon becoming:

Our 'new world': we have to realize to what degree we are the creators of our value feelings – and thus capable of projecting 'meaning' into history. This faith in truth attains its ultimate conclusion in us – you know what that is: that if there is anything that is to be worshipped it is *appearance* that must be worshipped, that the lie – and *not* the truth – is divine!

(Nietzsche 1968: §1011)

Ultimately then, Nietzsche's axiological transcoding of the cognitive crisis generated by the untrammelled potency of the will to truth, and the ensuing suggestion that transvaluation is the key to 'twisting free' (*Herausdrehen*) from nihilism, are predicated upon a generalized irrealism that denies autonomy to becoming as well as to being. Thus, Nietzsche's defusing of the will to nothingness depends upon his irrealism about becoming: since becoming is nothing in-itself, an act of evaluation suffices to transform it into something worthy of affirmation. But why should the thought that becoming aims at nothing and achieves nothing make a difference in the becoming that it affirms, effectively splitting it into a 'before' and an 'after'? Nietzsche's response is: because becoming is reflected into itself through this affirmation – since the will to power is at once evaluating and evaluated, becoming *evaluates itself* through the act that affirms its recurrence and bestows being upon it. This provides the conceptual underpinning for the claim that the eradication of value concomitant with the will to truth can be converted into a will capable of creating new values.

However, whether it is interpreted as the affirmation of identity, or as the affirmation of difference, Nietzsche's attempt to characterize the affirmation of recurrence as focal point of becoming faces insuperable difficulties. First, Nietzsche's irrealism about becoming threatens to restrict eternal recurrence understood as repetition of the same to the repetition of the present, for if the being of becoming orbits around its affirmation then it makes no sense to invoke a past or future dimension of becoming subsisting in-itself independently of the moment of its affirmation. The only sense in which the past and future of becoming recur is as fixed correlates of the *nunc stans*, the eternal now, of affirmation. Consequently, the affirmation of recurrence would render all the moments of becoming equivalent only insofar as it reduced them to *this* perpetually subsisting moment of affirmation. Second, the thought of eternal recurrence implies that becoming has never started or stopped; it is always repeating itself as what has already recurred an infinity of times. How then can history still harbour the possibility of a decisive turning point which divides the 'before' from the 'after' if every moment, and therefore *this* moment in which we are invited to affirm the repetition of the entire series of moments, has already recurred, and is already repeating itself, an infinity of times? What possible difference can affirmation make if it has already recurred an infinity of times? No doubt these and other difficulties attendant upon the interpretation of recurrence as repetition of the same tend to encourage the Deleuzean interpretation of the doctrine as repetition of difference. However, aside from the fact that there seems to be little support for it in Nietzsche's own texts, Deleuze's interpretation is vitiated by conceptual inconsistencies of its own – inconsistencies which are not just peculiar to Deleuze's Nietzsche, but inherent in any philosophy that would privilege becoming over stasis and creative affirmation over representation. Thus, third and finally, if recurrence is construed as the repetition of difference, then being must be inherently self-differentiating. But if being is essentially active, affirmative, creative, and productive, then why does it ever become alienated from itself in reactivity, negation, sterility, and representation? The claim that the history of nihilism pivots around truth's turning against itself invites the obvious retort: why should the affirmative will to illusion require the negative will to truth to come into its own and attain its maximal potentiation? Moreover, why does affirmation need to make a difference between identity and difference if being as such is nothing but differentiation? The answer to both questions, as we have already suggested, is a direct corollary of Nietzsche's irrealism: becoming requires affirmation because it is nothing until it is reflected into itself via the intercession of an affirmative act. In this regard, Deleuze's characterization of Nietzsche's overcoming of nihilism amounts to an inverted Hegelianism, which pits the power of the positive against the labour of the negative only in order to convert difference-in-itself into difference-for-itself. Even so, a fundamental difficulty persists, for though affirmation distinguishes itself from negation, and difference from indifference, it was the *hybridization* of activity and reactivity that provided the precondition for the necessity of this distinction. Yet once affirmation has successfully separated itself from negation, and activity from reactivity, not only does it become impossible to account for the necessity of their intrication, this separation cancels it own precondition, since the very difference through which eternal recurrence affirms the unity of becoming obviates the recurrence of this very unity. Thus the affirmation of recurrence retroactively negates the indivisibility of becoming which was supposed to provide its motivation. For it was precisely the premise of the indivisibility of good and evil, noble and base, activity and reactivity, that provided the condition for the affirmative redemption of becoming.

Ultimately, the claim that the affirmation of recurrence marks the turning point in the history of nihilism generates more difficulties than it can possibly resolve. The conclusion to be drawn here is that being is no more susceptible to affirmation than to negation: there is no more reason to opt for its differentiation through affirmation than its identification through negation. Being-in-itself – which we characterized in Chapter 5 in terms of a degree-zero of being (being-nothing) – cannot be construed as an object of representation, but this is no reason to try to construe it as a power of affirmation instead. Once we have jettisoned Nietzsche's irrealist postulate that being can be the correlate of an affirmative act, it is clear that the becoming that 'aims at nothing and achieves nothing' is as heedless of affirmation as it is of negation. It is precisely the realist commitment to the truth of the in-itself, and the concomitant extension of the appearance–reality distinction into the phenomenal realm carried out by the science of cognition (cf. Chapter 1), which countermands the legitimacy of the axiological register with which Nietzsche would disarm the will to nothingness. In this regard, Nietzsche's claim that life cannot but be privileged over knowing, since it remains its precondition, underestimates the profundity of the challenge posed to life by the will to know. For as Nietzsche himself recognized, the allegedly absolute difference between life and death is among the metaphysical absolutes shaken by the untrammelled will to truth. Yet Nietzsche sides with vitalism in seeking to incorporate death into life, even going so far as to identify living and being: 'Being – we have no idea of it apart from the idea of "living." – How can anything dead "be"?' (Nietzsche 1968: §582).

However, if knowing undercuts the difference between life and death, it is not by reducing the former to the latter, or by privileging entropy over negentropy – a metaphysical gesture as arbitrary as its vitalist antithesis – but by identifying difference and indifference, life and death, without synthesizing them ontologically, as Heidegger and Deleuze do through finite transcendence and psychic individuation respectively. As we saw in Chapter 5, the knowing that is determined by its object can be characterized as a structure of *adequation without correspondence*; one which does not seek to make a difference in becoming, as Nietzsche sought to via affirmation, but rather to identify the objective matrix of order and disorder while unbinding the ontological syntheses which would reduce the latter to correlates of thought. Thus, there is a knowing *of* the real (objective genitive) which repudiates the subordination of knowledge to vital and/or organic interests, but also the need to redeem or otherwise *justify* reality in order to render it compatible with the putative interests of reason – or 'rationality' – as construed within the bounds of the manifest image.

We saw in the previous chapter how vitalism – specifically Deleuze's vitalism – characterizes the relation between death and time as a locus for the production of temporal difference: death is not the cancellation of vital difference, but rather its expressive intensification. For Deleuze, intensive death is a gateway onto a virtual realm of creative individuation suffused with pre-individual singularities. Ultimately then, vitalism pits the ineradicable difference of creative time against the physical erasure of annihilating space, which, as we saw in Chapters 2 and 6, is perceived as a threat to the life of the mind. In this regard, the privileging of time over space goes hand in hand with the spiritualization of death as a more rarefied form of life. Against this vitalist sublation of physical death, it is necessary to insist on the indivisibility of space and time and the ineradicability of physical annihilation. These provide the speculative markers for an objectification of thought that can be identified with a figure of death which is not the cancellation of difference but rather the non-dialectical identity of difference and indifference, of negentropy and entropy. We begin to broach the latter through questions such as: *How does thought think a world without thought?* Or more urgently: *How does thought think the death of thinking?*

7.3   Solar catastrophe: Lyotard

This latter question lies at the heart of Jean-François Lyotard's 'Can Thought go on Without a Body?', the opening chapter from his 1991 collection *The Inhuman*.[34] Lyotard invites us to ponder philosophy's relationship to the terrestrial horizon which, in the wake of the collapse of the metaphysical horizon called 'God' – whose dissolution spurred the Nietzschean injunction *'remain true to the earth!'* (Nietzsche 1969: 42) – has been endowed with a quasi-transcendental status, whether as the 'originary ark' (Husserl), the 'self-secluding' (Heidegger), or 'the deterritorialized' (Deleuze).[35] But as Lyotard points out, this terrestrial horizon will also be wiped away, when, roughly 4.5 billion years from now, the sun is extinguished, incinerating the 'originary ark', obliterating the 'self-secluding', and vaporizing 'the deterritorialized'. The extinction of the sun is a catastrophe, a mis-turning or over-turning (*kata-strophe*), because it blots out the terrestrial horizon of future possibility relative to which human existence, and hence philosophical questioning, have hitherto oriented themselves. Or as Lyotard himself puts it: '[E]verything's dead already if this infinite reserve from which you now draw energy to defer answers, if in short thought as quest, dies out with the sun' (Lyotard 1991: 9). *Everything is dead already.* Solar death is catastrophic because it vitiates ontological temporality as configured in terms of philosophical questioning's constitutive horizonal relationship to the future. But far from lying in wait in for us in the far distant future, on the other side of the terrestrial horizon, the solar catastrophe needs to be grasped as something that *has already happened*; as the aboriginal trauma driving the history of terrestrial life as an elaborately circuitous detour from stellar death. Terrestrial history occurs between the simultaneous strophes of a death which is at once *earlier* than the birth of the first unicellular organism, and *later* than the extinction of the last multicellular animal. Paraphrasing a remark Freud makes in *Beyond the Pleasure Principle*, we could say: 'In the last resort, what has left its mark on the development of thought must be the history of the earth we live on and its relation to the sun.'[36] This mark imprinted upon thought by its relation to the sun is the trace of stellar death, which precedes and succeeds, initiates and terminates, the life and death with which philosophers reckon.

Lyotard juxtaposes two antithetical perspectives on the relation between thought and embodiment prompted by the prospect of solar extinction: one for which the *inseparability* between thought and its material substrate necessitates *separating* thought from its rootedness in organic life in general, and the human organism in particular; another according to which it is the irreducible *separation* of the sexes that renders thought *inseparable* from organic embodiment, and human embodiment specifically. Although the prospect of solar death is in some sense little more than a pretext for Lyotard's ingenious dramatization of the *differend* between the extropian functionalism endorsed in the first perspective, and the phenomenological feminism espoused in the second perspective – a *differend* which Lyotard refuses to adjudicate – it is the former which is most significant for our purposes, for it suggests that the extinction of the sun challenges the prevalent philosophical understanding of death – more specifically, it shatters the existential conception of death codified in Heidegger's phenomenological analysis of 'dying', so that the latter can no longer be held up as what sets human existence apart by endowing it with a privileged relationship to the future. If the extinction of the sun cannot be construed in terms of any existential possibility concomitant with the human relationship to death, this is not so much because the sun is not the kind of entity that dies, so that to speak of its 'death' would constitute an illegitimate anthropomorphism, but on the contrary, because humans can no longer be described as the kinds of entities privileged by the relationship to their own inexistence: the sun is *dying* precisely to the same extent as human existence is bounded by *extinction*. Extinction is not to be understood here as the termination of a biological species, but rather as that which *levels* the transcendence ascribed to the human, whether it be that of consciousness or *Dasein*, stripping the latter of its privilege as the locus of correlation (cf. Chapter 3). Thus, if the extinction of the sun is catastrophic, this is because it *disarticulates* the correlation. Unlike the model of death which, at least since Hegel, has functioned as the motor of philosophical speculation, it does not constitute an internal limit for thought, providing the necessary spur for thought to overstep its own bounds and thereby incorporating what was supposed to be exterior to it. Thought is perfectly capable of transcending the limits it has posited for itself. But the extinction of the sun is not a limit *of* or *for* thought. In this regard, it annuls the relationship to death from which philosophical thought drew sustenance. Or as Lyotard puts it:

> With the disappearance of earth, thought will have stopped – leaving that disappearance absolutely unthought of. It's the horizon itself that will be abolished and, with its disappearance, [the phenomenologist's] transcendence in immanence as well. If, as a limit, death really is what escapes and is deferred and as a result what thought has to deal with, right from the beginning – this death is still only the life of our minds. But the death of the sun is a death of mind, because it is the death of death as the life of the mind.
>
> (Lyotard 1991: 10)

The only way of rendering this death conceivable, and hence of turning the death of death into a death like any other, is by separating the future of thought from the fate of the human body:

> Thought without a body is the prerequisite for thinking of the death of all bodies, solar or terrestrial, and of the death of thoughts that are inseparable from those bodies. But 'without a body' in this exact sense: without the complex living terrestrial organism known as the human body. Not without hardware, obviously.
>
> (Lyotard 1991: 14)

Accordingly, thought must be weaned from its organic habitat and transplanted to some alternative support system in order to ensure its survival after the destruction of its terrestrial shelter. Lyotard's protagonist suggests that this weaning process, which would provide cognitive software with a hardware that could continue to operate independently of the conditions of life on earth – ensuring the survival of morphological complexity by replacing its material substrate – has been underway ever since life emerged on earth. Thus, the contention is that the history of technology overlaps with the history of life understood as originary synthesis of *techné* and *physis*. There is no 'natural' realm subsisting in contradistinction to the domain of technological artifice because matter – whether organic or inorganic – already possesses an intrinsic propensity to self-organization. 'Technology' names the set of evolutionary strategies bent on ensuring that the negentropic momentum underway on earth these last few billion years will not be eradicated by the imminent entropic tidal wave of extinction.

This narration of terrestrial history in terms of a trajectory of ever-increasing complexification is a now-familiar trope of vitalist eschatology, and one which remains vulnerable to Stephen Jay Gould's criticism of the 'fallacy of reified variation': the privileging of an idealized average at the expense of the full range of variations in a whole system. This is the fallacy that underlies the widely prevalent 'progressivist' interpretation of evolutionary history. In trying to gauge the underlying tendency of evolutionary variation we must distinguish between the *mean, median,* and *modal* values of variation. The mean or average value is obtained by adding all the values and dividing by the number of cases. The median is the halfway point in a graded array of values. But the mode is the most common value. In symmetrical distributions (as exemplified by the idealized figure of the 'bell curve'), all three values coincide. But many actual distributions – and the distribution of evolutionary complexity is among them – are asymmetrical because they are limited in the extent of potential spread in one direction by some fundament constraint or 'wall', which may be logical or empirical in nature, while remaining much freer to develop in the other direction. In the case of life, this wall is a function of the basic constraints of physics and chemistry: life can only begin at some minimal degree of complexity determined by the workings of physics and chemistry. Variations are subject to a left or right skew depending on the direction in which potential development is less constrained. But in skewed distributions, the values of the mean, the median, and the modal no longer coincide. Thus, the distribution of complexity over the course of evolutionary history can be charted by measuring the degree of complexity against its frequency of occurrence. Given a vertical axis measuring frequency of occurrence, and a horizontal axis measuring degree of complexity, the left wall of minimal complexity represented by the point of origin entails that the only direction open for the development of life is along the right axis of increasing complexity. But although the frequency distribution for life's complexity becomes increasingly right skewed over time, with complexity becoming ever more preponderant as the *mean* value represented by the continually expanding right tail of the distribution, the *modal* value remains more or less constant very close to the left wall of minimal complexity. Thus, Gould argues, although life's mean complexity may have increased, as represented by the development of increasingly sophisticated multicellular organisms, its modal complexity, as exemplified by bacteria, has remained more or less constant. Yet the latter outstrip the former not only in terms of frequency of occurrence – total bacterial biomass continues to exceed that of all other life combined – but also in terms of variation. Thus, out of the three most fundamental evolutionary domains, *Bacteria*, *Archea*, and *Eucarya*, two consist entirely of prokaryotes, which are the simplest unicellular organisms, devoid of nuclei, mitochondria, and chloroplasts. Moreover, the third domain, which is that of the eukaryotes (cells that *do* possess nuclei, chromosomes, etc.) comprises 13 kingdoms, among which are the three kingdoms that include all multicellular life – fungi, plants, and animals. More significantly, the extent of genetic diversity exhibited within the unicellular domains simply dwarfs that exhibited in the multicellular realm. Thus, the former comprises 23 kingdoms in all, while the latter consists of only 3; yet there is as much genetic distance between a *cynobacteria* and a *flavobacteria* as between a carrot and a zebra.

The 'progressivist' interpretation of evolutionary history assumes that the expanding 'right tail' of increasing complexity can be taken to be representative of the tendency exhibited by the continuum of variation considered as a whole. But this is a fallacy, for not only does the right tail merely represent a minuscule fraction of the total number of species, those species occupying the tip of the tail do not even form a continuous evolutionary lineage: thus, trilobites, dinosaurs, and *Homo sapiens* are completely different species which have stumbled into this position one after the other, and since no genetic continuity links these successive occupants of the tip of the tail, occupancy should not be attributed to any particular variety of adaptive prowess, but should rather be understood to be a consequence of the blind vagaries of evolutionary history. Ultimately then, as Gould puts it: 'The vaunted progress of life is really random motion away from simple beginnings, not directed impetus towards inherently advantageous complexity' (Gould 1996: 173).[37]

Thus, like the dialectical eschatology which is its principal rival (even if the latter codes its horizon of ultimate reconciliation as 'negative', and hence as a necessarily unattainable, perpetually deferred 'hope' – cf. Chapter 2), vitalist eschatology continues to evade the levelling force of extinction. For if the latter implies that 'everything is dead already', this is not only because extinction obliterates the earth construed as an inexhaustible reservoir of becoming, but also because, as Nietzsche provocatively suggested, the will to *know*, in its antagonism with the so-called will to live, is driven by the will to nothingness, understood as the compunction to become equal to the in-itself. Vitalism wants to have done with the will to nothingness, but believes it can do so by placing its faith in creative evolution, and by insisting that solar extinction is merely a local and temporary setback, which life will overcome by transforming its conditions of embodiment, whether by shifting from a carbon to a silicon-based substrate, or through some other, as yet unenvisaged strategy. But this is only to postpone the day of reckoning, because sooner or later both life and mind will have to reckon with the disintegration of the ultimate horizon, when, roughly one trillion, trillion, trillion (10^{1728}) years from now, the accelerating expansion of the universe will have disintegrated the fabric of matter itself, terminating the possibility of embodiment. Every star in the universe will have burnt out, plunging the cosmos into a state of absolute darkness and leaving behind nothing but spent husks of collapsed matter. All free matter, whether on planetary surfaces or in interstellar space, will have decayed, eradicating any remnants of life based in protons and chemistry, and erasing every vestige of sentience – irrespective of its physical basis. Finally, in a state cosmologists call 'asymptopia', the stellar corpses littering the empty universe will evaporate into a brief hailstorm of elementary particles. Atoms themselves will cease to exist. Only the implacable gravitational expansion will continue, driven by the currently inexplicable force called 'dark energy', which will keep pushing the extinguished universe deeper and deeper into an eternal and unfathomable blackness.[38]

Vitalism would restrict the scope of extinction by relocating the infinite horizonal reserve that fuels philosophical questioning from the local, terrestrial scale, to the global, cosmic scale. But given the aforementioned prospect of universal annihilation, this attempt to evade the levelling power of extinction – understood as the corollary of the claim that 'everything is dead already' – by expanding the horizon of creative becoming from a terrestrial to a cosmic habitat, reveals the spiritualist rationale behind the vitalist's denial of the possibility of physical annihilation – for what else is the assertion that the termination of physical existence *as such* presents no obstacle to the continuing evolution of life, if not a spiritualist declaration? Since cosmic extinction is just as much of an irrecusable factum for philosophy as biological death – although curiously, philosophers seem to assume that the latter is somehow more relevant than the former, as though familiarity were a criterion of philosophical relevance – every horizonal reserve upon which embodied thought draws to fuel its quest will be necessarily finite. Why then should thought continue investing in an account whose dwindling reserves are circumscribed by the temporary parameters of embodiment? Why keep playing for time? A change of body is just a way of postponing thought's inevitable encounter with the death that drives it in the form of the will to know. And a change of horizon is just a means of occluding the *transcendental* scope of extinction, precisely insofar as it levels the difference between life and death, time and space, revoking the ontological potency attributed to temporalizing thought in its alleged invulnerability to physical death.

Extinction portends a physical annihilation which negates the difference between mind and world, but which can no longer be construed as a limit internal to the transcendence of mind – an internalized exteriority, as death is for *Geist* or *Dasein* – because it implies an exteriority which *unfolds* or *externalizes* the internalization of exteriority concomitant with consciousness and its surrogates, whether *Geist* or *Dasein*. Extinction turns thinking inside out, objectifying it as a perishable thing in the world like any other (and no longer the imperishable condition of perishing). This is an externalization that cannot be appropriated by thought – not because it harbours some sort of transcendence that defies rational comprehension, but, on the contrary, because it indexes the autonomy of the object in its capacity to transform thought itself into a thing.

In this regard, extinction is a symptom of the *posteriority* which is the direct counterpart to the ancestrality discussed in Chapter 3. But we saw there how the premise of ancestrality alone does not suffice to disqualify the pretensions of correlationism, since the alleged incommensurability between ancestral and anthropomorphic time continues to assume a chronological framework which can be appropriated by the correlationist. Thus, ancestral anteriority can too easily be converted into anteriority *for us*. By way of contrast, the posteriority of extinction indexes a physical annihilation which no amount of chronological tinkering can transform into a correlate 'for us', because no matter how proximal or how distal the position allocated to it in space-time, it has *already* cancelled the sufficiency of the correlation. What defies correlation is the thought that 'after the sun's death, there will be no thought left to know its death took place' (Lyotard 1991: 9). Thus the thought of extinction undoes the correlation while avoiding any resort to intellectual intuition because it turns the absence of correlation – rather than ancestral reality – into an object of thought, but one which transforms thought itself into an object. There is no intellectual intuition of posteriority, since extinction does not index posterior reality – if it did, it would be necessary to account for this indicative relation, and this would reintroduce the dichotomy between correlation and intuition, which, as we saw in Chapter 3, threatens to remain intractable. Rather, extinction indexes the thought of the absence of thought. This is why it represents an objectification of thought, but one wherein the thought of the object is reversed by the object itself, rather than by the thought of the object. For the difference between the thought of the object and the object itself is no longer a function of thought, which is to say, of transcendence, but of the object understood as immanent *identity*, which, as we saw in Chapter 5, must be understood as the non-dialectical identity of the distinction between relation and non-relation. Thus, the object's difference from the concept is given ('without-givenness', which is to say, without-correlation) in such a way as to obviate the need for an account of the nature or genesis of this difference – something which neither intuitionism nor representationalism can do without turning this difference into a function of thought.

Consequently, there is a basic asymmetry in the relation between anteriority and posteriority: whereas the disjunction between ancestral time and anthropomorphic time was construed as a function of chronology – on the basis of the empirical assumption that the former preceded and will succeed the latter – there is an absolute disjunction between correlational time and the time of extinction, precisely insofar as the latter is not just a localizable spatiotemporal occurrence, and hence something that could be chronologically manipulated (although it is certainly *also* this), but rather *the extinction of space-time*. Thus, it is not so much that extinction *will* terminate the correlation, but that it *has already* retroactively terminated it. Extinction seizes the present of the correlation between the double pincers of a future that *has always already been*, and a past that is *perpetually yet to be*. Accordingly, there can be no 'afterwards' of extinction, since it already corrodes the efficacy of the projection through which correlational synthesis would assimilate its reality to that of a phenomenon dependent upon conditions of manifestation. Extinction has a transcendental efficacy precisely insofar as it tokens an annihilation which is neither a possibility towards which actual existence could orient itself, nor a given datum from which future existence could proceed. It retroactively disables projection, just as it pre-emptively abolishes retention. In this regard, extinction unfolds in an 'anterior posteriority' which usurps the 'future anteriority' of human existence.

7.4   The seizure of phenomenology: Levinas

The former is of course a key trope in Levinas's phenomenology of absolute alterity, wherein the radical passivity associated with the immemorial trace of the 'other in me' is associated with an 'impossibility of possibility' which disables intentional apprehension and *ekstatic* projection.

And in fact, Lyotard's 'solar catastrophe' effectively *transposes* Levinas's theologically inflected 'impossibility of possibility' into a natural-scientific register, so that it is no longer the death of the Other that usurps the sovereignty of consciousness, but the extinction of the sun. Significantly, this transposition occurs at the historical juncture wherein elements of the scientific image have begun to bleed into those philosophical discourses probing the extremities of the manifest image – which is to say, the discourses of post-Kantian continental philosophy – generating increasingly complex patterns of dissonance within the latter. For just as the phenomenon of death indexes an anomalous zone in the conceptual fabric of the manifest image – the point at which our everyday concepts and categories begin to break down, which is why it remains a privileged topic for philosophers exploring the outer limits of the manifest image – so, by the same token, the concept of extinction represents an aberration for the phenomenological discourse which sought to transcendentalize the infrastructure of the manifest image precisely in order to safeguard the latter from the incursions of positivism and naturalism. Yet it is precisely insofar as the concept of extinction expresses a dissonance resulting from the interference between the manifest and scientific images that it could not have been generated from within the latter; it is manufactured by deploying the manifest image's most sophisticated conceptual resources (in conjunction with elements of scientific discourse) against that image's own phenomenological self-understanding. At this particular historical juncture, philosophy should resist the temptation to install itself within one of the rival images, just as it should refuse the forced choice between the reactionary authoritarianism of manifest normativism, and the metaphysical conservatism of scientific naturalism. Rather, it should exploit the mobility that is one of the rare advantages of abstraction in order to shuttle back and forth between images, establishing conditions of transposition, rather than synthesis, between the speculative anomalies thrown up within the order of phenomenal manifestation, and the metaphysical quandaries generated by the sciences' challenge to the manifest order. In this regard, the concept of extinction is necessarily equivocal precisely insofar as it crystallizes the interference between the two discourses. Thus, the equivalence that obtained between the existential-phenomenological characterization of death, and the natural-scientific phenomenon of extinction, is reiterated in the reversibility between the phenomenology of trauma and the extinction of phenomenology, so that the catastrophic nature of extinction, its overturning of origin and end, empirical and transcendental, follows directly from its being at once a *naturalization of eschatology* and a *theologization of cosmology*. Fittingly, it is precisely the discourse of phenomenology that is best suited to registering the trauma that portends the disintegration of the manifest image.

In this regard, Levinas's hyperbolic phenomenology provides the perfect lexicon with which to describe extinction as a traumatic *seizure* of phenomenology. The hyperbolic emphasis of Levinas's discourse is the result of his attempt to excavate the meta-ontological and meta-categorical significance of a transcendence beyond being. Levinas proposes to decipher the latter via a set of signifying tropes, which, he claims, already animate the pre-ontological understanding of being sought for by the early Heidegger:

> Emphasis means both a rhetorical figure, a means of self-exaggeration, and a way of showing oneself. The word is a good one, as is the word 'hyperbole': there are hyperboles wherein notions transmute themselves. To describe this transmutation is also a way of doing phenomenology. Exasperation as philosophical method!
>
> (Levinas 1992: 142)[39]

Thus, Levinas's phenomenological method is one of *emphatic exasperation*, and he insists that it alone is capable of articulating the enigmatic and epiphenomenal 'sense of sense' harboured by the radically non-ontological transcendence he ascribes to the 'wholly other'. But the only register of phenomenological sense commensurate with the punishing alterity of this infinite transcendence is that of violation. More precisely, Levinas engages in an emphatic exasperation of phenomenology the better to describe the originary ethical sense proper to the phenomenon of trauma. Accordingly, infinite alterity is characterized as a 'wounding' and 'haemorrhaging' of subjectivity, just as the ethical subject is described as a 'hostage' who is 'traumatized' and 'persecuted' by the Other (indeed, for Levinas, excruciation seems to be the ethical trope *par excellence*).[40] The 'impossibility of possibility', which is the signature of the wholly other in Levinas's work, is both an impossibility *of* being and an impossibility *in* being. Dying as the impossibility of death is an impossibility *of* being, insofar as the latter is conceived as the interminable and anonymous rumble of the 'il y a' – Levinas's mischievous subreption of Heidegger's *Es gibt* ('there is') – from which there is no escape.[41] But it is simultaneously an impossibility *in* being, insofar as it points to the intolerable excess of passive suffering whereby the self is accused in responsibility by the infinitely Other. It is this traumatic accusation that prevents the self from being able to persist in its own being. For Levinas, the two senses of impossibility – the impossibility of ceasing to be and the impossibility of beginning to be – are absolutely different yet indissociable. Thus absolute alterity is traumatic precisely insofar as it combines the horror of sense and the horror of non-sense: it means at once the horror of non-sense as eternal persistence in being, with no possibility of escape (the *il y a*); and the horror of sense, understood as the infinite ethical interruption of being, which indefinitely postpones our ability to be (the wounding transcendence of *illeity*). As a result, the anterior posteriority concomitant with the impossibility of possibility gives rise to a traumatic double bind: we can neither begin to be, nor cease to be. Subjectivity is paralysed by an alterity that has 'always already' dispossessed it of its own substance, an alterity embedded 'in its skin', but which thereby renders it 'ill at ease in its own skin':

> as though encumbered and blocked by itself, suffocating beneath itself, insufficiently open, forced to unburden itself of itself, to breathe in more deeply, to the limit of its breath; forced to dis-possess itself until it loses itself. Does this loss have the void, the zero-point and quiet of the grave, as its term, as if the subjectivity of the subject signified nothing?
>
> (1990: 175)

Levinas's question is supposed to highlight the enigmatic character of the meaning of alterity. Were we in possession of a criterion allowing us to distinguish the ethical sense of our dispossession 'for the Other' from the ontological non-sense of our dispossession 'for nothing' (insofar as we remain trapped by the anonymous persistence of the *il y a*), then the 'anarchy' which Levinas ascribes to ethical significance – the enigma of the trace – would be betrayed. The ethical meaning of the 'for the Other' is kept open precisely insofar as it remains *ontologically* indistinguishable from the 'for nothing': the non-sense of being. Without this ambiguity, the excess which Levinas ascribes to ethical sense vis-à-vis the ontological economy of meaning would be cancelled and its alterity reinscribed within the theodicy of the logos. Consequently, the difference between the 'for the other' and the 'for nothing', or between the Other and the Same, must 'come to the same' (*revenir au même*) *within* being precisely in order to ensure the possibility – or what Levinas calls 'chance' – that the difference between ethical sense and ontological non-sense may not 'return to the Same', but rather point *beyond* being. However, given that Levinas's entire project proceeds from the prior stipulation that the transcendence of the infinitely Other *means* the 'good beyond being', it is difficult to see how this purported ambiguity could be anything more than a sham. Levinas has already answered his own question in the negative: subjectivity will not have the zero-point and quiet of the grave as its term, precisely because the subjectivity of the subject *does* mean something, and that something is 'the good beyond being'. Contra Levinas then, it is necessary to insist that the phenomenology of trauma also entails a trauma for phenomenology: subjectivity as understood by the latter has already been terminated, it already means nothing. The necessary obverse of Levinas's insistence on the inherently equivocal sense of trauma is the claim that the latter itself entails the extinction of phenomenological sense (and *a fortiori* of the ethical sense to which Levinas would subordinate it). It is in this regard that extinction is a transcendental trauma: it is the conceptual transposition of a physical phenomenon which undoes the phenomenological resources through which the manifest image would *make sense* of it. Moreover, by overturning the hierarchy of empirical and a priori, along with the phenomenological complicity between sense and nonsense, the catastrophe of extinction reiterates the trauma at the origin of life, which Freud in *Beyond the Pleasure Principle* construes in terms of the scission between the organic and inorganic.

7.5   The trauma of life: Freud

The phenomenon that motivates Freud's investigation in *Beyond the Pleasure Principle* is that of traumatic neurosis. The latter gives rise to a 'compulsion to repeat', wherein the sufferer compulsively relives the traumatic incident in his or her dreams. Yet if the function of dreams is primarily that of wish-fulfilment, in conformity with the pleasure principle, which strives to maximize pleasure – where pleasure is defined as a diminution of excitation – and to minimize displeasure – where displeasure is defined as an increase in excitation – then traumatic neurosis poses a problem for psychoanalysis because it resists explanation in terms of the pleasure principle: why is the patient compelled to relive a shatteringly unpleasurable experience? Freud's answer is that through this repetition, the psyche is striving to muster the anxiety required in order to achieve a successful *binding* (*Besetzung*) of the excess of excitation released by the traumatic breaching of its defences. It is this binding that lies 'beyond the pleasure principle'. The compulsion to repeat consists in an attempt on the part of the unconscious to relive the traumatic incident in a condition of anxious anticipation that will allow it to buffer the shock, thereby compensating for the impotent terror that

disabled the organism and staunching the excessive influx of excita-
tions brought about by a massive psychic wound.

Moreover, insofar as the manifestations of the compulsion to repeat
'give the appearance of some "daemonic" force at work' (Freud 1991:
307), this is due to their inherently 'instinctual' (*Triebhaft*) character. In
this regard, says Freud, the compulsion to repeat harbours the key to
understanding the nature of the 'drive' (*Trieb*) as such:

> It seems then that a drive is an urge inherent in organic life to restore
> an earlier state of things which the living entity has been obliged to
> abandon under the pressure of external disturbing forces; that is, a
> kind of organic elasticity, or, to put it another way, the expression of
> the inertia inherent in organic life. [...] It is possible to specify this
> final goal of all organic striving. It would be in contradiction to the
> conservative nature of the instincts if the goal of life were a state of
> things which had never been yet attained. On the contrary, it must
> be an old state of things, an initial state from which the living entity
> has at one time or another departed and to which it is striving to
> return by the circuitous paths along which its development leads. If
> we are to take it as a truth that knows no exception that everything
> living dies for internal reasons – becomes inorganic once again –
> then we shall be compelled to say that '*the aim of all life is death*' and
> looking backwards, that '*inanimate things existed before living ones*'.
>
> (Freud 1991: 309–11)

Thus, the fundamental tendency of the 'drive' or 'instinct' is the primordial pull back towards the inorganic. Although life diverges from
the inorganic in ever more circuitous detours, these are no more than
temporary extensions of the latter, which will eventually contract back
to their original inorganic condition, understood as the zero-degree of
contraction, or *decontraction*. But if death constitutes the 'aim of all life',
an aim which, according to Freud, is in some sense 'internal' to living
organisms, this cannot simply be understood in Aristotelian terms as a
telos, an intrinsic purpose orienting the development of the entity from
within. A *telos* has no reality independently of the entities whose existence it governs; thus, if the inorganic were merely the *telos* of the
organic in this conventional sense, it could not possibly have existed
before it. Yet Freud maintains the realist thesis according to which
'inanimate things existed *before* living ones' (my emphasis), and uses it
to underwrite the reality of the death-drive. Consequently, the inorganic as 'initial state' and 'aim' of life cannot simply be understood as a

condition internal to the development of life, whether as the *essence* that life has been, or the *telos* which it will be. Just as the reality of the inorganic is not merely a function of the existence of the organic, so the reality of death is not merely a function of life's past, or of its future. Death, understood as the principle of decontraction driving the contractions of organic life is not a past or future state towards which life tends, but rather the originary *purposelessness* which compels all purposefulness, whether organic or psychological.

With the thesis that 'the aim of all life is death', Freud defuses Nietzsche's metaphysics of the will: the life that wills power is merely a contraction of the death that wants nothing. The will to nothingness is not an avatar of the will to power; rather, the will to power is merely a mask of the will to nothingness. But this 'nothingness' cannot be retrojected into the past or projected into the future; the only temporality commensurate with it is that of the 'anterior posteriority' proper to physical death as that which seizes organic temporality, but which cannot be seized by it. Thus, the repetition which is driven by death does not repeat the latter as though it were an earlier state of affairs experienced by life or consciousness, for the trauma which drives repetition is precisely what cannot be lived or consciously apprehended. Though trauma is real, its reality cannot be calibrated by the life of the organism, just as it cannot be commensurated with the resources of consciousness. It can only be registered as a dysfunctioning of the organism, or as an interruption of consciousness, and it is this dysfunction and this interruption that is repeated. Accordingly, it is because the 'originary' traumatic occurrence was only ever registered in the unconscious, rather than experienced, that there is a compulsion to (re-)experience it. But it can only be re-experienced as something that was neither lived nor experienced, since trauma marks the obliteration of life and experience. Nevertheless, the fact that experience cannot obliterate itself points to the reality of trauma, which cannot simply be construed as a function of experience.

The reality of trauma is registered as an unconscious wound, which continues to resonate in the psychic economy as an unresolved disturbance, an un-dampened excess of excitation. And it is because it indexes an influx of excitation vastly in excess of the binding capacities exercised by what Freud calls 'the perception-consciousness system' that trauma leaves behind this permanent imprint in the unconscious, since consciousness always arises *instead of* a memory trace.[42] Thus, it is not the traumatic experience (which never occurred), but rather this unconscious trace whose demand to be renegotiated gives rise to compulsive repetition. Trauma is constitutively unconscious: it only exists as a trace. Yet this traumatic trace persists as a permanent and indelible imprint in the unconscious because it testifies to something unmanageable for the filtering apparatus of the perception-consciousness system: a haemorrhaging of the psyche.

Freud then proposes a remarkable speculative hypothesis linking the origins of this filtering apparatus to the genesis of organic individuation. A primitive organic vesicle (that is, a small bladder, cell, bubble or hollow structure) becomes capable of filtering the continuous and potentially lethal torrent of external stimuli by sacrificing part of itself in order to erect a protective shield against excessive influxes of excitation. In doing so, it effects a definitive separation between organic interiority and inorganic exteriority:

> [The vesicle] acquires the shield in this way: its outermost surface ceases to have the structure proper to living matter, becomes to some degree inorganic and thenceforth functions as a special envelope or membrane resistant to stimuli. In consequence, the energies of the external world are able to pass into the next underlying layers, which have remained living, with only a fragment of their original intensity [...] By its death the outer layer has saved all the deeper ones from a similar fate – unless, that is to say, stimuli reach it which are so strong that they break through the protective shield. *Protection against* stimuli is an almost more important function for the living organism than *reception of* stimuli [...] In highly developed organisms the receptive cortical layers of the former vesicle has long been withdrawn into the depths of the interior of the body, though portions of it have been left behind on the surface immediately beneath the shield against stimuli.
>
> (Freud 1991: 299)

Accordingly, the separation between organic interiority and inorganic exteriority is won at the cost of the death of part of the primitive organism itself, and it is this death that gives rise to the protective shield filtering out the potentially lethal influxes of external energy. Thus, individuated organic life is won at the cost of this aboriginal death whereby the organism first becomes capable of separating itself from the inorganic outside (cf. Chapter 2). This death, which gives birth to organic individuation, thereby conditions the possibility of organic phylogenesis, as well as of sexual reproduction. Consequently, not only does this death precede the organism, it is the precondition for the organism's ability to reproduce and die. If the death-drive qua compulsion to repeat is the originary, primordial motive force driving organic life, this is because the motor of repetition – the repeating instance – is this trace of the aboriginal trauma of organic individuation. The death-drive understood as repetition of the inorganic is the repetition of the death which gave birth to the organism – a death that cannot be satisfactorily repeated, not only because the organism which bears its trace did not yet exist to experience it, but also because that trace is the marker of an exorbitant death, one that even in dying, the organism cannot successfully repeat. Thus, the trace of aboriginal death harbours an impossible demand for organic life: it is the trace of a trauma that demands to be integrated into the psychic economy of the organism, but which cannot because it expresses the originary traumatic scission between organic and inorganic. The organism cannot live the death that gives rise to the difference between life and death. The death-drive is the trace of this scission: a scission that will never be successfully *bound* (invested) because it remains the *unbindable* excess that makes binding possible. It is as the bearer of this scission and this excess that physical death cannot be located either at the origin or end of life. Decontraction is not a negentropic starting point to which one could return, or an entropic terminus towards which one could hasten. Its reality is that of the 'being-nothing' whose anterior posteriority expresses the identity of entropic indifference and negentropic difference, an identity which is given to thought as the objective reality that already determines it. This determination occurs through philosophy's binding of the trauma of extinction, which persists as an un-conscious and un-bound disturbance of phenomenal consciousness, fuelling the will to know.

7.6   Binding extinction

Extinction is real yet not empirical, since it is not of the order of experience. It is transcendental yet not ideal, since it coincides with the external objectification of thought unfolding at a specific historical juncture when the resources of intelligibility, and hence the lexicon of ideality, are being renegotiated. In this regard, it is precisely the extinction of meaning that clears the way for the intelligibility of extinction. Senselessness and purposelessness are not merely privative; they represent a gain in intelligibility. The cancellation of sense, purpose, and possibility marks the point at which the 'horror' concomitant with the impossibility of either being or not-being becomes intelligible. Thus, if everything is dead already, this is not only because extinction disables those possibilities which were taken to be constitutive of life and existence, but also because the will to know is driven by the traumatic reality of extinction, and strives to become equal to the trauma of the in-itself whose trace it bears. In becoming equal to it, philosophy achieves a binding of extinction, through which the will to know is finally rendered commensurate with the in-itself. This binding coincides with the objectification of thinking understood as the *adequation without correspondence* between the objective reality of extinction and the subjective knowledge of the trauma to which it gives rise. It is this adequation that constitutes the truth of extinction. But to acknowledge this truth, the subject of philosophy must also recognize that he or she is already dead, and that philosophy is neither a medium of affirmation nor a source of justification, but rather the organon of extinction.

Notes

Preface

1. Friedrich Nietzsche, *The Will to Power*, ed. W. Kaufman, New York: Vintage, 1967, §1.
2. Steven Weinberg, *The First Three Minutes*, London: Flamingo, 1983, 149.
3. Jonathan Israel, *Radical Enlightenment: Philosophy and the Making of Modernity 1650–1750*, Oxford: Oxford University Press, 2001; *Enlightenment Contested: Philosophy, Modernity and the Emancipation of Man 1670–1752*, Oxford: Oxford University Press, 2006.

1   The *Apoptosis* of Belief

1. 'Apoptosis: a type of cell death in which the cell uses specialized cellular machinery to kill itself; a cell suicide mechanism that enables metazoans to control cell number and eliminate cells that threaten the animal's survival.' American Psychological Association (APA): apoptosis (n.d.), WordNet® 2.1, Dictionary.com website: http://dictionary.reference.com/browse/apoptosis.
2. Wilfrid Sellars, 'Philosophy and the Scientific Image of Man' in *Science, Perception and Reality*, London: Routledge and Kegan Paul, 1963a, 1–40.
3. Originally published in 1956 as Vol. I of *Minnesota Studies in the Philosophy of Science*, H. Feigl and M. Scriven (eds); reprinted in 1963 in Sellars's *Science, Perception, and Reality*, Routledge & Kegan Paul; and again in 1997 as *Empiricism and the Philosophy of Mind*, Cambridge MA: Harvard University Press.
4. See Paul Churchland, 'Folk Psychology' in P. M. Churchland and P. S. Churchland, *On the Contrary: Critical Essays 1987–1997*, Cambridge, MA: MIT Press, 1998, 4–5.
5. Originally published in the *Journal of Philosophy*, Vol. 78, No. 2, February 1981: 76–90. Reprinted in P. M. Churchland, *A Neurocomputational Perspective: The Nature of Mind and the Structure of Science*, London: MIT, 1989, 1–22.
6. J. Fodor, *Psychosemantics*, Cambridge, MA: MIT, 1987, xii.
7. There are other versions: Paul Feyerabend, 'Materialism and the Mind-Body Problem' in *Review of Metaphysics* XVII 1, 65 (September 1963), 49–66; Richard Rorty, 'Mind-Body Identity, Privacy, and Categories', *Review of Metaphysics* XIX, 1, 73 (September 1965), 24–54; Stephen P. Stich, *From Folk Psychology to Cognitive Science: The Case against Belief*, Cambridge, MA: MIT Press, 1983; Patricia S. Churchland, *Neurophilosophy: Toward a Unified Science of the Mind-Brain*, Cambridge, MA: MIT Press, 1986; Patricia S. Churchland and Terrence Sejnowski, *The Computational Brain*, Cambridge, MA: MIT Press, 1992.
8. For a comprehensive anthology of these and other critiques of EM, see R. N. McCauley ed., *The Churchlands and Their Critics*, Oxford: Blackwell, 1996.

9. J. Marshall and J. Gurd, 'The Furniture of Mind' in McCauley ed. *The Church-lands*, 176–91.

10. In this regard, the 'state space semantics' which Churchland has elaborated on the basis of his PVA model has been attacked on the grounds that it represents a regression to pre-Kantian empiricism. Thus Fodor and Lepore have argued that Churchland cannot provide conditions of individuation for concepts, which is to say, a criterion for identity of meaning. Consequently he must make do with a criterion of similarity. But he cannot provide a criterion of similarity of meaning for his psychological prototypes without surreptitiously resorting to an empiricist account of the identity conditions for concepts. As a result, the semantic dimensions which are supposed to individuate concepts are simply stipulated with reference to empirical features of the environment, and concepts become compositionally defined on the basis of empirical simples. According to Fodor and Lepore, this presents Churchland with the following dilemma: he can either re-invoke some version of the analytic–synthetic distinction or embrace Humean 'blank slate' empiricism. Churchland has retorted that his account can indeed provide a robust notion of functional similarity for prototypes via discriminatory mechanisms while avoiding the twin perils of associationism and the analytic a priori. Cf. J. Fodor and E. Lepore (1996a), 'Churchland and State Space Semantics' in McCauley ed. 1996, 145–58; P. M. Churchland (1996a), 'Fodor and Lepore: State Space Semantics and Meaning Holism' in McCauley ed. 1996, 273–7; J. Fodor and E. Lepore (1996b), 'Reply to Churchland' in McCauley ed. 1996, 159–62; P. M. Churchland (1996b), 'Second Reply to Fodor and Lepore' in McCauley ed. 1996, 278–83; and P. M. Churchland (1998a) 'Conceptual Similarity across Sensory and Neural Diversity: The Fodor–Lepore Challenge Answered' in P. M. Churchland and P. S. Churchland 1998, 81–112. For a defence of Churchland in this controversy, see Jesse J. Prinz, 'Empiricism and State Space Semantics' in *Paul Churchland*, Brian L. Keeley ed. Cambridge: Cambridge University Press, 2006, 88–112.

11. A version of this so-called *reductio* of EM is expounded at length by Lynn Rudder-Baker in *Saving Belief: A Critique of Physicalism*, Princeton, NJ: Princeton University Press, 1987. Michael Devitt – an ardent opponent of eliminativism – provides a convincing refutation of this line of attack in his 1990 article 'Transcendentalism about Content', *Pacific Philosophical Quaterly*, Vol. 71, No. 2, 247–63. Despite this and several equally decisive refutations by both Paul Churchland (cf. 1981, 1993) and Patricia Churchland (1981), the 'self-defeating' objection is regularly trotted out by foes of eliminativism.

12. The example is from Patricia Churchland, 'Is Determinism Self-Refuting?' in *Mind*, 90, 1981, 99–101; cited in P. M. Churchland (1989), 22.

13. In his 'Reply to Glymour', Churchland expands on this claim: 'Ceteris paribus, an activated prototype [i.e. an explanation] is better if it is part of the most unified conceptual configuration [...] networks that have formed the simplest or most unified partitions across their activation space are networks that do much better at generalising their knowledge to novel cases. Very briefly, they do better at recognising novel situations for what they are because they have generated a relevantly unified similarity gradient that will catch novel cases in the same subvolume that catches the training case' (P. M. Churchland, 1998c: 286).

14. 'FP, like any other theory, is a family of learned vectorial prototypes, prototypes that sustain recognition of current reality, anticipation of future reality, and manipulation of ongoing reality' (P. M. Churchland, 1998b: 15).
15. 'Whether FP is false and whether it will fail to reduce are empirical issues whose decisive settlement must flow from experimental research and theoretical development, not from any arguments a priori' (P. M. Churchland, 1998b: 10).
16. '[T]he folk-semantical notion of "reference" is without any real integrity. Reference is uniquely fixed neither by networks of belief, nor by causal relations, nor by anything else, because there is no single uniform relation that connects each descriptive term to the world in anything like the fashion that common sense supposes' (P. M. Churchland, 1989: 276–7).
17. Thus, Churchland invokes Einstein's Special Theory of Relativity to underline the extent to which 'new theories often bring with them a novel and proprietary vocabulary for describing the observable world, a vocabulary that can augment or even displace the old observational vocabulary' (P. M. Churchland 1998b: 18).
18. Churchland himself frequently adduces the argument that Ptolemaic astronomy could have happily continued 'explaining' and accommodating recalcitrant astronomical data by piling virtual epicycle upon virtual epicycle. Cf. for instance P. M. Churchland's 'Densmore and Dennett on Virtual Machines and Consciousness' in *Philosophy and Phenomenological Research*, Vol. LIX, No. 3, 1999, 767.
19. Cf. Thomas Kuhn, *The Structure of Scientific Revolutions*, Chicago: University of Chicago Press, 1962; and P. M. Churchland 1989: 191.
20. Since writing the above, I have learnt that a very similar criticism of Churchland has already been formulated (with far greater concision) by Teed Rockwell in his 1995 paper 'Beyond Eliminative Materialism: Some Unnoticed Implications of Churchland's Pragmatic Pluralism', available at http://cogprints.org/379/00/BeyondEM.html. Cf. also Rockwell's *Neither Brain nor Ghost: A Non-Dualist Alternative to Mind–Brain Identity Theory*, Cambridge, MA: MIT, 2005.
21. See especially the following texts by Fodor: 'Review of Dawkin's *Climbing Mount Improbable*', 'Deconstructing Dennett's Darwin', 'Is Science Biologically Possible? Comments on Some Arguments of Patricia Churchland and of Alvin Plantinga', and 'Review of Stephen Pinker's *How the Mind Works* and Henry Plotkin's *Evolution in Mind*'. All four essays can be found in Fodor's *In Critical Condition: Polemical Essays on Cognitive Science and the Philosophy of Mind*, Cambridge, MA: MIT, 2000.
22. Cf. Andy Clark, 'Dealing in Futures: Folk Psychology and the Role of Representation in Cognitive Science' in McCauley ed., 1996, 86–101; and also Floris van der Burg and Michael Eardley, 'Does the Man on the Clapham Omnibus Have a Labcoat in his Pocket? Eliminative Materialism is Based on a Valid Argument from the False Premise That Folk-Psychology is an Empirical Theory', in *PLI: The Warwick Journal of Philosophy, Vol. 9. Parallel Processes: Philosophy and Science*, 139–55, 2000.
23. Edmund Husserl, *Ideas Pertaining to a Pure Phenomenology and to a Phenomenological Philosophy. First Book*, tr. F. Kersten, London: Kluwer, 1982.
24. J. Searle, *The Rediscovery of the Mind*, Cambridge, MA: MIT Press, 1992, 121.

25. D. Dennett, *Sweet Dreams: Philosophical Obstacles to a Science of Consciousness*, Cambridge, MA: MIT Press, 2006.

26. J. Derrida, *Speech and Phenomena and Other Essays on Husserl's Theory of Signs*, tr. David B. Allison, Evanston, IL: Northwestern University Press, 1973.

27. Cf. M. Henry, *The Essence of Manifestation*, tr. G. Etskorn, The Hague: Martinus Nijhoff, 1973. We will return to Heidegger, Henry, and phenomenology in chapters 5 and 6.

28. Cf. T. Metzinger, *Being No-One: The Self-Model Theory of Subjectivity*, London: MIT Press, 2004.

2   The *Thanatosis* of Enlightenment

1. Theodore Adorno and Max Horkheimer, *Dialectic of Enlightenment* tr. Edmund Jephcott, Stanford, CA: Stanford University Press, 2002.

2. Andreas Huyssen distinguishes these five registers as follows: '[F]irst, in relation to the critique of the commodity form and its powers of reification and deception, a thoroughly negative form of mimesis [*Mimesis ans Verhärtete*]; secondly, in relation to the anthropological grounding of human nature which, as Adorno insists in *Minima Moralia*, is 'indissolubly linked to imitation'; third, in a biological somatic sense geared toward survival, as Adorno had encountered it in Roger Caillois's work [...]; fourth, in the Freudian sense of identification and projection indebted to *Totem and Taboo*; and, lastly, in an aesthetic sense that resonates strongly with Benjamin's language theory, as it relates to the role of word and image in the evolution of signifying systems.' Andreas Huyssen, 'Of Mice and Mimesis', *New German Critique*, No. 81, Dialectic of Enlightenment (Autumn 2000), 66–7.

3. Adorno had reviewed Caillois's 1934 text 'La Mante religieuse' (originally published in *Minotaure* 5 [1934]: 23–6) in the *Zeitschrift für Sozialforschung* 7 (1938): 410–11. Also relevant in this regard is Caillois's 'Mimétisme et psychasthénie légendaire', originally published in *Minotaure* 7 (1935): 4–10, which we will discuss below. Both texts are included in Caillois's *L'Homme et le sacré*, Paris: Gallimard, Folio/Éssais, 1988 (first published in 1938). English versions can be found in *On the Edge of Surrealism: A Roger Caillois Reader*, C. Frank and C. Nash (eds), Durham: Duke University Press, 2003.

4. We will return to *Beyond the Pleasure Principle* in Chapter 7, where we will reconsider Freud's account of the death-drive.

5. Cf. Sigmund Freud, 'Beyond the Pleasure Principle' in *The Penguin Freud Library. Vol. 11: On Metapsychology*, Harmondsworth, Middlesex: Penguin, 1991, 270–338.

6. The implication, more pathetic than provocative, is unavoidable: Einstein and Himmler are separated merely by degrees, not kind.

7. Jay Bernstein, *Adorno: Disenchantment and Ethics*, Cambridge: CUP, 2001, 191.

8. Roger Caillois, *L'Homme et le sacré*, Gallimard, Folio/Éssais 1988, 86–122.

9. I owe this formulation to Nigel Cooke's remarkable essay 'The Language of Insects' in *Sandwich 1: Autumn* , London: SecMoCo Publishing, 2004.

10. E. Minkowski, 'Le problème du temps en psychopathologie' in *Recherches Philosophiques*, 1932–33, 239; *Le Temps vécue. Études phénoménologiques et psychopathologiques*, Paris: L'évolution Psychiatrique, 1933; *Lived Time*,

tr. N. Metzel, Evanston: Northwestern University Press, 1970; *La Schizophrénie*, Paris: Payot, Rivages, 1997 (originally published 1927).
11. *Phagocytosis* is a process describing the engulfment and destruction of extra-cellularly derived materials by phagocytic cells, such as macrophages and neutrophils.
12. Roger Caillois, 'Mimétisme et psychasthénie légendaire' in *L'Homme et le sacré*, Gallimard, Folio/Éssais, 1988.
13. In this regard, the veritable analogue for the dialectic of enlightenment is not Homer's *Odyssey* but rather David Cronenberg's *The Fly* (1986), whose protagonist declares: 'I was an insect who dreamed he was a man – and loved it – but now the dream is over and the insect is awake.'

3   The Enigma of Realism

1. Q. Meillassoux, *Après la finitude. Éssai sur la nécéssité de la contingence*, Paris: Seuil, 2006, 39.
2. 'Billion' and 'trillion' will be used throughout, following their now interna-tionally accepted US usage, as meaning a thousand million and a million, million respectively.
3. Graham Harman has elaborated a profound critique of this tendency in con-temporary philosophy, seeing in it an avatar of a generalized anti-realism. Whether the relation in question is the epistemological relation between mind and world, the phenomenological relation between noesis and noema, the ekstatic relation between *Sein* and *Dasein*, the prehensive relation between event-objects, or the processual relation between matter and mem-ory, Harman argues that this premium on relationality occludes the discon-tinuous reality of objects in favour of their reciprocal idealizations. Harman's startlingly original interpretation of Heidegger provides the point of depar-ture for his complete re-orientation of phenomenology away from the pri-macy of the human relation to things and towards things themselves considered independently of their relation to humans or each other. Accordingly, the fundamental task for this 'object-oriented philosophy' con-sists in explaining how autonomous objects can ever interact with each other, and to that end Harman has developed a particularly ingenious the-ory of 'vicarious causation'. Harman first outlines the rudiments of this project in *Tool-Being: Heidegger and the Metaphysics of Objects*, Chicago: Open Court, 2002 and develops it further in *Guerrilla Metaphysics: Phenomenology and the Carpentry of Things*, Chicago: Open Court, 2005.
4. Here are some paradigmatic expressions of the correlationist credo from three canonical continental philosophers: Nietzsche, Husserl, and Heidegger:

> Against the scientific prejudice – The biggest fable of all is the fable of knowledge. One would like to know what things-in-themselves are; but behold, there are no things-in-themselves! But even supposing there were an in-itself, an unconditioned thing, it would for that very reason be unknowable! [...] [S]omething that is of no concern to anyone *is* not at all.
>
> (Nietzsche 1968: §555)

The existence of Nature *cannot* be the condition for the existence of consciousness, since Nature itself turns out to be a correlate of consciousness: Nature *is* only as being constituted in regular concatenations of consciousness.

(Husserl 1982: 116)

Given in and through this liberation [from the natural attitude] is the discovery of the universal, absolutely self-enclosed and absolutely self-sufficient correlation between the world itself and world-consciousness [...] the absolute correlation between beings of every sort and every meaning, on the one hand, and absolute subjectivity, as constituting meaning and ontic validity in this broadest manner, on the other hand. [...] [D]uring the consistently carried-out epochē, [the world] is under our gaze purely as the correlate of the subjectivity which gives it ontic meaning, through whose validities the world 'is' at all.

(Husserl 1970: 151–2)

Of course only as long as Dasein *is* (that is, as long as an understanding of Being is ontically possible), 'is there' Being. When Dasein does not exist, 'independence' 'is' not either, nor 'is' the 'in-itself'. In such a case this sort of thing can be neither understood nor not understood. In such a case even entities within-the-world can neither be discovered nor lie hidden. *In such a case* it cannot be said that entities are, nor can it be said that they are not.

(Heidegger 1962: 255)

5. Q. Meillassoux, *After Finitude: An Essay on the Necessity of Contingency*, tr. R. Brassier, London: Continuum 2008.
6. At the time of writing (2007), these objections have only been communicated verbally or in writing to Meillassoux; they have yet to appear in print.
7. This is essentially Slavoj Žižek's position: '[T]he only way effectively to account for the status of (self-)consciousness is to assert the ontological incompleteness of "reality" itself; there is "reality" only insofar as there is an ontological "gap", a "crack", in its very heart, that is to say, a traumatic excess, a foreign body which cannot be integrated into it' (Žižek 2006: 242). The thesis that consciousness or subjectivity is not a substantial entity but rather an insubstantial gap fissuring the ontological order lies at the heart of Žižek's (brilliant) hybridization of Lacan and Hegel. To his considerable credit, and in conformity with his commitment to a 'dialectical materialism', Žižek has consistently engaged with cognitive science (cf. Žižek 2006: 146–250). However, it is difficult to square Žižek's putative 'materialism' with his assertion that reality itself is structured around the traumatic kernel of subjectivity. If reality in-itself is necessarily constituted in relation to the fissure of self-consciousness, then all those material processes which, according to Darwin, preceded the emergence of self-consciousness, must be dismissed as phantasmatic 'false memories' generated by a delirious transcendental subject.
8. I am indebted to Graham Harman, Robin Mackay, and Damian Veal for all these critical points.
9. Though Kant would certainly not endorse an instrumentalist conception of science, it is his formula which most succinctly summarizes the way in

which correlationists render the empirical reality of scientific objects dependent upon transcendental conditions of objectivation: 'The conditions of the possibility of experience in general are likewise conditions of the possibility of the objects of experience' (Kant: A 158/B 197).

10. I owe this expression to Graham Harman.

11. We shall attempt to elaborate some of the conceptual resources required for such a task via a critical discussion of the work of François Laruelle in Chapter 5.

12. 'In general, our consideration of the nature of contradiction has shown that it is not, so to speak, a blemish, an imperfection or a defect in something if a contradiction can be pointed out in it. On the contrary, every concrete thing, every Notion, is essentially a unity of distinguished and distinguishable moments, which by virtue of their determinate, essential difference, pass over into contradictory moments. This contradictory side of course resolves itself into nothing, it withdraws into its negative unity. Now the thing, the subject, the Notion, is just this negative unity itself; it is inherently self-contradictory, but is no less the contradiction resolved: it is the ground that contains and supports its determinations' (Hegel 1989: 442).

13. Indeed, though Heidegger and Wittgenstein are probably the most renowned exemplars of this resurgence of religiosity in twentieth-century European philosophy, they are far from unusual in this regard. Twentieth-Century European philosophy harbours what can only be described as a profoundly conflicted attitude towards Judeo-Christian monotheism. Thus the avowed atheism of figures such as Bachelard, Badiou, Carnap, Cavailles, Neurath, Reichenbach, Sartre, Schlick, Deleuze, and Waismann is more than counterbalanced by the theological overtones in the works of Adorno, Benjamin, Bloch, Derrida, Gadamer, Henry, Horkheimer, Jaspers, Levinas, Marion, Merleau-Ponty, Ricoeur, and Scheler. The latter all seem to hold Judaeo-Christian theology in far higher philosophical regard than the cognitive achievements of modern scientific rationality. Husserl and the neo-Kantians hold an equivocal position here: like Kant before them, they declared their allegiance to the ideals of scientific rationality; yet at the same time their understanding of the latter seems to have been wholly compatible with, or at least did not rule out, an embrace of Judaeo-Christian monotheism – hence Cohen's Judaism, Husserl's Lutheranism, and so on. In this regard, their stance typifies post-Kantian fideism: since neither God's existence nor his non-existence can be rationally demonstrated, it is perfectly possible to reconcile a commitment to scientific rationality with a commitment to Judaism or Christianity. It is worth mentioning in this connection the striking similarities between Meillassoux's attack on correlationist fideism in *Après la finitude* and Lenin's assault on clericalist idealism in *Materialism and Empirio-criticism* (originally published 1908, tr. A. Fineberg, Peking: Foreign Languages Press, 1972); especially in Chapter 1, sections 2 and 3, where Lenin lambasts the 'correlativist' theory of subject and object which he explicitly connects to 'fideism'. My thanks to Damian Veal for pointing these parallels out to me. Though he does not mention him, Lenin's tract may well have provided a source of inspiration for Meillassoux's book. That the 'correlativism' excoriated by Lenin in 1908 remains in full force a hundred years later is both a testament to the continuing relevance

of Lenin's intervention and a depressing reminder of mainstream academic philosophy's seemingly imperturbable idealism. Whether or not *Après la finitude* was partly inspired by *Materialism and Empirio-Criticism*, Meillassoux's profoundly original speculative alternative to correlationism quells any suggestion of imitation.

14. In Meillassoux's eyes, the fact that the third thesis is not derived directly from the principle of factuality but relies on independent considerations renders it considerably more precarious than the first two. Meillassoux makes it clear that he views this as a shortcoming which he hopes to remedy in future work. Cf. Meillasoux, *Après la finitude*, 152–3.

15. 'Freedom is not simply the opposite of deterministic causal necessity: as Kant knew, it means a specific mode of causality; the agent's self-determination. There is in fact a kind of Kantian antinomy of freedom: if an act is fully determined by preceding causes, it is, of course, not free; if, however, it depends on the pure contingency which momentarily severs the full causal chain, it is also not free. The only way to resolve this antinomy is to introduce a second-order reflexive causality: I am determined by causes (be it direct brute natural causes or motivations), and the space of freedom is not a magic gap in this first-level causal chain but my ability retroactively to choose/determine which causes will determine me' (Žižek 2006: 203). In Žižek's Hegelianism, the subject achieves its autonomy by retroactively positing/reintegrating its own contingent material determinants: freedom is the subjective necessity of objective contingency. But by dissolving the idea of a necessary connection between cause and effect, Meillassoux's absolutization of contingency not only destroys materialist 'determinism' understood as the exceptionless continuity of the causal nexus, but also the idealist conception of subjective 'freedom' understood in terms of the second-order reflexive causality described by Žižek. The subject cannot 'choose' or determine its own objective determination when the contingency of all determination implies the equal arbitrariness of every choice, effectively erasing the distinction between forced and un-forced choice. Thus it becomes impossible to distinguish between objective compulsion and subjective reflexion, phenomenal heteronomy and noumenal autonomy. The principle of factuality collapses the distinction between first and second order levels of determination, thereby undermining any attempt to distinguish between objective heteronomy and subjective autonomy.

16. 'Nothingness' is here understood as the simple negation of all determinate existence. We shall see in Chapters 5 and 6 that there is an alternative definition of nothingness in terms of the determinate identity of 'being-nothing' and we will try to show why this is perfectly conceivable.

17. Cf. M. Heidegger, *Introduction to Metaphysics*, tr. G. Fried & R. Polt, New Haven: Yale University Press, 2000; and *The Principle of Reason*, tr. R. Lilly, Bloomington and Indianapolis: Indiana University Press, 1996.

18. L. Wittgenstein, *Tractatus Logico-Philosophicus*, tr. D. F. Pears & B. F. McGuinness, London: Routledge, 1974.

19. Cf. D. Hume, *A Treatise of Human Nature*, ed. C. Mossner, Harmondsworth: Penguin, 1984, Book I, Part III, 117–229.

20. Though Meillassoux states unequivocally that Popper's anti-inductivism continues to assume the principle of the uniformity of nature, this is debatable.

In fact, Popper's position is far more nuanced than Meillassoux makes out. Popper seems to distinguish between the metaphysical interpretation of the principle as a thesis about reality, which is unfalsifiable, and its scientific function as a methodological rule which makes no substantial assumptions about the nature of reality. Thus in *The Logic of Scientific Discovery* Popper writes:

> Consistently with my attitude toward other metaphysical questions, I abstain from arguing for or against faith in the existence of regularities [...] This principle [of the uniformity of nature], it seems to me, expresses in a very superficial way an important methodological rule, and one which might be derived, with advantage, precisely from a consideration of the non-verifiability of theories. [...] I think [...] that it would be a mistake to assert that natural regularities do not change (This would be a kind of statement that can neither be argued against nor argued for.) What we should say is, rather, that it is part of our *definition* of natural laws if we postulate that they are to be invariant with respect to space and time; and also if we postulate that they are to have no exceptions. Thus from a methodological point of view, the possibility of falsifying a corroborated law is by no means without significance. It helps us to find out what we demand and expect from natural laws. And the 'principle of the uniformity of nature' can again be regarded as a metaphysical interpretation of a methodological rule – like its near relative the 'law of causality'.
>
> (Popper 2002a: 250–1)

Elsewhere, Popper seems to reject the principle on the grounds that it is identical with the principle of induction. Thus in *Conjectures and Refutations*, he writes:

> [T]here is a third way of violating the principle of empiricism. We have seen how it can be violated by constructing a theory of knowledge which cannot do without a principle of induction – a principle that tells us in effect that the world is (or very probably is) a place in which men can learn from experience; and that it will remain (or very probably remain) so in future.
>
> (Popper 2002b: 394)

A world in which learning is possible is a uniform world; where uniformity defaults, learning, and a fortiori science, becomes impossible. Yet far from ruling it out, this is precisely a possibility which Popper claims rationalism must embrace. Thus David Miller strongly denies that Popperian critical rationalism is committed to any metaphysical version of the principle of uniformity: 'Science does not presuppose uniformity, it proposes it, and then attempts to dispose of its proposals' (Miller 2004: §1). Whether this distinction between scientific proposing and metaphysical presupposing is viable is a complex issue which I shall not pursue further here. But cf. Miller, 1994: Ch. 2, §2a and Miller 2006: esp. Ch. 4, §3.

21. Meillassoux borrows this reconstruction of the frequentialist argument from Jean-René Vernes's *Critique de la raison aléatoire, ou Descartes contre Kant*, Paris: Aubier, 1982. However, where Vernes endorses the argument, Meillassoux opposes it.
22. This is the upshot of Heidegger's reinterpretation of Kant in his *Kant and the Problem of Metaphysics*, tr. R. Taft, Indianapolis: Indiana University Press, 1990.
23. Cf. Meillasoux 2006: 164. Though Meillassoux does not cite him, Bertrand Russell makes precisely the same point in the opening paragraphs of his *Human Knowledge: Its Scope and Limits*:

> Ever since Kant [...] there has been what I regard as a mistaken tendency among philosophers to allow the description of the world to be influenced unduly by considerations derived from the nature of human knowledge. To scientific common sense (which I accept) it is plain that only an infinitesimal part of the universe is known, that there were countless ages during which there was no knowledge, and that there probably will be countless ages without knowledge in the future. Cosmically and causally, knowledge is an unimportant feature of the universe; a science which omitted to mention its occurrence might, from an impersonal point of view, suffer only a very trivial imperfection. In describing the world, subjectivity is a vice. Kant spoke of himself as having effected a 'Copernican revolution', but he would have been more accurate if he had spoken of a 'Ptolemaic counter-revolution', since he put Man back at the centre from which Copernicus had dethroned him.
>
> (Russell 1948: 9)

24. I have substituted 'ancestral phenomenon' for 'accretion' in the original passage. Since the accretion of the earth is obviously an example of an ancestral phenomenon, this substitution is intended to clarify the philosophical import of the passage without overly distorting the meaning of the original text.
25. Cf. Hilary Putnam's 'The Meaning of "Meaning"' in *Mind, Language, and Reality: Philosophical Papers Volume 2*, Cambridge: Cambridge University Press, 1975, 236.

4 Unbinding the Void

1. Cf. A. Badiou, *Manifeste pour la philosophie*, Paris: Seuil, 1989; *Manifesto for Philosophy* tr. Norman Madarasz, Albany, NY: SUNY, 1999; 'Philosophy and Mathematics: Infinity and the End of Romanticism' in *Theoretical Writings* ed. R. Brassier and A. Toscano, London and New York: Continuum, 2004, 21–38.
2. A. Badiou, *L'être et l'événement*, Paris: Seuil, 1988; *Being and Event*, tr. Oliver Feltham, London and New York: Continuum, 2006.
3. For an illuminating examination of the relation between Aristotle's and Badiou's characterizations of the task of ontology, cf. Jean-Toussaint Desanti's 'Some Remarks on the Intrinsic Ontology of Alain Badiou' in *Think Again: Alain Badiou and the Future of Philosophy*, ed. Peter Hallward, London: Continuum, 2004, 59–66.

4. This is a point made by Peter Hallward in *Badiou: A Subject to Truth,* Minneapolis: University of Minnesota Press, 2003, 276.
5. Cf. Badiou, *Being and Event,* Meditation 7. This 'greater than' is to be understood in terms of the concept of quantity, which is defined in terms of cardinality. Badiou establishes the concept of cardinality and the immeasurability of the excess of inclusion over belonging with reference to the Cohen–Easton theorem in Meditation 26 of *Being and Event* (Badiou 1988: 293–309, 2006a: 265–280).
6. For Badiou, ontology is necessarily indifferent to spatio-temporal categories: being qua being has nothing to do with space and/or time – this is of a piece with his Platonism.
7. The void only becomes discernible within a situation as a result of the dysfunctioning of the count which gives rise to the 'ultra-one' of the event; cf. *Being and Event,* Meditations 17 and 18.
8. Cf. Badiou, *Being and Event,* Meditation 3.
9. Cf. Wahl's incisive paper 'Presentation, Representation, Appearance' in *Alain Badiou. Penser le multiple* ed. Charles Ramond, Paris: L'Harmattan, 2002, 169–87.
10. These metaontological concepts must be distinguished from the metaontological use of the term 'being', which Badiou is careful not to reify into a concept. 'Being' is simply a proper name – that of the empty set, Ø – for the unpresentable.
11. Cf. Badiou, *Manifeste pour la philosophie,* 69.
12. For the distinction between truth and knowledge, cf. *Being and Event,* Meditations 31 to 36, and also 'On Subtraction' and 'Truth: Forcing and the Unnameable' in *Theoretical Writings,* 103–33.
13. Cf. Badiou, *Being and Event,* Meditation 16.
14. Cf. Badiou, *Being and Event,* Meditation 35.
15. For Badiou's account of the impasse of ontology cf. *Being and Event,* Meditation 26. Badiou seems to disavow the appeal to transcendence insofar as he aligns it with the onto-theological orientation which he sees exemplified in the theory of 'large cardinals'. A large cardinal is one whose existence is not deducible from the axioms of set-theory and hence requires the assertion of a supplementary axiom. Such an axiom is stronger than the one which guarantees the existence of a limit-ordinal and the succession of transfinite alephs. The theory of large cardinals fends off the measurelessness of ontological excess by positing the existence of super-alephs that circumscribe it 'from above'. But it is necessary to distinguish between the assertion of the existence of transcendent objects, such as the super-alephs, which do not acknowledge the impasse of ontology, since they do not force a decision as to the value of the power-set of the smallest denumerable infinity, alephnull; and the assertion of unobjectifiable transcendence, which is precisely the transcendence of decision, i.e. subjective intervention, vis-à-vis the immanent objective parameters of ontological discourse. It is insofar as he endorses the latter option that Badiou can be described as an advocate of radical transcendence.
16. This is the crux of the distinction between natural situations, which are characterized by the maximal equilibrium between presentation and re-presentation and circumscribed by aleph-null, smallest denumerable infinity; and historical

situations, for which that transitivity no longer obtains since they harbour singularities (evental sites) which are potential loci for the singularization of excess. Cf. *Being and Event*, Meditations 11–16.

17. A. Badiou, *Le Concept de modèle. Introduction a une épistémologie matérialiste des mathématiques*, Paris: Maspero, 1969. I have discussed the latter in 'Badiou's Materialist Epistemology of Mathematics' in *Angelaki: Journal of the Theoretical Humanities*, Vol. 10, No. 2, August 2005, 135–49.

18. This is François Wahl's recommendation. He argues that Badiou fails to establish a necessary link between the inconsistency of being and the consistency of presentation and concludes that subtractive ontology remains insufficient. Thus, he suggests 'the ontology of presentation and of beings, the ontology of the multiple determinations of being, still remains to be done' (Wahl 2002: 187).

19. A. Badiou, *Logiques des mondes. L'être et l'événement*, 2, Paris: Seuil, 2006.

5 Being Nothing

1. For a detailed bibliography see Laruelle 2003 in *Angelaki, Vol. 8, No. 2: The One or the Other: French Philosophy Today*, August 2003, 188–9.

2. 'The Transcendental Method' is an article which Laruelle contributed to the *Universal Philosophical Encyclopedia* Vol. 1, ed. André Jacob, Paris: PUF, 1989b, 71–80.

3. In *Angelaki, Vol. 8, No. 2: The One or the Other: French Philosophy Today*, 2003, 173–88.

4. Cf. for instance Laruelle 1989a.

5. Cf. particularly *Philosophy and Non-philosophy*. I have tried to provide a fuller (and uncritical) account of the scope and remit of non-philosophy as Laruelle sees it in 'Axiomatic Heresy: The Non-Philosophy of François Laruelle', *Radical Philosophy* 121, September/October 2003, 24–35.

6. See for instance Laruelle 1986, Ch. VII, 213–40. As an assiduous student of Heidegger and Derrida, Laruelle is careful to avoid casual uses of the term 'essence' (unless it is to speak of an 'essence-without-essence'), preferring to talk of the 'identity' of philosophy instead. But what he calls 'identity' or 'radical immanence' amounts to a non-metaphysical conceptualization of essence which, for present purposes, retains most of the characteristic functional features associated with the concept of 'essence' in its philosophical acceptation. Thus when Laruelle speaks of the 'identity' of philosophy, he has in mind something which is a formal invariant, a necessary but non-sufficient condition, and multiply instantiable.

7. Graham Harman has argued that the *Vorhandenheit/Zuzandenheit* distinction not only provides the key to understanding the ontic-ontological difference in *Being and Time*, but ultimately underlies all of Heidegger's thinking, particularly his critique of metaphysics. Cf. *Tool-Being: Heidegger and the Metaphysics of Objects*, Chicago: Open Court, 2002.

8. Cf. Laruelle 1986 and 1989, 104–9.

9. Though this reading is supplemented and informed by parallel readings of Plato, Kant, Hegel, Nietzsche, Husserl, Deleuze, and Michel Henry, Laruelle's identification of philosophy as 'decision' is nevertheless primarily indebted

to Heidegger and Derrida, in whom one can already discern the former's pre-occupation with uncovering the conditions of reality for conditions of possibility, and in whose work the notions of 'decision' (*Entscheidung*) and of the 'undecidable' first become privileged as clues to the essence of philosophy.

10. Cf. Kant 1929: B33–B116, 65–119.

11. Cf. Kant 1929: A95–A130 and B129–B169, 129–75.

12. Kant 1929: A84–A130, B116–B169, 120–75. Laruelle's account, indebted to his reading of neo-Kantianism, and particularly to Hermann Cohen's *Kant's Theory of Experience* (2nd edn, 1885), which puts the onus of the first *Critique* squarely on the principles of the pure understanding, provides an interesting contrast to certain influential interpretations of Kant which locate the essence of transcendental synthesis in the schematism of the imagination, most famously Heidegger (in *Kant and the Problem of Metaphysics*, Indianapolis: Indiana University Press, 1990a), whose interpretation of Kant was developed in explicit opposition to that of Cohen and the Marburg School.

13. In *The Philosophies of Difference* Laruelle explicitly identifies the Heideggerian shift from being as ontic-ontological *Differenz* to the 'event of appropriation' (*Ereignis*) as *Unterschied* with the decisional transition from metaphysical to transcendental difference (see Laruelle 1986: 48–120). On the Heideggerian notion of 'the turning' (*die Kehre*) see, for example, M. Heidegger, 'The Turning' in *The Question Concerning Technology and Other Essays*, tr. W. Lovitt, New York: Harper and Row, 1977a, 36–49; and §255 in Heidegger's *Contributions to Philosophy*, tr. P. Emad and K. Maly, Indianapolis: Indiana University Press, 1999, 286–8.

14. See, for example, Miklos Vetö, *De Kant à Schelling. Les deux voix de l'Idéalisme allemand. Tome 1*, Grenoble: Jérôme Millon, 1998, 61–85 and passim; F. W. J. Schelling, *On the History of Modern Philosophy*, tr. A. Bowie, Cambridge: Cambridge University Press, 1993, 95–163; Hegel, *Science of Logic*, op. cit., 209.

15. See in particular M. Henry, *L'essence de la manifestation*, Paris: PUF, 1963; *The Essence of Manifestation*, tr. G. Etzkorn, The Hague: Nijhoff, 1973.

16. See Heidegger 1999, especially 60–71 for an explicit account of thinking as 'decision' and of the link between being's 'essential unfolding' as *Ereignis* and the 'leap' or 'crossing over' enacted by 'inceptual' (i.e. non-metaphysical) thinking from what Heidegger calls philosophy's 'first' to its 'other' beginning.

17. Cf. in particular Chapters III and IV of *The Philosophies of Difference*.

18. F. Laruelle, *La Lutte et l'utopie à la fin des temps philosophiques* [*Struggle and Utopia in the Endtimes of Philosophy*], Paris: Kimé, 2004.

19. Thus in his book on ethics (*Éthique de l'étranger* [*Ethics of the Stranger*], Paris: Kimé, 2000b) Laruelle does not actually provide anything like a substantive conceptual analysis of ethical tropes in contemporary philosophy; he simply uses potted versions of Plato, Kant, and Levinas to sketch what a non-philosophical theory of 'the ethical' would look like. Similarly, in his *Introduction to Non-Marxism* he does not actually engage in an analysis of Marxist theory and practice; he simply uses two idiosyncratic philosophical readings of Marx, those of Althusser and Henry, as the basis for outlining what a non-philosophical theory of Marxism would look like.

20. For an account of 'negative dialectics' cf. Adorno's *Negative Dialectics*, tr. E. B. Ashton, London: Routledge, 1973.

21. Laruelle defends this privileging of the 'name-of-man' over other nominations of the real in *Struggle and Utopia*, 54–9.
22. This indifference is largely feigned, as evinced by Laruelle's occasional displays of indulgence towards Heidegger and Derrida, and his notable impatience with Nietzsche and Deleuze. It becomes difficult to credit Laruelle's pretension to complete impartiality vis-à-vis philosophical disputation when one compares, for example, his devastatingly thorough but relatively sympathetic critiques of Heidegger and Derrida in *The Philosophies of Difference* with his rather severe and unforgiving attitude towards Deleuze. Cf. 'Reply to Deleuze' in *La non-philosophie des contemporains* [*The Non-Philosophy of Contemporaries*], *Non-Philosophie. Le Collectif*, Paris: Kimé, 1995, 49–78. This collective volume also contains Laruelle's appraisal of Badiou: 'Badiou and Non-Philosophy: A Comparison', 37–46 (written under the pseudonym 'Tristan Aguilar').

6 The Pure and Empty Form of Death

1. Martin Heidegger, *The Concept of Time* tr. William McNeill, Oxford: Blackwell, 1992.
2. Gadamer, quoted by Theodore Kisiel, *The Genesis of Heidegger's Being and Time*, London: University of California Press, 1993, 315.
3. Martin Heidegger, *Being and Time*, tr. J. Macquarrie and E. Robinson, Oxford: Blackwell, 1962.
4. Kisiel 1993: 23–5.
5. '*Augenblick*' is of course Nietzsche's term to describe the moment wherein eternal recurrence is confronted. We shall discuss Deleuze's account of the relation between eternal recurrence and ontological transcendence below.
6. Heidegger will contrast *Dasein*'s radically individuated, unobjectifiable 'self' to the impersonal anonymity of the metaphysical or transcendental subject.
7. M. Heidegger, *The Basic Problems of Phenomenology*, tr. A. Hofstader Bloomington & Indianapolis: Indiana University Press, 1982.
8. Cf. Françoise Dastur,'The Ekstatico-Horizonal Constitution of Temporality' in C. Macann, ed. *Critical Heidegger*, London: Routledge, 1996, 158–71.
9. No doubt this difficulty had something to do with Heidegger's abandonment of the project of fundamental ontology. But why does the latter unravel precisely at that point where the existential analytic, outlining *Dasein's* ekstatic structure of transcendence, was to be surpassed towards an account of the temporality proper to being as such? Heidegger's retrieval of the ontological problematic in *Being and Time* was to be effected via a critical radicalization of transcendental philosophy. The fundamental question is not just of being but of our access to being: how do we originally access the being of phenomena? *Dasein* is in the world but also not just something in the world. Herein lies the rub: where Kantian transcendentalism cultivated suspicion of unmediated access to phenomena, transcendental phenomenology countered with the revelation that the mediation is immediate, i.e. unmediated. That which is accessed is mediated, but the access as such is not, whether it be intentionality or finite transcendence. Finite transcendence is the condition of possibility for all access to the being of phenomena – indeed, according to Heidegger, it is the condition of possibility for those merely metaphysical

conditions of possibility identified by the ontotheological tradition – but this condition of conditions is necessarily unconditioned: it is 'the ekstatikon in and for itself'. Recognizing the taint of idealist subjectivism in this latter, Heidegger went on to seek an even more originary access to the primordial 'happening', and ever more radical means of unearthing the conditions for conditions: *Ereignis*, the fourfold, etc. The phenomenological radicalization of transcendentalism initiated by Heidegger finds itself excavating deeper and deeper into the primordial: uncovering the conditions for the conditions of the conditions, etc. Yet the deeper it digs towards the pre-originary, the greater its remove from 'things themselves' and the more impoverished its resources become. Heidegger and his successors – up to and including Laruelle – end up burrowing ever deeper into reflexivity in order to unearth the pre-reflexive, exacerbating abstraction until it becomes reduced to plying its own exorbitant vacuity. Derrida introduces both a healthy measure of scepticism and a fatal dose of irony into this meta-transcendental problematic by revealing how the immediacy of access was 'always already' contaminated by *différance* as inclusive disjunction of mediation and immediacy. But he is trumped by Laruelle, who unveils the unobjectifiable immediacy of 'man' as that which is always already presupposed by and hence the ultimate determinant for *différance's* inclusive disjunction of mediation and immediacy (cf. Chapter 5). Once the problematic of access, and of the access to access, has reached its absurd denouement in the claim that this 'man without qualities' is the primal phenomenon determining the conditions of the conditions of access, it is no surprise to see the very notion of a world indifferent to our access to it recede into unintelligibility. But if the idea of a world independent of our access to it becomes unintelligible, then perhaps the fault lies with the correlational criteria of intelligibility stipulated by the philosophy of access, rather than with the world. One cannot but be struck by the comic spectacle of the later Heidegger trying to uncover the roots of the primal phenomenon, the *Ur-etwas*, in old Greek words. The phenomenology that sought to begin again with 'the things themselves' is redirected by Heidegger and ends up poring over words, nothing but words ...... Perhaps this is the inevitable fate of the philosophy of access.

10. This disjunction will provide Heidegger's heirs, such as Levinas, Blanchot, and Derrida, with the ever-popular theme of 'the impossibility of death'.

11. Cf. M. Heidegger, *The Fundamental Problems of Metaphysics: World, Finitude, Solitude*, tr. W. McNeill, Bloomington & Indianapolis: Indiana University Press, 1995. Heidegger's attempt to wriggle out of this dichotomy by claiming that the distinction at issue is not between having or not having a world but rather between entities that are 'rich in world' (i.e. human beings) and those that are 'poor in world' (such as animals) is a desperate sophism since he makes it perfectly clear that there can be no common measure for degrees of 'richness' or 'poverty' in world and hence no possible transition from one to the other. The fact that such transitions frequently occur within the realm of *Dasein* – e.g. in cases of brain-damage or dementia – only underlines the explanatory poverty of Heidegger's distinction.

12. It is important to register the way in which Heidegger's ontologization of *Dasein*'s 'historicality' licenses a total disregard for the merely 'ontic' details of *Dasein*'s empirical and/or natural history – and it is precisely this disregard which will provide the precondition for Heidegger's 'history of being'.

13. G. Deleuze, *Différence et répétition*, Paris: PUF, 1968; *Difference and Repetition*, tr. Paul Patton, New York: Columbia University Press, 1994.
14. Already in 1956's 'Bergson's Conception of Difference', Deleuze is arguing that to conceive of being as pure self-differentiation is to conceive of it in Bergsonian terms as duration: 'Duration, tendency, is self-differentiating; and what differs from itself is *immediately* the unity of substance and subject'. G. Deleuze, 'La conception de la différence chez Bergson' in *L'île déserte et autres textes*, Paris: Minuit, 2002a, 52. As we shall see, though *Difference and Repetition* will qualify and complicate this claim about the 'immediate' unity of substance and subject, or being and thought, in its account of the third synthesis, the re-inscription of Hegel persists.
15. Deleuze attributes the distinction between death as personal possibility and dying as impersonal impossibility of possibility (the death of the Other in me) to Blanchot, citing three works: *The Space of Literature* (originally published 1955; tr. A. Smock, Nebraska: University of Nebraska Press, 1982); *The Book to Come* (originally published 1959, tr. C. Mandell, Stanford: Stanford University Press, 2002); and 'The Laughter of the Gods' (originally published 1965; included in *Friendship*, tr. E. Rottenberg, Stanford: Stanford University Press, 1997). But though Deleuze may not have been aware of it, Blanchot derives this distinction more or less directly from Levinas, whose influence thoroughly pervades Blanchot's *oeuvre*. Indeed, it would be difficult to overestimate the influence of Levinas's key tropes upon Blanchot's thinking – the impersonal anonymity of the '*il y a*', radical passivity, the Other, etc. Thus Blanchot's version of the distinction between death and dying comes from Levinas's critique of Heidegger in *Time and the Other*, originally published in 1948 (tr. R. Cohen, Pittsburgh: Dusquesne University Press, 1987). However, Levinas's inversion of the relation between possibility and impossibility in *Being and Time* remains entirely dependent upon the conceptual machinery of Heidegger's text, and it is arguable that far from subverting the latter, this reversibility between possibility and impossibility is one of its enabling conditions.
16. H. Bergson, *Matter and Memory*, tr. N. M. Paul and W. S. Palmer, New York: Zone Books, 1991.
17. Curiously, this is rendered as 'Ideas and the Synthesis of Difference' in Paul Patton's English translation.
18. Timothy Murphy has pointed out that Deleuze's contrast between *répétition nue* and *répétition vétue* must be understood in terms of the theatrical metaphorics which run throughout *Difference and Repetition*. In French, *répétition vétue* also means 'dress rehearsal'. Cf. Timothy Murphy, 'The Theatre of (the Philosophy of) Cruelty in *Difference and Repetition*' in *Pli: The Warwick Journal of Philosophy*, Vol. 5. *Deleuze and the Transcendental Unconscious*, ed. J. Broadhurst-Dixon, Coventry: University of Warwick, 1992, 105–35.
19. Though Badiou tends to privilege *Difference and Repetition* (alongside Deleuze's two *Cinema* volumes) to the detriment of both volumes of 'Capitalism and Schizophrenia' in his critique of Deleuze, he seems to disregard the role of the third synthesis as locus of thought's conversion from contemplation to production, which at the very least problematizes his depiction of Deleuze's philosophy as essentially contemplative. Cf. A. Badiou, *Deleuze: The Clamour of Being*, tr. L. Burchill, Minneapolis: University of Minnesota Press, 2002.
20. Deleuze's account is heavily indebted to Gilbert Simondon's *L'Individu et sa genèse physico-biologique*, Paris: PUF, 1964.

21. Cf. G. Deleuze, 'La méthode de dramatisation' in *L'île déserte et autres textes*, Paris: Minuit, 2002b, 131–62.
22. I owe this crucial insight to Alberto Toscano's indispensable study, *The Theatre of Production: Philosophy and Individuation between Kant and Deleuze*, Basingstoke: Palgrave Macmillan, 2006. Cf. especially Chapter 6 and the Conclusion, 157–201.
23. For accounts of the role of 'expression' in Deleuze's thought which differ from the one presented here, see Len Lawlor, 'The End of Phenomenology: Expressionism in Deleuze and Merleau-Ponty' in *Continental Philosophy Review*, Vol. 31, No. 1, 1998, 15–34; and Simon Duffy, 'The Logic of Expression in Deleuze's *Expressionism in Philosophy: Spinoza*: A Strategy of Engagement' in *International Journal of Philosophical Studies*, Vol. 12, No. 1, 2004, 47–60.
24. 'We call this dark precursor, this difference in itself or second-degree difference, which relates disparate or heterogeneous series to one another, "the disparate"' (Deleuze 1968: 157, 1994: 120 tm). 'We call "disparity" this infinitely redoubled, infinitely resonating state of difference. Disparity, i.e. difference or intensity (difference of intensity), is the sufficient reason of the phenomenon, the condition of that which appears. [...] The reason of the sensible, the condition of that which appears, is not space and time, but the Unequal in itself, or *disparateness* such as is comprised and determined in difference of intensity, in intensity as difference' (Deleuze 1968: 287, 1994: 222–3 tm).
25. 'A distribution conforms to good sense when it tends by itself to banish difference in the distributed' (Deleuze 1968: 289, 1994: 224 tm).
26. It is this supplementary dimension constituted by reflection and inherent in representation which Deleuze will denounce ever more emphatically in all his subsequent work. Thus his increasing insistence upon the 'immanence' which is the proper element of philosophical thought, and upon the necessity of simultaneously constructing and expressing it, follows directly from this critical circumscription of the secondary and derivative nature of reflexive consciousness in *Difference and Repetition*.
27. 'Sense is like the Idea which is developed through sub-representative determinations' (Deleuze 1968: 201, 1994: 155 tm).
28. Cf. Keith Ansell-Pearson, 'Dead or Alive' in *Viroid Life: Perspectives on Nietzsche and the Transhuman Condition*, London: Routledge, 1997, 57–83.
29. 'Every phenomenon flashes forth in a signal-sign system. We call 'signal' the system such as it is constituted by or bounded by at least two heterogeneous series; two disparate orders capable of entering into communication; the phenomenon is a sign, i.e. that which flashes forth in the system when these disparates enter into communication' (Deleuze 1968: 286–7, 1994: 222 tm). Cf. Daniel W. Smith, 'Deleuze's Theory of Sensation: Overcoming the Kantian Duality' in *Deleuze: A Critical Reader*, ed. P. Patton, Oxford: Blackwell, 1995, 34.
30. Cf. D. Deleuze and C. Parnet, *Dialogues*, Paris: Flammarion, 1977, 68–72.
31. '[P]roblematic Ideas are at once the ultimate elements of nature and the subliminal object of small perceptions. Learning always proceeds through the unconscious; it always takes place in the unconscious, thereby establishing the bond of a profound complicity between nature and mind' (Deleuze 1968: 214, 1994: 165 tm).
32. 'Unlike the physico-chemical sphere, where the "code" that underlies forms or qualities is distributed throughout the three-dimensionality of a structure,

in the organic sphere this code becomes detached as a separate one-dimensional structure: the linear sequence of nucleic acids constituting the genetic code.' Manuel De Landa, *Intensive Science and Virtual Philosophy*, London: Continuum, 2002, 163–4. While this is in many ways a very useful gloss, the claim that individuating factors constitute a 'code' is problematic on two counts. First, it seems to ignore Deleuze's distinction between individuating and individual differences, which is the distinction between enveloping intensity as clear expression of a distinct difference in the Idea and enveloped intensity as confused expression of the Idea's obscure perplication: 'Two individuating intensities may be abstractly the same by virtue of what they clearly express; they are never the same on account of the order of intensities which they envelop or the relations which they obscurely express' (Deleuze 1968: 326, 1994: 253 tm). This irreducible variability in the correlation between individuating differences and pre-individual singularities would seem to indicate an order of complexity which is difficult to codify in an information-theoretic register. Second, it is not clear how individuating factors could become detached as a 'separate one-dimensional structure' without themselves becoming individuated. Intensive individuation was supposed to provide part of the 'sufficient reason' for actualization (Deleuze 1968: 285, 1994: 221), not its cause in extensity, and if the individuating factors invoked in order to account for actualization are themselves already individuated then the virtual–actual distinction collapses and an infinite regress looms.

33. '"Possible" here is not to be understood as implying resemblance, but rather as the state of the implicated or the enveloped in its heterogeneity with that which envelops it' (Deleuze 1968: 334, 1994: 260 tm).

34. The proximity to Levinas and Blanchot regarding the theme of 'the death of the Other' has already been noted. Where Deleuze's account differs conspicuously from both, however is in the notable paucity of references to 'radical passivity', a recurring trope whenever Blanchot or Levinas discuss the relation between death and alterity. For Deleuze, by way of contrast, dying seems rather to be a function of *the act* of thinking.

35. 'The indivisibility of the individual pertains exclusively to the property whereby intensive quantities cannot divide without changing in nature' (Deleuze 1968: 327, 1994: 254 tm). The latter is precisely Bergson's definition of duration as qualitative multiplicity, which he contrasts to the quantitative multiplicities proper to space.

36. Cf. Alfred North Whitehead, *Process and Reality*, London and New York: The Free Press, 1978; David Chalmers, 'Is Experience Ubiquitous?' in Chapter 8 of Chalmers's *The Conscious Mind*, Oxford: Oxford University Press, 1996.

37. Thus De Landa (2002), for instance, proposes a reading of Deleuze wherein virtuality becomes the preserve of theoretical entities such as phase spaces and dynamic attractors. But as Alberto Toscano has pointed out, he does so at the cost of eliding Deleuze's fundamental distinction between virtuality and possibility. Cf. Toscano (2006), 184–7.

38. 'Sense is the genesis or production of the true, and truth is merely the empirical result of sense. [...] Nevertheless, the Idea which traverses all the faculties is not reducible to sense. For it is just as much non-sense; and there is no difficulty reconciling this double-aspect through which the Idea is constituted

by structural elements which have no sense in themselves, while constituting the sense of everything it produces (structure and genesis)' (Deleuze
1968: 200, 1994: 154 tm).

7 The Truth of Extinction

1. F.Nietzsche, 'On Truth and Lies in a Nonmoral Sense' in *Philosophy and Truth: Selections from Nietzsche's Notebooks of the Early 1870s*, ed. and tr. D. Breazeale, Atlantic Highlands, New Jersey: Humanities Press, 1979a, 79.
2. F. Nietzsche, *The Gay Science*, tr. W. Kaufman, New York: Vintage, 1974, §109.
3. F. Nietzsche, *The Will to Power*, ed. W. Kaufman, New York: Vintage, 1968, §12.
4. *Grossoktavausgabe*, Leipzig, 1905, XII, 64; cited in Heidegger, *Nietzsche. Vol. II: The Eternal Recurrence of the Same*, ed. D. F. Krell, New York: HarperSanFrancisco, 1990, 23.
5. Nietzsche, *Will to Power*, §1057.
6. Cf. Nietzsche, *Will to Power*, §5.
7. Nietzsche, *The Will to Power*, §15; cf. Heidegger, *Nietzsche. Vol. II: The Eternal Recurrence of the Same*, 121–32.
8. 'We have abolished the real world: what world is left? The apparent one per-haps? … But no! *With the real world we have also abolished the apparent world!* (Mid-day; moment of the shortest shadow; end of the longest error; zenith of mankind; INCIPIT ZARATHUSTRA.' *Twilight of the Idols*, tr. R. J. Hollingdale, Harmondsworth: Penguin, 1990, 'How the "Real World" at Last Became a Myth', 51.
9. Nietzsche, *The Will to Power*, Preface, 3.
10. As is well known, there are only three explicit mentions of 'eternal recur-rence' in Nietzsche's published works: *The Gay Science*, IV, §341, 'The Heaviest Burden'; *Thus Spake Zarathustra*, III, 'Of the Vision and the Riddle' and 'The Convalescent'; and *Beyond Good and Evil*, III, §56. However, some inkling of its importance for Nietzsche is given by the frequency with which it is invoked in his unpublished notebooks. Thus *The Will to Power* contains not only numerous references but also several explicit discussions of the idea: specifically, in sections 617, 708, 1057, 1058, 1059, 1060, 1062, and 1066. Despite their sometimes controversial interpretations, it is to the credit of the 'strong' readings of Nietzsche proposed by Heidegger and Deleuze that they position the doctrine of eternal recurrence (along with the concept of will to power) at the very heart of Nietzsche's philosophy.
11. Nietzsche, 1968: §54, cf. also §708 and §1062.
12. Translated by Hugh Tomlinson, London: Athlone, 1983. Deleuze's famous (not to say notorious) interpretation of eternal recurrence in this book insists that it is not identity – the world as yoked beneath the iron collar of representation – that returns, but rather difference – the world as dynamic flux of pre-individual singularities and impersonal individuations. The trou-ble with this audacious proposal is that it flies in the face of Nietzsche's own understanding of the nature of eternal recurrence. Nietzsche insists that it is precisely the moment as apprehended from the perspective of the individu-ated self that will be eternally repeated, not the world as experienced by Deleuze's anonymous, intensive individual, who cannot be confined by the form of the I or the matter of the self (cf. Chapter 6). Zarathustra could not

be more explicit: 'I shall return, with this sun, with this earth, with this eagle, with this serpent – not to a new life or a better life or a similar life: I shall return eternally to this identical and self-same life, in the greatest things and in the smallest, to teach once more the eternal recurrence of things.' (*Thus Spake Zarathustra*, tr. R. J. Hollingdale, Harmondsworth: Penguin, 1969, 237–8.) Elsewhere Nietzsche explicitly evokes the 'infinite recurrence of *identical* cases' (1968: §1066, emphasis added) – just as he insists that the hypothesis proceeds on the assumption that the world comprises 'a certain *definite quantity* of force and a certain *definite number* of certain *centers* of force' (ibid., emphasis added) – in other words, individuated loci of will to power, and not the process of intensive individuation privileged by Deleuze in *Difference and Repetition*. Here we may detect a tension between Deleuze's anti-mechanistic conception of will to power in terms of quanta of force which are inherently unequalizable and hence beyond the reach of scientific quantification (cf. Deleuze 1983: 42–6), and Nietzsche's own blunt avowal that he wishes to reconcile mechanism and Platonism (cf. 1968: §1061) – precisely the arch-representatives of identitarian thinking to which Deleuze's Nietzsche is supposed to be opposed. Moreover, for Nietzsche, it is the *finitude* of force in conjunction with the *infinity* of time that necessitates the hypothesis of eternal recurrence (cf. 1968: §1066). Thus, in §1062 of *Will to Power*, Nietzsche warns against the temptation to conclude from the disqualification of teleology that becoming harbours a 'miraculous power of infinite novelty in its form and states'. In what effectively amounts to a pre-emptive critique of Deleuze's subsequent attempt to align the notion of will to power with Spinoza's *natura naturans* and Bergson's *élan vital*, Nietzsche writes: '[This] is still the old religious way of thinking and desiring, a kind of longing to believe that *in some way* the world is like the old beloved, infinite, boundlessly creative God – that in some way, "the old God still lives" – that longing of Spinoza which was expressed in the words "*deus sive natura*" (he even felt "*natura sive deus*")' (1968: §1062). Keith Ansell-Pearson provides a critically nuanced appraisal of Deleuze's Nietzsche, specifically with regard to the topic of eternal recurrence, in his *Viroid Life: Perspectives on Nietzsche and the Transhuman Condition*, London: Routledge, 1997, esp. 42–7. However, elsewhere in the same book, Ansell-Pearson seems to endorse the Deleuzean interpretation of recurrence: 'The repetition implicated in the eternal return is not the repeating of an original model since there is no original moment which can be subjected to a law of repetition. Eternal return already takes place within the element of difference and simulacra' (Ansell-Pearson 1997: 62). It is precisely this Deleuzean characterization of eternal recurrence – as the repetition of difference rather than identity – which we believe to be incompatible with Nietzsche's own understanding of the doctrine.

13. This is undoubtedly why it is a demon who first broaches the idea under the heading 'The Heaviest Burden' in *The Gay Science*, IV, §341.
14. '[M]y world has just become perfect, midnight is also midday, pain is also a joy, a curse is also a blessing, the night is also a sun' *Thus Spake Zarathustra*, IV, 'The Intoxicated Song' (1969: 331).
15. Nietzsche 1968: §664–7.
16. Nietzsche 1968: §1011.
17. Nietzsche 1968: §1067.

18. Cf. Deleuze, *Nietzsche and Philosophy*, 171–5.
19. '[T]he world of "phenomena" is the adapted world which we feel to be real. The "reality" lies in the continual recurrence of identical, familiar, related things in their logicized character, in the belief that here we are able to reckon and calculate. [...] The antithesis of this phenomenal world is not "the true world", but the formless, unformulable world of the chaos of sensations – another kind of phenomenal world, a kind "unknowable" for us; [...] [Q]uestions, what things in themselves may be like, apart from our sense receptivity and the activity of our understanding, must be rebutted with the question: how could we know that things exist? "Thingness" was first created by us' (Nietzsche 1968: §569). Such remarks provoke an obvious rejoinder: if, as Nietzsche so often insists, it makes no sense to talk about what the world is like independently of our relation to it, and ergo in abstraction from those things with which our senses and understanding reckon and calculate, then why even suppose there to be a 'formless, unformulable' and hence unknowable world beyond the world of identical, familiar, related, logicized things? Why suppose that a 'chaos' of sensations prior to their logicization as things exists? Moreover, the premise that this 'chaos' must be assumed to be the cause of our orderly, logicized sensations is insupportable given Nietzsche's critiques of causality and his restriction of the notion of cause to the realm of logicized sensation.
20. Nietzsche himself seems to have been perfectly aware of this: 'What actually arouses indignation over suffering is not the suffering itself but the *senselessness* of suffering: but neither for the Christian, who saw in suffering a whole hidden machinery of salvation, nor for naïve man in ancient times, who saw all suffering in relation to spectators or to instigators of suffering, was there any such *senseless* suffering. [...] "All evil is justified if a God takes pleasure in it": so ran the primitive logic of feeling – and was this logic really restricted to primitive times? The gods viewed as the friends of *cruel* spectacles – how deeply this primeval concept still penetrates into our European civilization!' (Nietzsche 1994: 48).
21. Cf. Nietzsche 1969: 45–7.
22. Cf. Deleuze 1983: 68.
23. On the will to power as 'will to will' cf. Heidegger (1990c) *Nietzsche. Vol. III: The Will to Power as Knowledge and as Metaphysics*, ed. D. F. Krell, HarperSanFrancisco, 1990, 196.
24. Cf. Nietzsche 1968, §617, 330–1.
25. Cf. *Thus Spake Zarathustra*, IV, 'The Ass-Festival', 321–6.
26. Cf. Deleuze 1983: 186.
27. For a trenchant critique of this Nietzschean–Deleuzean motif, cf. Peter Hallward's *Out of This World: Deleuze and the Philosophy of Creation*, London: Verso, 2006.
28. 'Judgements, value judgements concerning life, for or against, can in the last resort never be true: they possess value only as symptoms, they come into consideration only as symptoms – in themselves such judgements are stupidities. One must reach out and try to reach this astonishing finesse, that the value of life cannot be estimated. Not by a living man, because he is a party to the dispute, indeed its object, and not the judge of it; not by a dead one, for another reason. For a philosopher to see a problem in the value of

life thus even constitutes an objection to him, a question mark as to his wisdom, a piece of un-wisdom.' 'The Problem of Socrates' in *Twilight of the Idols*, tr. R. J. Hollingdale, Harmondsworth: Penguin, 1990, 40.
29. Cf. Deleuze 1983: 171–94.
30. F. Nietzsche, *Ecce Homo*, tr. R. J. Hollingdale, Harmondsworth: Penguin 1979b XV, §8.
31. 'To redeem the past and transform every "it was" into an "I wanted it thus" – that alone do I call redemption!' (Nietzsche 1969: 161).
32. Cf. Hegel 1989: 390–408.
33. Realism of any sort never seems to have been a serious option for Nietzsche, even after his break with Schopenhauer. As he himself puts it in a remark from 1872: 'Time in itself is nonsense: time exists only for a sensate creature. The same is true for space. Every structure appertains to the subject' (Nietzsche 1995: 46). In many regards, Nietzsche's perspectivism is simply an exacerbation of his mentor's transcendental idealism: just as the will to life subtends the relation between knowing subject and known object for Schopenhauer, the will to power is at once the agent and patient of evaluation for Nietzsche.
34. J-F. Lyotard, *The Inhuman: Reflections on Time*, tr. G. Bennington and R. Bowlby, Stanford, CA: Stanford University Press, 1991.
35. Cf. Edmund Husserl, 'The Originary Ark: The Earth Does Not Move' in *Husserl at the Limits of Phenomenology*, ed. L. Lawlor with B. Bergo, Evanston, IL: Northwestern University Press, 2002; Martin Heidegger, 'The Origin of the Work of Art' in *Basic Writings*, ed. D. F. Krell, HarperSanFrancisco, 1977b; Gilles Deleuze and Felix Guattari, *A Thousand Plateaus*, tr. B. Massumi, London: Athlone, 1988.
36. S. Freud, 'Beyond the Pleasure Principle' in *The Penguin Freud Library Vol. 11: On Metapsychology*, Harmondsworth, Middlesex: Penguin, 1991: 310.
37. Stephen Jay Gould, *Life's Grandeur: The Spread of Excellence from Plato to Darwin*, London: Jonathan Cape, 1996, 173.
38. Cf. S. Odenwald, *Patterns in the Void: Why Nothing is Important*, S. F. Odenwald, Boulder, Colorado: Westview Press, 2002, 163; and L. Krauss and G. Starkman, 'Life, The Universe, and Nothing: Life and Death in an Ever Expanding Universe' in *The Astrophysical Journal* Vol. 531, No. 1 (2000), 22–30.
39. E. Levinas, *De Dieu qui vient a l'idée*, Paris: Vrin, 1992.
40. Cf. E. Levinas, *Autrement qu'être ou au-dela de l'essence*, Folio/Livre de Poche, 1990; *Otherwise than Being or Beyond Essence*, tr. A. Lingis, Pittsburg, PA: Duquesne University Press, 1998.
41. Cf. E. Levinas, *De l'existence à l'existant*, Paris: Vrin, 1993.
42. Cf. S. Freud, 'Beyond the Pleasure Principle' in *The Penguin Freud Library. Vol. 11: On Metapsychology*, Harmondsworth, Middlesex: Penguin, 1991, 296, and 'The "Mystic Writing-Pad"', op. cit., 430.

Bibliography

Adorno, T. (1973) *Negative Dialectics*, tr. E.B. Ashton (London: Routledge).

Adorno, T. and Horkheimer, M. (2002) *Dialectic of Enlightenment*, tr. E. Jephcott (Stanford, CA: Stanford University Press).

Aldapuerta, J.I. (1995) *The Eyes*, ed. and tr. L. Teodora (Stockport: Critical Vision).

Allison, H. (1983) *Kant's Transcendental Idealism* (New Haven: Yale University Press).

Ansell-Pearson, K. (1997) *Viroid Life: Perspectives on Nietzsche and the Transhuman Condition* (London: Routledge).

Badiou, A. (1969) *Le Concept de modèle. Introduction a une épistémologie matérialiste des mathématiques* (Paris: Maspero).

Badiou, A. (1988) *L'être et l'événement* (Paris: Seuil).

Badiou, A. (1989) *Manifeste pour la philosophie* (Paris: Seuil).

Badiou, A. (1999) *Manifesto for Philosophy*, tr. N. Madarasz (Albany, NY: SUNY).

Badiou, A. (2002) *Deleuze: The Clamour of Being*, tr. L. Burchill (Minneapolis: University of Minnesota Press).

Badiou, A. (2004) *Theoretical Writings*, ed. R. Brassier and A. Toscano (London and New York: Continuum).

Badiou, A. (2004a) 'Philosophy and Mathematics: Infinity and the End of Romanticism' in *Theoretical Writings* (London and New York: Continuum).

Badiou, A. (2004b) 'On Subtraction' in *Theoretical Writings* (London and New York: Continuum).

Badiou, A. (2004c) 'Truth: Forcing and the Unnameable' in *Theoretical Writings* (London and New York: Continuum).

Badiou, A. (2006a) *Being and Event*, tr. O. Feltham (London and New York: Continuum).

Badiou, A. (2006b) *Logiques des mondes. L'être et l'événement, 2* (Paris: Seuil).

Bergson, H. (1991) *Matter and Memory*, tr. N.M. Paul and W.S. Palmer (New York: Zone Books).

Bernstein, J. (2001) *Adorno: Disenchantment and Ethics* (Cambridge: Cambridge University Press).

Blanchot, M. (1982) *The Space of Literature*, tr. A. Smock (Nebraska: University of Nebraska Press).

Blanchot, M. (1997) *Friendship*, tr. E. Rottenberg (Stanford: Stanford University Press).

Blanchot, M. (2002) *The Book to Come*, tr. C. Mandell (Stanford: Stanford University Press).

Brassier, R. (2003) 'Axiomatic Heresy: The Non-Philosophy of François Laruelle' in *Radical Philosophy* 121, September/October, 24–35.

Brassier, R. (2005) 'Badiou's Materialist Epistemology of Mathematics' in *Angelaki: Journal of the Theoretical Humanities*, Vol. 10, No. 2, 135–49.

Caillois, R. (1988) *L'Homme et le sacré* (La Flèche: Folio/Éssais).

Chalmers, D. (1996) *The Conscious Mind* (Oxford: Oxford University Press).

Churchland, P.M. (1981) 'Eliminative Materialism and the Propositional Attitudes', *Journal of Philosophy*, Vol. 78, No. 2, 76–90. Reprinted in *The Philosophy of Science* eds R. Boyd, P. Gaspar, J. D. Trout (Cambridge, MA: MIT Press, 1991) 615–30.

Churchland, P.M. (1989) *A Neurocomputational Perspective: The Nature of Mind and the Structure of Science* (London: MIT Press).

Churchland, P.M. (1996a) 'Fodor and Lepore: State Space Semantics and Meaning Holism' in R.N. McCauley ed. *The Churchlands and Their Critics* (Oxford: Blackwell) 273–7.

Churchland, P.M. (1996b) 'Second Reply to Fodor and Lepore' in R.N. McCauley ed. *The Churchlands and Their Critics* (Oxford: Blackwell) 278–83.

Churchland, P.M. (1998a) 'Conceptual Similarity across Sensory and Neural Diversity: The Fodor-Lepore Challenge Answered' in P.M. Churchland and P.S. Churchland *On the Contrary: Critical Essays 1987–1997* (Cambridge, MA: MIT Press) 81–112.

Churchland, P.M. (1998b) 'Folk Psychology' in P.M. Churchland and P.S. Churchland *On the Contrary: Critical Essays 1987–1997*. (Cambridge, MA: MIT Press) 3–15.

Churchland, P.M. (1998c) 'Reply to Glymour' in P.M. Churchland and P.S. Churchland *On the Contrary: Critical Essays 1987–1997* (Cambridge, MA: MIT Press) 281–7.

Churchland P.M. and Churchland P.S. (1998) *On the Contrary: Critical Essays 1987–1997* (Cambridge, MA: MIT Press).

Churchland, P.M. (1999) 'Densmore and Dennett on Virtual Machines and Consciousness' in *Philosophy and Phenomenological Research*, Vol. LIX, No. 3.

Churchland, P.S. (1981) 'Is Determinism Self-Refuting?' in *Mind*, Vol. 90, 99–101.

Churchland, P.S. (1986) *Neurophilosophy: Toward a Unified Science of the Mind-Brain* (Cambridge, MA: MIT Press).

Churchland, P.S. and Sejnowski, T. (1992) *The Computational Brain* (Cambridge, MA: MIT Press).

Clark, A. (1996) 'Dealing in Futures: Folk Psychology and the Role of Representation in Cognitive Science' in R.N. McCauley ed. *The Churchlands and Their Critics* (Oxford: Blackwell) 86–101.

Cohen, H. (2001) *La théorie Kantienne de l'expérience*, tr. E. Dufour and J. Servois (Paris: Cerf).

Cooke, N. (2004) 'The Language of Insects' in *Sandwich 1* (London: SecMoCo Publishing).

Critchley, S. (1997) *Very Little, Almost Nothing* (London: Routledge).

Cunningham, C. (2002) *Genealogy of Nihilism: Philosophies of Nothing and the Difference of Theology* (London: Routledge).

Dastur, F. (1996) 'The Ekstatico-Horizonal Constitution of Temporality' in C. Macann ed. *Critical Heidegger* (London: Routledge) 158–71.

De Landa, M. (2002) *Intensive Science and Virtual Philosophy* (London: Continuum).

Deleuze, G. (1968) *Différence et répétition* (Paris: PUF).

Deleuze, G. and Parnet, C. (1977) *Dialogues* (Paris: Flammarion).

Deleuze. G. (1983) *Nietzsche and Philosophy*, tr. H. Tomlinson (London: Athlone).

Deleuze, G. and Guattari, F. (1988) *A Thousand Plateaus*, tr. B. Massumi (London: Athlone).

Deleuze, G. (1994) *Difference and Repetition*, tr. P. Patton, (New York: Columbia University Press).

Deleuze, G. (2002a) 'La conception de la différence chez Bergson' in *L'île déserte et autres textes* (Paris: Minuit) 43–72.

Deleuze, G. (2002b) 'La méthode de dramatisation' in *L'île déserte et autres textes* (Paris: Minuit) 131–62.

Dennett, D. (2006) *Sweet Dreams: Philosophical Obstacles to a Science of Consciousness* (Cambridge, MA: MIT Press).

Derrida, J. (1973) *Speech and Phenomena and Other Essays on Husserl's Theory of Signs*, tr. D.B. Allison (Evanston, IL: Northwestern University Press).

Desanti, J-T. (2004) 'Some Remarks on the Intrinsic Ontology of Alain Badiou' in P. Hallward ed. *Think Again: Alain Badiou and the Future of Philosophy* (London: Continuum) 59–66.

Devitt, M. (1990) 'Transcendentalism about Content' *Pacific Philosophical Quarterly*, Vol. 71, No. 2, 247–63.

Duffy, S. (2004) 'The Logic of Expression in Deleuze's *Expressionism in Philosophy: Spinoza*: A Strategy of Engagement' in *International Journal of Philosophical Studies*, Vol. 12, No. 1, 47–60.

Feyerabend, P. (1963) 'Materialism and the Mind-Body Problem', *Review of Metaphysics*, Vol. XVII, No. 1, Issue 65, 49–66.

Fodor, J. (1987) *Psychosemantics* (Cambridge. MA: MIT Press).

Fodor, J. (2000) *In Critical Condition: Polemical Essays on Cognitive Science and the Philosophy of Mind* (Cambridge, MA: MIT Press).

Fodor, J. and Lepore, E. (1996a) 'Churchland and State Space Semantics' in R.N. McCauley ed. *The Churchlands and Their Critics* (Oxford: Blackwell) 145–58.

Fodor, J. and Lepore, E. (1996b) 'Reply to Churchland' in R.N. McCauley ed. *The Churchlands and Their Critics* (Oxford: Blackwell) 159–62.

Frank, C. and Nash, C. eds (2003) *On the Edge of Surrealism: A Roger Caillois Reader* (Durham: Duke University Press).

Freud, S. (1991) 'Beyond the Pleasure Principle' in *The Penguin Freud Library Vol. 11: On Metapsychology*, (Harmondsworth, Middlesex: Penguin).

Freud, S. (1991a) 'The Mystic Writing-Pad' in *The Penguin Freud Library Vol. 11: On Metapsychology*, (Harmondsworth, Middlesex: Penguin).

Gillespie, M.A. (1996) *Nihilism before Nietzsche* (Chicago: University of Chicago Press).

Gould, S.J. (1996) *Life's Grandeur: The Spread of Excellence from Plato to Darwin* (London: Jonathan Cape).

Hallward, P. (2003) *Badiou: A Subject to Truth* (Minneapolis: University of Minnesota Press).

Hallward, P. ed. (2004) *Think Again: Alain Badiou and the Future of Philosophy* (London: Continuum).

Hallward, P. (2006) *Out of This World: Deleuze and the Philosophy of Creation* (London: Verso).

Harman, G. (2002) *Tool-Being: Heidegger and the Metaphysics of Objects* (Chicago: Open Court).

Harman, G. (2005) *Guerrilla Metaphysics: Phenomenology and the Carpentry of Things* (Chicago: Open Court).

Haugeland, J. (1985) *Artificial Intelligence: The Very Idea* (Cambridge, MA: MIT Press).

Hegel, G.W.F. (1989) *Science of Logic*, tr. A.V. Miller (New Jersey: Humanities Press).

Heidegger, M. (1962) *Being and Time*, tr. E. Macquarrie and J. Robinson (Oxford: Blackwell).

Heidegger, M. (1977a) 'The Turning' in *The Question Concerning Technology and Other Essays*, tr. W. Lovitt (New York: Harper and Row) 36–52.

Heidegger, M. (1977b) 'The Origin of the Work of Art' in D.F. Krell ed. *Basic Writings* (San Francisco: Harper) 149–87.

Heidegger, M. (1982) *The Basic Problems of Phenomenology*, tr. A. Hofstader (Bloomington & Indianapolis: Indiana University Press).

Heidegger, M. (1990a) *Kant and the Problem of Metaphysics*, tr. R. Taft (Indianapolis: Indiana University Press).

Heidegger, M. (1990b) *Nietzsche Vol. II: The Eternal Recurrence of the Same*, ed. D.F. Krell (New York: HarperSanFrancisco).

Heidegger, M. (1990c) *Nietzsche Vol. III: The Will to Power as Knowledge and as Metaphysics*, ed. D.F. Krell (New York: HarperSanFrancisco).

Heidegger, M. (1990d) *Nietzsche Vol. IV: Nihilism*, ed. D.F. Krell (New York: HarperSanFrancisco).

Heidegger, M. (1992) *The Concept of Time*, tr. W. McNeill (Oxford: Blackwell).

Heidegger, M. (1995) *The Fundamental Problems of Metaphysics: World, Finitude, Solitude*, tr. W. McNeill (Bloomington & Indianapolis: Indiana University Press).

Heidegger, M. (1996) *The Principle of Reason*, tr. R. Lilly (Bloomington and Indianapolis: Indiana University Press).

Heidegger, M. (1999) *Contributions to Philosophy*, tr. P. Emad and K. Maly (Indianapolis: Indiana University Press).

Heidegger, M. (2000) *Introduction to Metaphysics*, tr. G. Fried & R. Polt (New Haven: Yale University Press).

Henry, M. (1963) *L'essence de la manifestation* (Paris: PUF).

Henry, M. (1973) *The Essence of Manifestation*, tr. G. Etzkorn (The Hague: Nijhoff).

Hume, D. (1957) *Enquiry Concerning Human Understanding*, ed. C.W. Hendel (New York: The Liberal Arts Press).

Hume. D. (1984) *A Treatise of Human Nature*, ed. C. Mossner (Harmondsworth, Middlesex: Penguin).

Husserl, E. (1970) *The Crisis of the European Sciences and Transcendental Phenomenology*, tr. David Carr (Evanston, IL: Northwestern University Press).

Husserl, E. (1982) *Ideas Pertaining to a Pure Phenomenology and to a Phenomenological Philosophy. First Book*, tr. F. Kersten (London: Kluwer).

Husserl, E. (2002) 'The Originary Ark: The Earth Does Not Move' in *Husserl at the Limits of Phenomenology*, ed. L. Lawlor with B. Bergo (Evanston, IL: Northwestern University Press).

Huyssen, A. (2000) 'Of Mice and Mimesis' *New German Critique, No. 81, Dialectic of Enlightenment*, 66–7.

Israel, J. (2001) *Radical Enlightenment: Philosophy and the Making of Modernity 1650–1750* (Oxford: Oxford University Press).

Israel, J. (2006) *Enlightenment Contested: Philosophy, Modernity and the Emancipation of Man 1670–1752* (Oxford: Oxford University Press).

Kant, I. (1929) *Critique of Pure Reason*, tr. N.K. Smith (London: Macmillan)

Kisiel, T. (1993) *The Genesis of Heidegger's Being and Time* (London: University of California Press).

Krauss, L. M. and Starkman, G. D. (2000) 'Life, The Universe, and Nothing: Life and Death in an Ever Expanding Universe' in *The Astrophysical Journal* Vol. 531, No. 1, 22–30.

Kuhn, T.S. (1962) *The Structure of Scientific Revolutions* (Chicago: University of Chicago Press).

Laruelle, F. (1985) *Une biographie de l'homme ordinaire* (Paris: Aubier).

Laruelle, F. (1986) *Les Philosophies de la différence. Introduction critique* (Paris: PUF).

Laruelle, F. (1989a) *Philosophie et non-philosophie* (Liège/Bruxelles: Mardaga).

Laruelle, F. (1989b) 'La méthode transcendantale' in *Encyclopédie Philosophique Universelle*. Vol. 1, ed. André Jacob (Paris: PUF) 71–80.

Laruelle, F. (1991) *En tant qu'un* (Paris: Aubier).

Laruelle, F. (1995) 'Réponse à Deleuze' in *La non-philosophie des contemporains* (Paris: Kimé). 49–78.

Laruelle, F. (1996) *Principes de la non-philosophie* (Paris: PUF).

Laruelle, F. (1998) ed. *Dictionnaire de la non-philosophie* (Paris: Kimé).

Laruelle, F. (2000a) *Introduction au non-marxisme* (Paris: PUF).

Laruelle, F. (2000b) *Éthique de l'Étranger, Du crime contre l'humanité* (Paris: Kimé).

Laruelle, F. (2003) 'What Can Non-Philosophy Do?' *Angelaki: Journal of the Theoretical Humanities*, Vol. 8, No. 2, 169–90.

Laruelle, F. (2004) *La Lutte et l'utopie à la fin des temps philosophiques* (Paris: Kimé).

Lawlor, L. (1998) 'The End of Phenomenology: Expressionism in Deleuze and Merleau-Ponty' in *Continental Philosophy Review*, Vol. 31 No. 1, 15–34.

Lenin, V.I. (1972) *Materialism and Empirio-Criticism* (originally published 1908, tr. A. Fineberg (Peking: Foreign Languages Press).

Levinas. E. (1987) *Time and the Other*, tr. R. Cohen (Pittsburgh: Duquesne University Press).

Levinas, E. (1990) *Autrement qu'être ou au-dela de l'essence* (Livre de Poche/Biblio Éssais).

Levinas, E. (1993) *De l'existence à l'existant* (Paris: Vrin).

Levinas, E. (1998) *Otherwise than Being or Beyond Essence*, tr. A. Lingis (Pittsburg, PA: Duquesne University Press).

Lyotard, J-F. (1991) *The Inhuman* (Stanford, CA: Stanford University Press).

Marshall, J. and Gurd, J. (1996) 'The Furniture of Mind' in R.N. McCauley ed. *The Churchlands and Their Critics* (Oxford: Blackwell) 176–91.

McCauley, R.N. ed. (1996) *The Churchlands and Their Critics* (Oxford: Blackwell).

Meillassoux, Q. (2006) *Après la finitude. Éssai sur la nécéssité de la contingence* (Paris: Seuil).

Metzinger, T. (2004) *Being No-One: The Self-Model Theory of Subjectivity* (London: MIT Press).

Miller, D.W. (1994) *Critical Rationalism: A Re-statement and Defence* (Chicago: Open Court).

Miller, D.W. (2004) 'The Uniformity of Nature: What Purpose Does It Serve? Comments on Karl Milford's "Inductivism in 19th Century German Economics"' in Friedrich Stadler ed. *Induction & Deduction in the Sciences* (Dordrecht: Kluwer Academic Publishers) 293–7.

Miller, D.W. (2006) *Out of Error: Further Essays on Critical Rationalism* (Aldershot: Ashgate).

Minkowski, E. (1932–3) 'Le problème du temps en psychopathologie' in *Recherches Philosophiques*.

Minkowski, E. (1933) *Le Temps vécue. Études phénoménologiques et psychopathologiques* (Paris: L'évolution Psychiatrique).

Minkowski, E. (1970) *Lived Time*, tr. N. Metzel (Evanston: Northwestern University Press).

Minkowski, E. (1997) *La Schizophrénie* (Paris: Payot, Rivages) (originally published 1927).

Murphy, T. (1992) 'The Theatre of (the Philosophy of) Cruelty in Difference and Repetition' in *Pli: The Warwick Journal of Philosophy Vol. 5. Deleuze and the Transcendental Unconscious*, ed. J. Broadhurst-Dixon (Coventry: University of Warwick) 105–35.

Nietzsche, F. (1968) *The Will to Power*, ed. and tr. W. Kaufman (New York: Vintage).

Nietzsche, F. (1969) *Thus Spake Zarathustra*, tr. R.J. Hollingdale (Harmondsworth: Penguin).

Nietzsche, F. (1974) *The Gay Science*, tr. W. Kaufman (New York: Vintage).

Nietzsche, F. (1979a) 'On Truth and Lies in a Nonmoral Sense' in *Philosophy and Truth: Selections from Nietzsche's Notebooks of the Early 1870s* tr. Daniel Breazeale (Atlantic Highlands, New Jersey: Humanities Press) 79–97.

Nietzsche, F. (1979b) *Ecce Homo*, tr. R.J. Hollingdale (Harmondsworth: Penguin).

Nietzsche, F. (1990) *Twilight of the Idols/The Anti-Christ*, tr. R.J. Hollingdale (Harmondsworth: Penguin).

Nietzsche, F. (1990b) *Beyond Good and Evil*, tr. R.J. Hollingdale (Harmondsworth: Penguin).

Nietzsche, F. (1994) *On the Genealogy of Morality*, ed. K.A. Pearson, tr. C. Diethe (Cambridge: Cambridge University Press).

Nietzsche, F. (1995) *Unpublished Writings from the Period of Unfashionable Observations*, tr. R. Gray (Stanford, California: Stanford University Press).

Odenwald, S. (2002) *Patterns in the Void: Why Nothing is Important* (Boulder, Colorado: Westview Press).

Osborne, P. (1995) *The Politics of Time: Modernity and Avant-Garde* (London: Verso).

Pieper, J. (1954) *The End of Time: A Meditation on the Philosophy of History*, tr. M. Bullock (New York: Pantheon Books).

Popper, K. (2002a) *The Logic of Scientific Discovery* (London: Routledge).

Popper, K. (2002b) *Conjectures and Refutations* (London: Routledge).

Putnam, H. (1975) 'The Meaning of "Meaning"' in *Mind, Language, and Reality: Philosophical Papers Volume 2* (Cambridge: Cambridge University Press) 215–71.

Prinz, J.J. (2006) 'Empiricism and State Space Semantics' in B.L. Keeley ed. *Paul Churchland* (Cambridge: Cambridge University Press) 88–112.

Rockwell, T. (1998) 'Beyond Eliminative Materialism: Some Unnoticed Implications of Churchland's Pragmatic Pluralism' available at http://cogprints.org/379/00/BeyondEM.html

Rockwell, T. (2005) *Neither Brain nor Ghost: A Non-Dualist Alternative to Mind-Brain Identity Theory* (Cambridge, MA: MIT Press).

Rorty, R. (1965) 'Mind-Body Identity, Privacy, and Categories' *Review of Metaphysics*, Vol. XIX, No. 1, Issue 73, 24–54.

Rose, G. (1984) *Dialectic of Nihilism: Post-Structuralism and Law* (Oxford: Blackwell).

Rosen, S. (2000) *Nihilism: A Philosophical Essay* (New York: St. Augustine's Press).

Rudder-Baker, L. (1987) *Saving Belief: A Critique of Physicalism* (Princeton, NJ: Princeton University Press).

Russell, B. (1948) *Human Knowledge: Its Scope and Limits* (London: George Allen and Unwin Ltd).

Schelling, F. (1993) *On the History of Modern Philosophy*, tr. A. Bowie (Cambridge: Cambridge University Press).

Searle, J. (1992) *The Rediscovery of the Mind* (Cambridge, MA: MIT Press).

Sellars, W. (1963a) 'Philosophy and the Scientific Image of Man' in *Science, Perception and Reality* (London: Routledge and Kegan Paul) 1–40.

Sellars, W. (1963b) *Science, Perception, and Reality* (London: Routledge & Kegan Paul).

Sellars, W. (1997) *Empiricism and the Philosophy of Mind* (Cambridge, MA: Harvard University Press).

Simondon, G. (1964) *L'Individu et sa genèse physico-biologique* (Paris: PUF).

Smith, D.W. (1995) 'Deleuze's Theory of Sensation: Overcoming the Kantian Duality' in P. Patton ed. *Deleuze: A Critical Reader* (Oxford: Blackwell) 34.

Souche-Dagues, D. (1996) *Nihilismes* (Paris: PUF).

Stich, S. (1983) *From Folk Psychology to Cognitive Science: The Case against Belief* (Cambridge, MA: MIT Press).

Toscano, A. (2006) *The Theatre of Production: Philosophy and Individuation between Kant and Deleuze* (Basingstoke: Palgrave Macmillan).

Van der Burg, F. and Eardley, M. (2000) 'Does the Man on the Clapham Omnibus Have a Labcoat in His Pocket? Eliminative Materialism is Based on a Valid Argument from the False Premise That Folk-Psychology is an Empirical Theory', in *PLI: The Warwick Journal of Philosophy, Vol. 9. Parallel Processes: Philosophy and Science*, (Coventry: University of Warwick) 139–55.

Vattimo, G. (1991) *The End of Modernity: Nihilism and Hermeneutics in Postmodern Culture* (Baltimore: John Hopkins).

Vattimo, G. (2004) *Nihilism and Emancipation* (New York: Columbia University Press).

Vernes, J.-R. (1982) *Critique de la raison aléatoire, ou Descartes contre Kant* (Paris: Aubier).

Vetö, Miklos. (1998) *De Kant à Schelling: Les deux voies de l'Idéalisme allemand. Tome I.* (Grenoble: Éditions Jérôme Millon).

Wahl, F. (2002) 'Présentation, représentation, apparaitre' in C. Ramond ed. *Alain Badiou. Penser le multiple* (Paris: L'Harmattan) 169–87.

Weinberg, S. (1978) *The First Three Minutes* (London: Flamingo).

Whitehead, A.N. (1978) *Process and Reality* (London and New York: The Free Press).

Wittgenstein, L. (1974) *Tractatus Logico-Philosophicus*, tr. D.F. Pears & B.F. McGuinness (London: Routledge).

Žižek, S. (2006) *The Parallax View* (London: MIT Press).

Index of Names

Adorno, T. W., 31–48, 129, 243, 246, 252
Allison, D., 243
Althusser, L., 252
Ansell-Pearson, K., 256, 259

Bachelard, G., 246
Badiou, A., 86–88, 94, 97–118, 134, 137, 147–148, 246, 249–251, 253, 255
Benjamin, W., 243, 246
Bergson, H., 163–165, 175–177, 196, 201–204, 255, 257, 259
Berkeley, G., 51
Bernstein, J., 40, 243
Blanchot, M., 185, 254–255, 257
Bloch, E., 246

Caillois, R., 33, 42–45, 243–244
Cantor, G., 81, 89
Carnap, R., 246
Cavailles, J., 246
Churchland, P. M., 8–14, 16–27, 134, 240–242
Churchland, P. S., 16, 240–242
Clark, A., 242
Cohen, H., 246, 252, 255
Cohen, P. J., 102, 250
Cooke, N., 63, 243
Copernicus, 249
Cronenberg, D., 244

Darwin, C. R., 40, 48, 242, 245, 261
Dastur, F., 253
De Landa, M., 257
Deleuze, G., 119, 126, 140, 150, 162–194, 196–200, 202–204, 208, 210, 215–217, 221–224, 246, 251, 253, 255–261
Dennett, D., 26, 29–30, 242
Derrida, J., 30, 119, 121, 129, 140, 243, 246, 251–254
Desanti, J.-T., 249

Descartes, R., 90, 249
Devitt, M., 241
Duffy, S., 256

Eardley, M., 242
Easton, W. B., 102, 250
Einstein, A., 58, 242–243

Feyerabend, P., 240
Fodor, J., 10, 25, 241–242
Freud, S., 33, 36, 47, 163, 186, 204, 223, 234–238, 243, 261

Gadamer, H.-G., 246, 253
Galilei, G., 40
Gould, S. J., 226, 228, 261
Gurd, J., 13, 241

Hallward, P., 249–250, 260
Harman, G., 245–246, 251
Hegel, G. W. F., 24, 31, 33, 36, 38, 41, 45, 48, 58, 65–66, 70–71, 125, 131, 134–135, 140, 147, 216, 218, 225, 245–246, 251–252, 255, 261
Heidegger, M., 7, 27–28, 51, 57, 65–66, 68, 73, 97–98, 119, 121, 124, 126–127, 129–132, 134–135, 137, 140, 150, 153–159, 161, 163, 170, 185, 195, 203, 208, 215, 222–223, 225, 232–233, 243, 245–246, 249, 251–252, 253–255, 258, 260–261
Henry, M., 30, 127, 135, 137, 145, 246, 251–252
Heraclitus, 121
Himmler, H., 243
Homer, 244
Horkheimer, M., 31–42, 44–48, 243, 246
Hume, D., 74–76, 78–80, 134, 196
Husserl, E., 26, 28, 30, 54, 57, 124, 126, 176, 223, 242–246, 251, 261
Huyssen, A., 32, 243

Index of Subjects

Made in the USA
Columbia, SC
22 March 2018